The Feminist Spectator as Critic

by
Jill Dolan

THE UNIVERSITY OF MICHIGAN PRESS

Ann Arbor

First published by the University of Michigan Press 1991
Copyright © by Jill Susan Dolan 1988
All rights reserved
Published in the United States of America by
The University of Michigan Press
Manufactured in the United States of America

1994   1993   1992   4   3

Library of Congress Cataloging-in-Publication Data

Dolan, Jill, 1957–'
     The feminist spectator as critic / by Jill Dolan.
         p.   cm.
     Reprint. Originally published: Ann Arbor, Mich. : UMI Research
Press, c1988.
     Includes bibliographical references (p.   ) and index.
     ISBN 0-472-08160-8 (paper : alk.)
     1. Feminist theater—United States.   2. Feminist Criticism.
3. Theater audiences.   4. Feminism.   I. Title.
[PN2270.F45D64   1991]
792'.015'082—dc20   91-11487
                                                    CIP

British Library Cataloguing in Publication Data

Dolan, Jill, *1957–*
     The feminist spectator as critic.
     I. Title
     792.015088042

     ISBN 0-472-08160-8

The Feminist Spectator
as Critic

For Cyma and Jerry Dolan,
Randee and Ann Beth Dolan,
and Bess Solomon,
whose love, support, and unwavering belief
made this possible
And in memory of
Rose Dolan and
Jake Dolan and Dave Solomon,
whose stories about vaudeville and "drama"
helped form my own tenacious commitment
to the power of performance

Contents

Preface   *ix*

Acknowledgments   *xi*

1   The Discourse of Feminisms: The Spectator and Representation   *1*

2   Feminism and the Canon: The Question of Universality   *19*

3   Ideology in Performance: Looking through the Male Gaze   *41*

4   The Dynamics of Desire: Sexuality and Gender in
    Pornography and Performance   *59*

5   Cultural Feminism and the Feminine Aesthetic   *83*

6   Materialist Feminism: Apparatus-Based Theory and Practice   *99*

Afterword   *119*

Notes   *123*

Bibliography   *145*

Index   *151*

Preface

This book is not meant to be a definitive study of feminist performance criticism. Rather, in some ways, it is a historical accounting of the different methodological and ideological pathways this criticism has taken over the last twenty-odd years, illustrated here by critical case studies. I do not mean to neutralize my own critical stance by that caveat; the following pages should be clearly understood as representing my own methodological and ideological position as a materialist feminist critic.

The book is organized as a series of essays that refract around the central topic, which is detailed in chapter 1. Taken together, the essays should provide a cumulative effect, rather than a necessarily linear one. The last chapter, however, does represent work that I feel is the most stimulating and provocative of contemporary feminist performance criticism.

Writing for people interested in a feminist approach to theatre and performance is a challenging task, since that constituency is large and varied from theoretical, political, and ideological perspectives. Any feminist endeavor in this area confronts the problem—and pleasure—of diversity among its audience. The Women and Theatre Program of the American Theatre in Higher Education organization, for example, is charged with appealing to academics and practitioners and a range of women who admit to very different stances vis-à-vis feminism. *Women & Performance Journal*—with which I was involved as managing editor and cofounder at its inception in the Performance Studies Department at New York University—worried at the outset about providing a forum for all women interested in performance.

As I hope to clarify in this study, I believe that such a committedly nonpartisan approach inevitably butts against its own limitations. How can an organization or a journal provide a kind of visionary leadership if it does not take a clear ideological and political stand on its own issues? In January 1988, the Women and Theatre Program created formal by-laws that at least set forth the organization's commitment to address and attempt to eradicate sexism, racism, and homophobia as part of its charter. This stated intent cannot help but focus, shape, and lend vitality to the group's future work.

In publication, it seems equally important to take a stand and to state it at the outset of one's writing. If part of the materialist feminist project is to demystify ideological authority in performance and in dramatic literary texts, it is necessary to guard against reinstituting the materialist feminist critic as the absent, naturalized authority. Demystifying the author and particularizing—instead of idealizing—the reader for whom she writes seems imperative as part of the critical process.

I have tried continually to clarify my stance and my ideological, political, and personal investments in the studies that follow. I write from my own perspective as a white, middle-class woman, with every effort to stay aware of and change my own racism and attitudes about class. As a Jew and as a lesbian, I also write from my own awareness of exclusion from dominant ethnic and heterosexual discourse. I hope that readers constituted across a diversity of race, class, ethnicity, gender, and sexual preference identities will find the ideas in these pages useful.

This text is written for practitioners and critics, historians and theorists, academics and professionals, and myriad other feminist spectators interested in what it means to combine feminism and performance. I see it as an introduction to feminist critical and theoretical ideas relevant to theatre and performance. Still, it straddles a somewhat precarious position in relation to its intended readership.

On one hand, although it is an introduction, it demands at least a cursory familiarity with post-structuralism, deconstruction, and semiotics. I have tried to refrain from needlessly opaque jargon. But formulating new critical theory demands a new critical language, which I do draw on here. On the other hand, in addition to introducing these ideas, I would like this work to challenge and provoke colleagues who are already breaking new ground in the field of feminist theatre criticism. I hope that both sets of readers will find their way here. With an eye toward provoking dialogue and debate, both are envisioned in these pages.

Acknowledgments

This book in some respects charts my own development as a feminist performance critic, and there are many people who in one way or another helped to shape my growth and its direction. The editorial board of *Women & Performance Journal*—which began meeting as an informal feminist support group in Performance Studies at New York University in Fall 1981—provided me with a continual sounding board during my graduate work. The Women and Theatre Program of the defunct American Theatre Association, now reconstituted as American Theatre in Higher Education, has given me a supportive forum for my thinking since I began attending their conferences in 1983. My personal sense of growth is justly shared by the members of that organization, as we move together toward a sophisticated, but accessible, political and theoretical, practice-oriented consideration of feminism and theatre.

Kate Davy's insight into body image and performance, and her comments on my work on Richard Foreman, were very helpful on initial drafts of chapters 2 and 3. Sue-Ellen Case and E. Beth Sullivan were instrumental in editing and refining an early version of chapter 4, which appeared in *Theatre Journal* (May 1987). Elin Diamond's brilliant insight into the possible connections between feminist poetics and Brecht was a primary inspiration for chapter 6.

The continuing discussions among my feminist colleagues—at conferences, through their published work, and through our informal but crucial national network—and my first group of students in feminist theory and theatre at the University of Washington in Seattle in Fall 1987 provided me with the constant and final impetus to think and to write this book. I would also like to thank Barbara Kirshenblatt-Gimblett, Susan Slyomovics, Brooks McNamara, and Michael Kirby for their comments on the manuscript.

Two people warrant special thanks. Personally, professionally, and politically, Sue-Ellen Case has been a continual source of inspiration. With her energy, commitment, and sense of purpose, she serves as an invaluable role model, and has blazed the trail for feminist theatre critics in the academy and in the theatre profession. Finally, Peggy Phelan's work on this manuscript as editor, advisor, and intellectual watchdog continually prompted me to challenge myself and to push further. I sincerely appreciate her dialogue with me around this work.

1

The Discourse of Feminisms: The Spectator and Representation

In the illusionist tradition that dominates American theatre practice, performers and spectators are separated by a curtain of light that helps maintain the fictitious fourth wall. Performers facing the audience are blinded by the workings of the apparatus that frames them. The blinding lights set them apart from the sea of silhouetted heads without faces toward whom their words flow. The spectators' individuality is subsumed under an assumption of commonality; their differences from each other are disguised by anonymity. The spectators become the audience whom the performers address—albeit obliquely, given realist theatre conventions—as a singular mass.

The performance apparatus that directs the performer's address, however, works to constitute that amorphous, anonymous mass as a particular subject position. The lighting, setting, costumes, blocking, text—all the material aspects of theatre—are manipulated so that the performance's meanings are intelligible to a particular spectator, constructed in a particular way by the terms of its address.[1] Historically, in North American culture, this spectator has been assumed to be white, middle-class, heterosexual, and male. That theatre creates an ideal spectator carved in the likeness of the dominant culture whose ideology he represents is the motivating assumption behind the discourse of feminist performance criticism.

Since the resurgence of American feminism in the 1960s, feminist theatre makers and critics have worked to expose the gender-specific nature of theatrical representation, and to radically modify its terms. Denaturalizing the position of the ideal spectator as a representative of the dominant culture enables the feminist critic to point out that every aspect of theatrical production, from the types of plays and performances produced to the texts that are ultimately canonized, is determined to reflect and perpetuate the ideal spectator's ideology.

Because its critique centers on the ideological assumptions that create an ideal spectator for representation, feminist performance criticism is subversive by nature. It is grounded in the belief that representation—visual art, theatre and performance, film and dance—creates from an ideological base meanings that have very specific, material consequences.

The feminist critic can be seen as a "resistant reader," who analyzes a performance's meaning by reading against the grain of stereotypes and resisting the manipulation of both the performance text and the cultural text that it helps to shape.[2] By exposing the ways in which dominant ideology is naturalized by the performance's address to the ideal spectator, feminist performance criticism works as political intervention in an effort toward cultural change.

This study concentrates on spectatorship. It represents an effort to bring up the lights in the theatre auditorium, as it were, to illuminate the differences between spectators positioned in front of the representational frame. Since it directs its address to a gender-specific spectator, most performance employs culturally determined gender codes that reinforce cultural conditioning. Performance usually addresses the male spectator as an active subject, and encourages him to identify with the male hero in the narrative.[3] The same representations tend to objectify women performers and female spectators as passive, invisible, unspoken subjects.

The feminist spectator viewing such a representation is necessarily in the outsider's critical position. She cannot find a comfortable way into the representation, since she finds herself, as a woman (and even more so, as a member of the working class, a lesbian, or a woman of color), excluded from its address. She sees in the performance frame representatives of her gender class with whom she might identify—if women are represented at all—acting passively before the specter of male authority.

She sees women as mothers, relegated to supporting roles that enable the more important action of the male protagonist. She sees attractive women performers made-up and dressed to seduce or be seduced by the male lead. While the men are generally active and involved, the women seem marginal and curiously irrelevant, except as a tacit support system or as decoration that enhances and directs the pleasure of the male spectator's gaze.

Finding her position compromised if she allows herself to identify with these women, the feminist spectator contemplates the option of participating in the play's narrative from the hero's point of view. She empathizes with his romantic exploits, or his activities in a more public sphere, but has a nagging suspicion that she has become complicit in the objectification or erasure of her own gender class.

Ruminating over these unsavory positions, the feminist spectator might find that her gender—and/or her race, class, or sexual preference—as well as her ideology and politics make the representation alien and even offensive. It seems that as a spectator she is far from ideal. Determined to draw larger conclusions from this experience, she leaves the theatre while the audience applauds at the curtain call and goes off to develop a theory of feminist performance criticism.

Feminism as the Site of Differences

Feminism begins with a keen awareness of exclusion from male cultural, social, sexual, political, and intellectual discourse. It is a critique of prevailing social conditions that formulate women's position as outside of dominant male discourse. Linda Gordon defines feminism in general as "a critique of male supremacy, formed and offered in the light of a will to change it, which in turn assumes a conviction that it is changeable."[4] The routes feminism takes to redress the fact of male dominance, however, are varied. Feminism has in fact given way more precisely to *feminisms,* each of which implies distinct ideological interpretations and political strategies.[5]

Attendant forms of feminist criticism theorize ways of exposing and changing women's subservient position as it is revealed in representation. But since feminism is not a monolithic discourse with a cohesive party line, its modes of criticism also take multiple forms. Some borrow from sociology, some from psychoanalysis, others from post-structuralist and deconstructive strategies, and all propose various ideological perspectives that elaborate on basic definitions of feminism.

The "playful pluralism" of early feminist criticism was accepted because it symbolized intellectual, ideological, and methodological freedom.[6] But feminist theorists have since recognized the dangers implicit in trumpeting a strictly nonsectarian approach to method and ideology. Feminism loses some of its polemical force if it is not linked to a coherent ideological structure. Therefore, it is crucial to identify common characteristics that describe the differences among the feminisms.

American feminism can be separated generally into liberal, cultural or radical, and materialist segments, each of which presents a different critical approach to the issue of exclusion from male discourse and the representations in which it is embodied. There are many gradations within and among these categories—some of which are socialist feminism, lesbian feminism, spiritualist feminism—but I find these three most inclusive and most useful for clarifying the different feminist ways of seeing.[7]

Liberal feminism takes its cues from liberal humanism. Rather than proposing radical structural change, it suggests that working within existing social and political organizations will eventually secure women social, political, and economic parity with men.[8] Alison Jaggar, in her work on feminist politics and epistemology, defines liberal feminism as "radically individualistic"; it relies on values claimed to be universally human, and in essence, demands that "everyone should receive equal consideration with no discrimination on the basis of sex."[9] The National Organization for Women and the National Women's Political Caucus are exemplary of liberal feminist work within American politics. These organizations lobby to create legislation that will promote parity between men and women within the dominant system.

The fight to ratify the Equal Rights Amendment, the effort to gain equal pay for equal work, a woman's right to control over her body and to choose abortion, childcare, and affirmative action are some of the issues that dominate liberal feminist discourse. The movement's general effort is to insert women into the mainstream of political and social life by changing the cultural perception of them as second-class citizens.

Over the last twenty years, liberal feminism has made strides toward this end. The increased number of women in the work force, a slightly higher percentage of women in corporate executive positions, and Geraldine Ferraro's position on the 1984 presidential ticket, for instance, all stand as evidence of liberal feminism's achievements in chipping away at male hegemony.

In theatre practice and criticism, liberal feminist efforts are responsible for the wider visibility of women playwrights, directors, producers, and designers, and the creation of richer roles for women performers. Organizations such as the Women's Project and the Women and Theatre Program of the American Theatre Association (now American Theatre in Higher Education) provide opportunities for women to refine their craft so that they can compete effectively in male-dominated production and academic contexts.[10] Broadway productions of plays by Marsha Norman, Beth Henley, and Emily Mann evince the greater visibility of particularly women playwrights in mainstream forums.

As liberal feminism gains a foothold for women in the male-dominated institutions of American theatre, however, an insidious backsliding sometimes occurs with regard to feminist politics. Some women in theatre suggest that women's advocacy groups and workshop spaces are temporary measures that will no longer be necessary when women truly achieve parity with men. Many working women playwrights vehemently resist the feminist appellation, because to survive economically their plays must be produced widely in commercial venues. The analogy between feminism and politics is seen as threatening to the universality of their work.[11]

Liberal feminist playwrights and critics accept the notion that theatre communicates universally and prefer not to be particularized as women. Sue-Ellen Case perceives a danger in their detachment from the movement that made their success possible:

> Without an answerability to the movement, does not the work of women in theatre become isolated from the community it represents? . . . Mainstream women playwrights regard political critique as an imposition or confinement of their creative processes. The old male model of the Romantic movement has re-emerged: the Artist is a Genius and the oppression of women

disappears before the "universal" and "eternal" qualities of art. These same qualities have been the ones employed to render women invisible in the traditional theatre, its history and the formation of the canon.[12]

Their desire to become part of the system that has historically excluded them forces some liberal feminists in theatre to acquiesce to their erasure as women. Little changes, even as stronger women characters are written into their plays, because the universal to which they write is still based on the male model.

Liberal feminist texts produced in mainstream theatre present a hoary problem, critically speaking. My discussion of the Broadway production of Marsha Norman's *'night, Mother* in chapter 2 looks at the ambivalent response to the play by mainstream male critics, who were forced to decide whether a play written by a woman about a mother/daughter relationship could be considered universal. The comparisons they made were to a canon of dramatic literature written by men, in which father/son relationships are privileged. *'night, Mother* takes place in a kitchen/livingroom, and its form is kitchen-sink realism. But because its author and characters are women, "kitchen-sink" took on different connotations for the male critics than it did when perceived in the context of *Death of a Salesman*, which was written by Arthur Miller, the father of American domestic drama. In fact, Miller's play serves as a useful counterpoint to *'night, Mother*, a comparison explored fully in chapter 2.

Thrown into relief by its comparison with the standard canon, the sex-based division of public and private spheres can suddenly be seen more clearly in terms of their relative worth as universal dramatic material. Chapter 2 looks at the ideological implications of the traditional critical search for universality and transcendance, and addresses the issue of canon formation.

Liberal feminists applauded what they saw as Norman's elevation into the canon when she won the Pulitzer Prize for drama in 1983. Other feminists debated whether Norman's play might form part of a female countercanon because of its gender differences from the male model. Cultural feminism, the second segment of American feminism I am delineating here, proposes that there are, and should be maintained, clear differences between men and women which might form the basis of separate cultural spheres.

Cultural feminism is sometimes called radical feminism. At the start of the second wave of American feminism in the late 1960s and early 1970s, radical feminism was based in a theoretical struggle to abolish gender as a defining category between men and women. Cultural feminism, on the contrary, bases its analysis in a reification of sexual difference based on absolute gender categories. Alice Echols comments that in the 1980s,

This perspective has gained legitimacy and achieved hegemony with the radical feminist movement. This view represents such a fundamental departure from the early radical feminist version that it is important to differentiate the two. I . . . therefore refer to this more recent strain of radical feminist as *cultural feminism* because it equates women's liberation with the development and preservation of a female counter-culture.[13]

Linda Gordon, too, finds a movement away from "androgyny to female uniqueness" in the shift from radical to cultural feminism: "The early women's liberation movement, both radical and liberal, emphasized equal rights and equal access for women to previously male privilege. In the past decade, we have seen . . . a celebration of women's unique and superior qualities with . . . an emphasis on mothering as both source and ultimate expression of these qualities."[14] Cultural feminism is founded on a reification of sexual difference that valorizes female biology, in which gender is an immutable, determining, and desirable category. Because I find Echol's and Gordon's definitions of this movement lucid and precise, I have chosen to use the term "cultural feminism" here.

An inquiry into sex and gender categories is the primary focus of feminism in general, but within each of the feminisms, the investigation manifests different ideology and different forms. Liberal feminism, as we have seen, would subsume the female gender into the (male) generic, or universal, category. Cultural feminism proposes instead a fundamental change in the nature of universality by suggesting that female gender values take the place of the generic male. It seeks to reverse the gender hierarchy by theorizing female values as superior to male values. The oppressions wrought by gender polarization constructed through dominant theories of sexual difference remain peculiarly unattacked in cultural feminist thought.

Gayle Rubin, whose influential article "The Traffic in Women: Notes on the 'Political Economy' of Sex" traces the causes of women's oppression through anthropological and psychoanalytical discourses, defines the sex/gender system as a "set of arrangements by which society transforms biological sexuality into products of human activity."[15] Sex is biological, based in genital differences between males and females. Gender, on the other hand, is a fashioning of maleness and femaleness into the cultural categories of masculinity and femininity. These adjectives describe cultural attributes that determine social roles. Sex is empirical, but gender is an interpretation that can only take place within a cultural space.

Cultural feminists, however, elide the difference between sex and gender. In their analysis, the biological base of women's difference from men—primarily focused on their reproductive capabilities—gives rise to a formulation of femininity as innate and inherently superior to masculinity. Jaggar describes the cultural feminist—although her preferred term is "radical feminist"—ethos:

Radical feminist epistemology starts from the belief that women know much of which men are ignorant, and it takes one of its main tasks as being to explain why this should be so. Radical feminist epistemology explores the strategies women have developed for obtaining reliable knowledge and for correcting the distortions of patriarchal ideology. One of the best known of these strategies is the "consciousness-raising" process, a process that is often considered paradigmatic of the feminist method of inquiry. . . . One of the faculties that radical feminism regards as a special source of knowledge for women is the faculty of intuition [and another is] the spiritual power of experiencing a mystical sense of connection or identification with other people.[16]

The revelation of women's experience and intuitive, spiritual connection with each other and the natural world is idealized as the basis of cultural feminist knowledge.

Because they can give birth, women are viewed as instinctually more natural, more closely related to life cycles mirrored in nature.[17] Men are seen as removed from nature, which they denigrate rapaciously. Since women are nurturers, they are seen as instinctively pacifistic. Men, on the other hand, are viewed as instinctually violent and aggressive. Women are spiritual; men have lost touch with their spirit in their all-encompassing drive to conquer and claim.

These equations might seem simplistic—in fact, Echols despairs that "cultural feminists reduce women and men to mere caricatures of themselves"[18]—but this formulation of sexual difference is the bedrock of cultural feminist thought. Echols writes that cultural feminists "discuss gender differences as though they reveal deep truths about the intractability of maleness and femaleness."[19] Since these values are considered innate, the cultural feminist political strategy is not to abolish gender categories, but to change the established gender hierarchy by situating female values as superior.

The notion of a female countercanon, then, is a response to the suppression of women's artistic achievements under millenia of male domination, and an effort to separate out female, or feminine, values from the male standard. Cultural feminist performance critics and practitioners are suspicious of both male forms and contents, since they equate them with male meanings that are alien and oppressive to women. These critics look instead to women's culture for female significations.

Cultural feminist theatre stands as a countertradition to theatre history. In what Rosemary Curb defines as "woman-conscious drama," "the necrophilia of the patriarchy is unmasked, that which confines and paralyzes women in cells of self-loathing leading to self-destruction."[20] The gender dichotomy is strictly adhered to: The death principle in patriarchy is replaced with the life-affirming ritual of cultural feminist theatre.

At the Foot of the Mountain Theatre in Minneapolis is one of the oldest American cultural feminist theatre ensembles. A brochure the company created in 1976 details its ideological and aesthetic stance:

> At the Foot of the Mountain is a women's theatre—emergent, struggling, angry, joyous. . . . We are asking: What is a woman's space? What is a women's ritual? How does it differ from the theatre of the patriarchy? We struggle to relinquish traditions such as linear plays, proscenium theatre, non-participatory ritual and seek to reveal theatre that is circular, intuitive, personal, involving. We are a theatre of protest, witnesses to the destructiveness of a society which is alienated from itself, and a theatre of celebration, participants in the prophesy of a new world which is emerging through the rebirth of women's consciousness.[21]

The statement implies that the replacement of male values with female values will heal society and allow its rebirth in a female form. Through formulating a feminine aesthetic, cultural feminist theatre lends its support to the larger cultural project.

Chapter 5 investigates this issue of a feminine aesthetic based in cultural feminist principles. The importation of *l'écriture féminine* from French pyschoanalytic feminist critics has helped theorize such an inscription of femininity in the representational space. *L'écriture féminine* focuses its debate in language, and proposes that biologically based differences in female sexuality give rise to a form of female textuality that can subvert male signification. Writing with the female body allows for an excessive flow of blood, birth, and sexual metaphors in a nonlinear, florid, stream-of-consciousness style that inscribes sexual difference as the content and form of cultural feminist theatre.

L'écriture féminine's theorization of the stage space harkens to Artaud's theatre of cruelty, which overturns the authority of the text to privilege the body and gesture as the primordial essence. Hélène Cixous' theatrical model suggests that if the "stage is woman," plots will no longer be necessary: "A single gesture is enough, but one that can transform the world. Take for example this movement of women towards life, passed on from one woman to another, this outstretched hand which touches and transmits meaning, a single gesture unfolding throughout the ages, and it is a different Story."[22]

This female-based exchange, however, has insidious implications for spectatorship. Linking women's sexuality to their textuality offers a subject position carved in transcendent universalisms. Ann Jones, in her critique of *l'écriture féminine*'s essentialist tendencies, asks: "If we define female subjectivity through universal biological/libidinal givens, what happens to the project of changing the world in feminist directions? Further, is women's sexuality so monolithic that a notion of a shared, typical femininity does justice to it? What about variations in class, in race, and in culture among women? How can one libidinal voice speak for all women?"[23] In cultural feminist theatre, the imaginary formation of "Woman" becomes the text's point of entry and the female spectator is constituted as the new ideal, generic spectator. But while her sexual difference from men is reified, her differences from other women are largely ignored. The flattening out of lived differences between women compromises the position of this transcendent female spectator. Case, for example, critiques the cultural feminist position as inherently racist and classist:

> With its sole focus on gender, it highlights the conflicts between "women" and men, while obfuscating the critical differences among women produced by class and race. As in the capitalist system, its theatre represents the dominant class, primarily dramatizing the experiences of upper-middle-class white women as if they were the problems of all women. . . . Feminist plays that dramatize racial relations among women and their attending class relations are very difficult to locate. . . . In spite of the increased visibility or vocality of women of color and working class women in the socialist feminist movement, radical feminism has at best moved only slightly away from the homogeneous transcendent female subject to a call for a heterogeneity within its system of representation.[24]

In their formulation of Woman as a transcendent, universal subject position, cultural feminism and *l'écriture féminine* erect a new monolith from which it becomes difficult to diverge. The hegemony of the feminine becomes invidious.

Echols feels that cultural feminism "encourages a dangerously elitist attitude among those who consider themselves 'woman-identified,' "[25] and that accounting for the class, race, and differences in sexual preference among women threatens the predominating notion of a homogeneously defined Woman. All difference, therefore, is framed in terms of sameness defined by women's separation from men.

The mother/daughter relationship becomes paradigmatic of the content of cultural feminist theatre. The female spectator is asked to situate herself as a woman vis-à-vis this relationship, which orders the representation's female meanings. Much of this work embodies what Jones calls a "coercive glorification of motherhood,"[26] which continually refers to the nuclear family system it wants to critique. Rather than deconstructing family-structured gender practices, cultural feminism is content to recuperate the female position as mother or daughter within the family. As we will see in chapter 5, the assumption of sameness among women based on the mother/daughter model is coercive, and marginalizes those women who prefer to cut loose from the continual reference to the family or to formulate their gender in other ways.

Teresa de Lauretis senses a shift away from sexual difference as the overriding principle of American feminism:

> Again I see a shift . . . in the feminist understanding of female subjectivity: a shift from the earlier view of woman defined purely by sexual difference (i.e., in relation to man) to the more difficult and complex notion that the female subject is a site of differences; differences that are not only sexual or only racial, economic, or (sub) cultural, but all of these together, and often enough at odds with one another.[27]

The shift de Lauretis observes moves toward the theory of materialist feminism, which I am demarcating as the third strain of American feminist thought.

I have found the materialist approach outlined below most reasonable and suitable to my own ideological beliefs. But in the discussions of liberal and particularly cultural feminism above and in the chapters that follow, my intent is not to "trash" the work or to imply that it is ranked lower on a political or theoretical hierarchy that elevates materialist feminism to its apex. My delineations of the feminisms have met with some resistance. Kendall, for example, writing for the *Women's Review of Books,* responded to a paper I delivered on the feminisms in theatre at the 1987 Themes in Drama Conference. Describing the three categories I use, she protested, "Clearly, the third is the only one to go for. Yet can it be that there are really only three ways to be a feminist, and two of them ugly?"[28] I hope this chapter and the studies that follow here will stand in response to Kendall's question.

Both liberal and cultural feminism speak to the ideologies of the social formations in the particular historical moment they address. The celebratory tone of cultural feminism is a corrective to female denigration under male domination. The fight for female visibility in a male world has helped liberal feminism open doors into mainstream activity for some women who once jealously peered in through the keyholes. Liberal feminist gains and cultural feminist recoveries of women's vitality cannot be viewed superficially or scorned.

Materialist feminism, however, frames the debate over gender in more gender-neutral terms than either liberal feminism, which would absorb women into the male universal, or cultural feminism, which would overturn the balance of power in favor of female supremacy. Materialist feminism deconstructs the mythic subject Woman to look at women as a class oppressed by material conditions and social relations.

Where cultural feminism sees knowledge as transcendent, ahistorical, and therefore universal, materialist feminism inquires into the flux and material conditions of history. It views women as historical subjects whose relation to prevailing social structures is also influenced by race, class, and sexual identification. Rather than considering gender polarization as the victimization of only women, materialist feminism considers it a social construct oppressive to both women and men.

In materialist discourse, gender is not innate. Rather, it is dictated through enculturation, as gender divisions are placed at the service of the dominant culture's ideology. Rubin clarifies the materialist position on gender: "A woman is a woman. She only becomes a domestic, a wife, a chattel, a playboy bunny, a prostitute, or a human dictaphone in certain relations. Torn from these relationships, she is no more the helpmate of man than gold in itself is money."[29]

Here, gender becomes a construct formed to support the structure of the dominant culture. Gender is a socially imposed division of the sexes, an arrangement of relationships that also prescribes sexuality. As another social construct, sexuality is also an expression of gender relationships within a power dynamic. The social relations of sexuality demand compulsory heterosexuality and the constraint of active female sexuality.[30] Rubin emphasizes that through a system of social relations, females are fashioned into genderized products that are exchanged on a political economy that benefits men. Far from reifying sexual difference, materialist feminism works to understand how women have been oppressed by gender categories. It attempts to denaturalize the dominant ideology that demands and maintains such oppressive social arrangements.

One of the tools of materialist feminist criticism is a systematic dismantling of the assumptions that underlie psychoanalysis. Rubin, for example, views Freudian and Lacanian psychoanalysis as theories that structure gender encultu-ration, mechanisms for the reproduction of sexual arrangements that teach gender conditioning and enforce sexual convention.[31]

Freudian psychoanalysis, for instance, insists that a girl child must learn several things to properly assume her feminine role. She must give up clitoral masturbation and channel her sexuality toward vaginal passivity, and she must reorient her sexuality away from her mother toward her father. Since the mother is the girl's first primary love object, Rubin, among others, observes that Freudian psychoanalysis must accomplish some imaginative theoretical leaps to explain the girl's progress toward heterosexuality within his paradigm.[32]

The penis envy that Freud believes motivates the girl's reorientation is, in Rubin's opinion, situational. Within the logic of heterosexual coupling that structures the family system and through which the girl assumes her feminine role, the little girl realizes she is genitally ill-equipped to satisfy her mother sexually. Penis envy is not innate, Rubin argues, but conferred situationally. The parents' heterosexuality produces the idea of the little girl's genital inferiority.[33]

When the little boy recognizes his mother's sexual lack, his fear that he will be similarly castrated encourages him to give up his sexual love for the mother and to ally himself with the father. His pleasure, however, is simply deferred. Someday, another woman will replace his mother as love object. Little girls, on the other hand, must give up all women and find fulfillment in the feminine role bestowed by male authority. Eventually, the girl's own mother-hood will provide her with a baby, a penis substitute theoretically provided by the father that begins the process over again. It is through mothering, Freud argues, that a woman achieves self-fulfillment. In Lacanian terms, mothering is the erasure of her lack.

Rubin and other theorists describe Lacanian psychoanalysis as an articulation of this Oedipal crisis in terms of language and cultural meanings.[34] The penis becomes the phallus in Lacanian theory—the organ comes to represent cultural information. The pre-Oedipal realm is Lacan's Imaginary, where the child exists before language acquisition in sensual unity with his mother. The recognition that the mother lacks the phallus persuades the child to ally himself with the father and accede to his rightful place in the phallologocentric order. The mirror stage is Lacan's term for this scene of sexual differentiation, the entry into a polarized gender structure, and into an articulation of subjectivity within language.

Phallologocentricism organizes phallic authority in language, and the phallus becomes the symbolic object of exchange in a family and social system that denies women agency. The phallus passes through women and settles upon men: "The phallus is more than a feature which distinguishes the sexes: it is the embodiment of the male status, to which men accede, and in which certain rights adhere—among them, the right to a woman. It is an expression of the transmission of male dominance. . . . The tracks which it leaves include gender identity, the division of the sexes."[35] The circulation of the phallus as meaning sketches a structure for language in which women are clearly outside of discourse. The phallus is exchanged between men.

Rubin also submits that women are exchanged between men in a political economy in which they have use-value.[36] Rubin deconstructs Levi-Strauss' studies on kinship systems to reveal the theory of women's oppression he tacitly constructs. Tracing the meanings of the incest taboo and gift exchange that constitutes women as social currency in a practice of male bonding, Rubin finds once again that women have no agency in an exchange in which they are objects, not subjects:

> If it is women who are being transacted, then it is the men who give and take them who are linked, the woman being a conduit of a relationship rather than a partner to it. . . . If women are the gifts, then it is men who are the exchange partners. And it is the partners, not the presents, upon whom reciprocal exchange confers its quasi-mystical power of social exchange. The relations of such a system are such that women are in no position to realize the benefits of their own circulation. As long as the relations specify that men exchange women, it is men who are the beneficiaries of the product of such exchanges—social organization.[37]

This paradigm becomes crucial to an understanding of materialist and psychoanalytic feminist readings of traditional representational strategies. The implications of subject-formation in representational processes are fully developed vis-à-vis Richard Foreman's work in chapter 3.

As many feminist film theorists have shown, it is the exchange of women between men—buttressed by psychoanalytic processes that reify gender positioning—that works to deliver gender enculturated meanings through representation. Although these theories have been worked out most fully in feminist film criticism, they have distinct and important applications for materialist feminist performance criticism developed in the chapters below.

In 1975, Laura Mulvey set the precedent for a psychoanalytic study of representational strategies. She proposes a way of looking at the classical cinema as a representation whose apparatus encodes ideologically gender-marked meanings by controlling the relationship between image and spectator. Using both Freudian and Lacanian psychoanalytic theory as a framework, she suggests that the cinematic apparatus mimics the identification processes that inform the male child's progress away from the mother toward the father and into the male realm of language.[38] Through scopophilia (pleasure derived from looking), voyeurism, and fetishism, the male spectator is able to identify with the film's active male protagonist and simultaneously disarm the threat posed by the image of the "castrated" female body.

Mulvey writes that the series of "looks" built into the structure of film—the pro-filmic look exchanged between the actors, the camera's gaze at the actor, and the projected, carefully constructed look assigned to the spectator—position the male spectator as a subject who is invited to identify with the film's male protagonist as the ego-ideal he saw in the mirror phase. Mulvey goes on to suggest the possibility that visual pleasure must be eradicated in order to inscribe women in representation. The implications of this position and its resonances with the theoretical stances of Richard Foreman and Bertolt Brecht are developed in chapters 3 and 6, respectively.

Other film theorists, such as Teresa de Lauretis, E. Ann Kaplan, and Mary Ann Doane, suggest that by objectifying the woman in the narrative as the passive object of his own active desire, the hero/spectator reenacts the realization of his mother's sexual lack and proceeds into the Symbolic register of language. The woman is left behind in the Imaginary, as a negative value expressed only by her lack. In Lacanian analysis, and its apt application to representational processes, women are given no opportunity to achieve subjectivity, because they are merely defined as "other" than the male referent.[39]

The male spectator's identification with the protagonist allows him a point of entry into the film's address, and allows the representation to replicate the process of sexual differentiation in the meanings it delivers. The male spectator's position is the point from which the text is most intelligible; the representation constructs the ideal (gendered) spectator at the point of its address.[40]

If, as de Lauretis argues, male desire drives all narrative and objectifies women, the female spectator is placed in an untenable relationship to representation.[41] If she identifies with the narrative's objectified, passive woman, she places herself in a masochistic position. If she identifies with the male hero, she becomes complicit in her own indirect objectification. If, as Doane argues, she admires the represented female body as a consumable object, she participates in her own commodification.[42] Within the conventions of filmic pleasure, these are the only positions available for the female spectator to assume.

The representation of woman is exchanged between the men in the narrative, and between the male hero and the male spectator. Women have use-value in the representational space, as they are the conduit through which the phallus passes. Women as spectators are not, however, considered as subjects by the classical film's address. The woman spectator finds herself, once again, the site of the conduit for an identificatory relationship between men, a gift in a male exchange that does not benefit her at all.

Some feminists argue that this psychoanalytic critical model tends to formulate transcendent subject positions. But its investigation of the genderized nature of the gaze in representation can be usefully applied to theatre and performance, while avoiding the pitfalls of universalism. The gaze in performance, although not as carefully controlled as in film, is also based in a narrative paradigm that presents gender and sexuality as a factor in the exchange of meanings between performers and spectators.

If Rubin's view of psychoanalysis as a theory of gender enculturation is maintained, it becomes clear that the implications of representation's complicity with psychoanalytic processes must be deconstructed as part of the solution to the crisis of women's place in representation. Part of the materialist critical project is to denaturalize the psychological identification processes implicit in representation. When the representational apparatus is foregrounded, its once mystified ideology becomes clear.

Here, the materialist critique has much to gain from the precedent of Brechtian theory, a connection which is discussed in detail in chapter 6. By denaturalizing the illusionist forms of traditional theatre, the smooth operation of psychoanalytical processes is thwarted. Rather than being seduced by the narrative that offers a comfortable gender position, the spectator is asked to pay critical attention to the gender ideology the representational process historically produces and the oppressive social relations it legitimizes.

Brecht's epic theatre is based in a Marxian analysis that meant to demystify the dominant ideology masked by conventional theatre. His alienation effect, his theory of the social *gestus,* and his description of an acting technique that asks a performer to quote, rather than psychologically become, a character, are formulated to provoke a political critique that will lead to a profitable change in class-based social relations.

Diverging from Brecht's theory, materialist feminist performance criticism is not strictly Marxian, as it focuses its analysis on material conditions of gender positioning, rather than privileging economic determinism. Some borrowing of Marxian terms, however, is apparent in materialist definitions of ideology that structure the critique of representation. Cultural production is viewed as a framework for the imposition of ideology, a framework which can be dissected and exposed as complicit in the formation of systems of social relations.

Michelle Barrett, for example, defines the intersection of ideology and representation:

Ideology is a generic term for the processes by which meaning is produced, challenged, reproduced, transformed. Since meaning is negotiated primarily through means of communication and signification, it is possible to suggest that cultural production provides an important site for the construction of ideological processes. . . . [L]iterature [read "theatre"] (for instance) can be usefully analysed as a paradigmatic case of ideology in particular social formations.[43]

Barrett's definition of cultural production—or representation—as producing ideology within a given social formation at a particular historical moment will inform the discussions of performance and criticism in the chapters below.

Materialist feminist criticism emphasizes the ideological nature of all cultural products. Dominant ideology has been naturalized as nonideology, since the perceptions of the more powerful have come to serve as standards for the less powerful, who do not have the same access to the media and artistic outlets that create public opinion. Lillian Robinson, working out the basic Marxist tenet of the relationship between base and superstructure, argues that through cultural production the ideas of the ruling class come to be considered normative for the culture at large. Less powerful people are subjected to social structures that benefit the interests of the more powerful.[44]

People of color, for instance, who do not have equal access to cultural production, are subject to dominant ideology as it appears in representation. Case introduces the "Theatre of Color" issue of *Theatre Journal* with a statement that illustrates this problem:

This special issue on "Theatre of Color" suggests that the regular fare of theatre production, academic study, and journals such as this one is "colorless theatre." The construction of the canon of plays, history, and theory rests upon the premise that the color of one's skin is not a constituent element in the mode of cultural production. What this really means is that the majority of our theatrical production, historical research, and critical attention is dedicated to white theatre.[45]

The same statement could be equally applied to an investigation of gender, class, and sexual identification which, along with race, are indeed constituent elements of cultural production.

Ideology is implicit in perception, and therefore in any critical or creative act—analysis, description, or interpretation. The study of Richard Foreman's work vis-à-vis ideology that forms the basis of chapter 3 reveals that the ideology of gender polarization continues to structure Foreman's work, even though he claims that his aesthetic breaks with the psychological pleasure of bourgeois theatre and is anti-ideological.

Foreman's work is typical of much of the postmodernist contemporary avant-garde. Although it deals in a rejection of traditional forms, it tends to abdicate responsibility for perpetuating or attacking dominant ideology. The intersection of materialist feminist criticism and postmodernism emphasizes that forms cannot be productively changed without an attendant change in ideology. Deconstructing the performance apparatus in postmodernist terms is not politically progressive unless the gender assumptions that underlie representation are also denaturalized and changed.[46]

The mystification of ideological processes that work to form cultural meanings make the feminist critical project one of careful excavation. Materialist feminists Judith Newton and Deborah Rosenfelt caution:

> Ideology . . . is not a set of deliberate distortions imposed on us from above, but a complex and contradictory system of representations (discourse, images, myths) through which we experience ourselves in relation to each other and to the social structures in which we live. Ideology is a system of representations through which we experience *ourselves* as well, for the work of ideology is to construct coherent subjects.[47]

Feminist theory suggests that representation offers or denies subjectivity by manipulating the terms of its discourse, images, and myths through ideology. As a system of representation, ideology is related to social structures not as a simple mimetic reflection, but as a force that participates in creating and maintaining social arrangements.

Neither is representation simple mimesis, to reverse the equation. The theatre, that is to say, is not really a mirror of reality. A mirror implies passivity and noninvolvement, an object used but never changed by the variety of people who hold it up and look into it. The theatre has in fact been much more active as an ideological force. Rozsika Parker and Griselda Pollock concur: "Art is not a mirror. It mediates and re-presents social relations in a schema of signs which require a receptive and preconditioned reader in order to be meaningful."[48]

Barrett, too, insists that representation is not simply a mimetic space, but one within which ideology is bounded as meaning:

> It is neither plausible nor possible to study literature [read "theatre"] for the purpose of berating morally reprehensible authors. Nor is it possible to take literary texts, or any other cultural products, as necessary reflections of the social reality of any particular period. . . . What they can offer, I suggest, is an indication of the bounds within which particular meanings are constructed and negotiated in a given social formation.[49]

Materialist feminism focuses on the construction of ideology in social formations influenced by gender, race, class, and categories of sexual preference. It views the power base in these relationships dialectically, as capable of change.

If power is a term that can be wielded fruitfully by women, as it sometimes is in materialist analysis, the passive, objectified nature of women as performers and spectators might be fundamentally changed. Chapter 4 looks at just such a possibility for change by proposing an alternative to narrative structured by male desire. This study recuperates the lesbian position from its desexualized stance in cultural feminism to suggest that if lesbian sexual desire motivates narrative, the lesbian spectator may be able to find a subject position vis-à-vis lesbian representation. The lesbian model of alternative spectatorship might hold clues to developing a more tenable position for feminist spectators of any ideological persuasion.

Toward Materialist Feminist Performance Criticism

A final note about criticism. This study is meant to outline cogent feminist critical approaches to all kinds of performance. It stresses the ideological nature of representation, and the necessity for alternative criticism provided by the feminisms to unmask the naturalized ideology of the dominant culture most theatre and performance represents. Terry Eagleton, in his monograph on the function of criticism, proposes that "criticism was only ever significant when it engaged with more than literary issues—when, for whatever historical reason, the 'literary' was suddenly foregrounded as the medium of vital concerns deeply rooted in the general intellectual, cultural, and political life of an epoch."[50] The bestowal of value judgments about aesthetic quality is at best a subsidiary issue here. As Barrett states concisely, "Preoccupation with the question of value ('quality,' 'standards') has been detrimental for feminist criticism. . . . This debate is fruitless . . . in that it reproduces the assumption that aesthetic judgement is independent of social and historical context."[51]

My point here is not to distinguish "good" theatre and performance from "bad," according to some prescriptive, transcendent, liberal, cultural, or materialist feminist aesthetic standard. Rather, my point is to conduct a feminist inquiry into representation as a form of cultural analysis. There is perhaps a moral imperative here; I admit that I think it is "bad" that so much of representation denies women subjectivity, and I do not think it is "good" that dominant cultural ideology relegates women to subservient roles. Robinson tells an anecdote that addresses the question of value judgments and ideology that is relevant here:

> Sartre once asked whether it would be possible to write a "good" anti-Semitic novel in the wake of Nazi genocide. I imagine we would all counter by asking, 'What do you mean 'good'?" A radical kind of textual criticism might well be able to answer that question. It could usefully study the way the texture of sentences, choice of metaphors, patterns of exposition and narrative relate to ideology.[52]

Likewise, my effort here is to ask questions about method. How does a given performance—the dialogue, choice of setting, narrative voice, form, content, casting, acting, blocking—deliver its ideological message? How does it convey its assumptions about its relation to social structures? My intent is to uncover ideological meanings that otherwise go unnoticed and continue to perpetuate cultural assumptions that are oppressive to women and other disenfranchized social groups.

The following chapters deconstruct the privileged position of the ideal white, middle-class, heterosexual male spectator from a feminist perspective. By displacing his hegemonic position and stealing his seat, as it were, for a feminist spectator who can cast an eye critical of dominant ideology, representation can be analysed more precisely for the meanings it produces and how those meanings can be changed. The intent, by extension, is to affect a larger cultural change in the ideological and material condition of women and men.

2

Feminism and the Canon:
The Question of Universality

The insistent work of liberal feminists to make visible the once-hidden talent of women in theatre has been primarily responsible for the growing number of women playwrights working in the professional arena. But the mainstream critical response to plays written by women continues to reveal deep-seated gender biases. By creating a different "horizon of expectations,"[1] these biases inform how male critics writing for influential daily newspapers or monthly magazines receive a play written by a woman, especially one that dramatizes concerns traditionally associated with women. Most mainstream critics are powerful enough to influence a production's success or failure in a given venue, and their response molds and to a certain extent predetermines the response of potential spectators for the play reviewed. Because it is such an important factor in the collective audience's interpretation of a play's meaning, mainstream criticism both shapes and reflects the ideological workings of the dominant culture whose concerns it represents.

The production history of Marsha Norman's *'night, Mother* is an excellent case study of the gender-biased politics of reception, since it is one of the first plays written by a woman and addressing women's concerns to gain widespread attention, critical acclaim, and economic success. When *'night, Mother* opened on Broadway in 1983, it provoked a media response polarized around gender differences.

On one hand, powerful male New York critics such as Frank Rich and Mel Gussow, writing for the *New York Times,* struggled to reconcile Norman's gender—and her female characters—with their desire to inscribe the play into the predominantly male canon of good American drama. On the other hand, the feminist press was split between claiming—or disclaiming—Norman as the vanguard of their own separate canon, and applauding her elevation into the dominant male realm.

Canon-formation and deconstruction is an issue currently debated in literary criticism as a result of the wider consideration of marginalized texts prompted by women's and black studies. The terms of the debate are governed by traditional critics—who jealously guard the historical canon as a necessary standard with which to compare any succeeding drama or literature—and by revisionist critics, who see the traditional canon and the literary history it enshrines as a project of a class of privileged, powerful, mostly white male subjects whose ideology it represents.[2]

Some feminist critics suggest that the inclusion of women's writing in the traditional canon is problematical, since female systems of signification are unavailable to men, who cannot read their signs and therefore dismiss their meanings.[3] Sue-Ellen Case takes a less biological than historical approach to the problem of women's place in the dramatic canon, using the example of Hrotsvit von Gandersheim. Case argues that the patriarchal biases of the cultural authorities caused them to deny a place in the canon for Hrotsvit as the first female playwright. By failing to allow her to set the precedent that canons intrinsically deem necessary, these cultural authorities left no standard of comparison within the canon for future women playwrights.

"The seemingly dramatic standards which select the playwrights in the canon are actually the same patriarchal biases which organize the economy and social organization of the culture at large," Case writes.[4] She adds that "exclusion from the canon of the greats suggests a failure on the part of the playwright to produce a dramatic experience which has important historical resonances."[5] The history of cultural authority and its charter to set transcendent literary and dramatic standards remains unimpugned by Hrotsvit's absence from the canon. Instead, the individual playwright is blamed for her inability to meet its criteria.

As the following analysis suggests, Marsha Norman took great pains to avoid Hrotsvit's alleged mistakes. Two questions are included within the parameters of my debate: If Marsha Norman's play is allowed into the traditional canon, will it establish a precedent for women playwrights to follow? Or, is *'night, Mother* read as a contender for membership in the canon because it so closely follows the male precedent the canon has already set?

The traditional dramatic canon that *'night, Mother* was measured against has certain explicit rules. First, a play must conform to the rule of universality by transcending the historical moment and speaking to a generic spectator. Also, as Janet Staiger, writing about canon-formation in cinema studies, points out, canons are formed to reinforce and reproduce "a hegemonic culture and economic structure."[6] For *'night, Mother* to be inserted into the canon, it should not substantially threaten the canon's dramatic or ideological values. And, to support the canon's economic imperatives in the context of late capitalism and twentieth-century Broadway play production, it also had to generate institutional recognition that would make it viable as a profitmaking product.

After *'night, Mother* received the 1983 Pulitzer Prize for drama, it became a profitable success on Broadway, meeting the canon's requirements for institutional and economic recognition. But some New York critics, such as Howard Kissel at *Women's Wear Daily,* remained ambivalent about Norman and the canonization of her play. Their hesitations turned on the issue of universality. Since women's concerns are not seen as generic to theatre, in which the active dramatic agents and the spectators to whom they play have historically been men, some critics doubted that the play qualified for the canon. Others insisted that its strict adherence to Aristotelian principles made it imminently eligible.

In feminist circles, *'night, Mother*'s canonization as prototypical good American drama or as the vanguard of the new feminist drama was seriously debated. Since one of the aims of feminist literary and dramatic criticism is to deconstruct the male canon and its underlying ideology, including a woman's text in the dominant canon is a complicated gesture. A popular alternative for some feminists is to construct a countercanon with feminist criteria for inclusion. The female version of the canon often rescues obscured women from literary or theatrical history, and replaces the generic male reader/spectator with a generic female. The universal qualities sought are those that might explain or describe what are considered prototypical female experiences.

But the female canon has its own ideological, critical, and aesthetic standards, however "playfully pluralistic."[7] While liberal feminists celebrated Norman's success in the dominant culture, and some cultural feminists wanted to canonize *'night, Mother* in a new, feminist "best of" list, many materialist feminists argued that any canon is by definition exclusionary, since it perpetuates only a particular ideological view. A materialist feminist perspective points out that both the dominant cultural and feminist dramatic canons tend to universalize and idealize subject positions.

The question to pose with regard to *'night, Mother*'s placement in any canon is how Norman's gender switch away from the theatre's usual male axis of categorization informed mainstream and feminist critical response. The canon-formation issue is crucial to this investigation because Norman's play was not presented as "women's theatre" in a 100-seat house in the West Village. The play moved through the proscribed hierarchy of regional theatre readings, workshops, and productions that culminate with a Broadway production. Broadway is the context from which plays become literature to canonize. The radical element of Norman's play was not that it was written by a woman about a mother/daughter relationship, but that it was performed in a space historically reserved for male playwrights to address father/son relationships.

A chronology of events in the play's production history will prove helpful to contextualize the assessment that will follow. *'night, Mother* was first produced at the American Repertory Theatre (ART) in Cambridge, Massachusetts, in December 1982. Robert Brustein, artistic director of ART and generally considered the "dean" of American theatre critics, was enthusiastic about the script and agreed to produce the play. After a successful and critically acclaimed run in Cambridge, the Broadway production opened March 31, 1983, to widely favorable reviews. Norman won the 1983 Pulitzer Prize for drama for *'night, Mother* on April 19, 1983. After 388 performances on Broadway (over a year's run), *'night, Mother* opened at the Cheryl Crawford Theatre of the Westside Arts Center, also in New York City, where it closed after 54 performances.

Certain features of this chronology are significant to the play's reception. Brustein's favorable disposition to Norman's work ensured its production at ART, where it was promoted as "an authentically American play but with the stark inevitability of Greek tragedy."[8] Even prior to its Broadway run, Brustein began *'night, Mother*'s comparison to the canon's Aristotelian criteria by emphasizing its adherence to the unities of time, space, and action. Under Brustein's leadership, the ART has become one of the most respected regional theatres in the country. *'night, Mother*'s success in Cambridge, with Brustein's blessing, brought the play to Broadway advertised primarily on the strength of good reviews from the ART production.[9]

After Norman won the Pulitzer Prize, the press documents the effect of the national attention the honor conferred.[10] *Variety* exclaimed, "What a difference a Pulitzer makes."[11] The reporter noted that *'night, Mother* had doubled its $5,000-per-day box office income and that advance sales were starting to build. The Pulitzer award had a favorable impact on the public's perception of the play and influenced spectators' expectations by validating and legitimizing the production.

Author's Intent

The unusual institutional approbation awarded Norman's play, in light of the historical lack of notice for women playwrights, makes it interesting to investigate from a feminist point of view the meanings Norman intended her work to communicate to spectators. While author's intent is a somewhat taboo factor in reception theory, which emphasizes the individualized exchange between culturally constituted readers and shifting texts, Norman's intentions with *'night, Mother* are somewhat illuminating. Norman did have a specific plan for the reception of her play. But her collaborators, in the process of reading and reconstructing her text as their production, imposed their own meanings. They created a performance text that diverged from the written text, and these new meanings ultimately influenced critics' and spectators' responses.

The dramaturgical process currently at work in American theatre impinges a priori on the issue of authorship. Since theatre is a collaborative art, the playwright's text is a schematic outline for other production elements. Often, the original script is cut, characters are changed or deleted, and dialogue is rewritten based on what the cast and director find will or will not "play." As

Elizabeth Wray writes in *Performing Arts Journal,* the playwright is "assigned a front row seat for watching layers of aesthetic preconceptions applied to her play by her director, designers, and producer. All too often, the finished product has little to do with her initial vision. She discovers too late that she has compromised her play away."[12] The performance text presented each evening is an amalgamation of the director's, actors', and designers' interpretations of the playwright's text.

Play publishing houses usually option scripts after their initial productions have received enough attention to be appealing to regional or community theatre groups. The acting script published and sold to other producing organizations when they request rights to the play solidifies performance decisions incorporated up to the Broadway production. Indicated stage directions range from movements ("Stands up, moves toward the phone") to qualities of vocal delivery ("Almost a whisper") that are a faithful record of the Broadway presentation, which as a result becomes the standard which all subsequent productions of the play will be modeled after, deviate from, or be compared to.

In addition to the expectations generated by critical response to previous productions, the spectator's reading of the performance text has been influenced before she or he arrives at the theatre by the producers' marketing and advertising strategies, by published reviews, and by her or his own ideological perceptions and cultural heritage. These combined expectations and spectators' subsequent individualized readings of the play can work to obscure the playwright's original intent.

Yet as the hoary question of authorship resurfaces, Marsha Norman is considered responsible for the entire presentation of the play *'night, Mother.* She, not director Tom Moore, receives the Pulitzer Prize and the press coverage. As Norman says wryly, "Most [critics] can't tell the difference between the play and the production. They don't understand that the director is the author of the production. It is a myth that playwrights have total control. . . . Of course, ultimately you end up taking *full* responsibility for the production."[13] This process of altering an author's text through a collaborative process, then attributing the final product to the playwright as "her" text, becomes significant to the play's reception.

Although Hill and Wang published an edition of the play, the acting version distributed by Dramatists Play Service, Inc., is more important to consult for guidelines to how the play is to be presented and received. The text sold for production includes a property plot and list, a costume plot, and a scene design rendering that are not included in Hill and Wang's version. The detail of these lists is intended to carefully control the play's presentation and thereby affect its reception.

'night, Mother is a one-act, two-character play. Jessie Cates, a woman in her late thirties or early forties, tells her mother, Thelma, that she intends to

commit suicide and proceeds to carry out her promise. Jessie insists she is telling Thelma in advance simply so the older woman will be prepared when it happens. Although Jessie wants her last evening with her mother to be calm and uneventful, a mirror image of all their evenings together, the night becomes a probing exploration into the reasons for Jessie's choice.

Jessie has been caring for Thelma and intends to relinquish her household duties in proper form. As Jessie delivers her instructions, it becomes clear that her life with her mother is routine and mundane, and probably will not change significantly until they die. Their conversation also reveals that under the domestic veneer lies a "problem" of the sort that propels many American family dramas. In Norman's published text, epilepsy is blamed as the prime motivating factor for Jessie's ruined life—her failed marriage, her delinquent son, her inability to hold a job, and ultimately, her decision to commit suicide.

This is a simple outline of Norman's plot devices, onto which she layers carefully constructed character portraits. Norman's notes on the characters are significant in light of critics' response to *'night, Mother*. Jessie is "pale and vaguely unsteady, physically. It is only in the last year that Jessie has gained control of her mind and body, and tonight, she is determined to hold onto that control."[14] Norman goes on to describe aspects of Jessie's personality, but gives no further information about Jessie's appearance. Norman continues: "Thelma is Jessie's mother, in her late fifties or early sixties. She has begun to feel her age, and so takes it easy when she can . . . she speaks quickly and enjoys talking. . . . Her sturdiness is more a mental quality than a physical one, finally. She is chatty and nosy and this is *her* house" (p. 5, italics in original).

Throughout the text, Norman assigns wry observations to Thelma. Her perspective is characteristically one of resignation, but she sees her condition as universally human, rather than personal. "Things happen," Thelma says. "You do what you can about them and you see what happens next" (p. 39). Jessie, on the other hand, is unremittingly personal. Her justification for suicide is "I'm just not having a very good time and I don't have any reason to think it'll get anything but worse" (p. 7).

At the Actors Theatre of Louisville, Norman had worked previously with both Anne Pitoniak, who would play Thelma, and Kathy Bates, who would play Jessie. In fact, while she was writing the play, Norman invited Pitoniak and Bates to her Manhattan apartment to read an unfinished version. In some sense, the play's casting must have influenced even the initial construction of Norman's script.

Although the actresses expected to be replaced by well-known performers when the play moved from ART to Broadway, both were retained. According to media interviews, Norman exerted a great deal of effort to ensure that less well-known performers would play the roles, so that spectators would not be distracted from her play's meaning by their expectations and knowledge of more familiar performers.[15]

Once the play hit the regional theatre circuit, however, the policy of casting unknown performers was for the most part discarded. Thelma, as opposed to Jessie, is generally cast with a star performer. For instance, Mercedes McCambridge played the role at the Arkansas Rep, and Sylvia Sidney played it at the Pittsburgh Public Theatre. Star-casting, as Norman feared, could substantially alter the play's reception.

In the acting edition of *'night, Mother,* Norman sets out very particular instructions about the play's presentation in the author's note that preceeds the script:

> The time is the present, with the action beginning about 8:15. Clocks onstage in the kitchen and on a table in the living room should run throughout the performance and be visible to the audience. There will be no intermission. The play takes place in a relatively new house built way out on a country road. . . . [U]nder no circumstances should the set and its dressing make a judgement about the intelligence or taste of Jessie and Thelma. It should simply indicate that they are very specific real people who happen to live in a particular part of the country. Heavy accents, which would further distance the audience from Jessie and Thelma are also wrong. (pp. 6–7)

Norman wants to avoid provoking a condescending response to Jessie and Thelma, although her desire that the set not comment on the women's intelligence or taste seems to anticipate such a response. She is misguided in thinking that the set for her play—or its entire presentation—can be detached from ideological readings, but her aim was the kind of transcendent universality that would seem to obscure these readings. Norman intends to keep audience identification primary by deleting any sense of regionalism. A note at the end of the property plot in the acting edition corroborates her approach: "All food, cleaning supply, refrigerator, and candy props should be national brands which do not indicate any specific area in the country" (p. 62).

Norman was striving for a reception of her play that would validate its aim toward universal meanings and transcendence, and that would inch it toward acceptance into the male realm of historically lasting drama. The Pulitzer Prize was not enough to secure this fate for her play. Beth Henley, with whom Norman was linked for a time in popular press reviews, won the Pulitzer Prize in 1981 for her comedy *Crimes of the Heart.* Henley, at 29 years of age, was the first woman to win the Pulitzer for drama in 23 years. The difference between *'night, Mother'*s reach for qualification as tragedy and *Crimes'* categorization as comedy helps to explain why critics grappled with canonizing Norman's play, and not Henley's.

Crimes of the Heart was generally received as a regional play—it was flavored with Southern dialect, ambiance, and eccentricities, and was not reviewed as making a universal statement. *Crimes* was a comedy people could laugh at (i.e., distance themselves from). Comedy usually resolves its problems in a conventional manner such as the reinscription of its protagonists and antagonists in the culturally sanctioned order of society or family.

The comparison between the two plays is worth noting, however, because of the similar circumstances of their productions and the similarity of the themes they address, albeit in different styles. Suicide, for example, is a recurring theme in *Crimes of the Heart*. The MaGrath sisters' mother has killed herself, and when Babe feels desperate over her dilemma, she, too, attempts first to hang herself then to gas herself in the family oven. But where Norman paints Jessie's suicide as an acceptable response to a pointless life, Henley gives her situations a comic turn that points out the absurdity of the whole enterprise. Mrs. MaGrath has hung not only herself, but the family cat as well; Babe can't find a rope strong enough to break her neck, and she bangs her head on an oven rack when she attempts to kill herself with gas. Meg MaGrath pulls Babe away from the oven and exclaims, "We've just got to learn how to get through these real bad days here. I mean, it's getting to be a thing in our family."[16]

Norman makes suicide a tragic act of heroism, but Henley discounts it as neither heroic nor an appropriate response to depression or anxiety. Norman's play presents the family as an inadequate life-supporting mechanism; Henley offers the reintegration of the MaGrath family as her play's happy ending. In both plays, the families are women-centered, yet for various reasons one can argue whether or not either play is definitively feminist. Neither *'night, Mother* nor *Crimes of the Heart*, however, was meant to be received as a feminist alternative to mainstream drama.

Both *'night, Mother* and *Crimes of the Heart* were released as films in 1986. *'night, Mother* was promoted on the strength of the play's notices three years before, although Sissy Spacek as Jessie and Anne Bancroft as Thelma were featured prominently in the advertisements. *Crimes'* advertisements ran a tag line that played up its absurdist comedy and featured a family-like portrait of the star performers Diane Keaton, Jessica Lange, and Sissy Spacek. No mention was made of its history as a play. *'night, Mother* failed at film box offices, while *Crimes* was very successful, gaining two Academy Award nominations.

Advertising good literature, it seems, does not necessarily guarantee economic success. Almost as Norman intended, her play and her film were contextualized as "art," and both had to struggle for the laurels that confer success within that realm. Although it dealt with similar issues, *Crimes of the Heart*, as a comedy, was always clear about its value as entertainment, and both the play and the film were highly successful in those terms.

Kitchen Drama versus Domestic Drama: The Mainstream Critical Response

Once '*night, Mother* was in production, press documentation makes it obvious that Norman's collaborators began to contradict her stated intent toward universal meanings, particularly with regard to the characters. For instance, despite Norman's insistence that the set not comment on the characters' intelligence or taste, designer Heidi Landesman had a very particular response to Thelma and Jessie, which she chose—appropriately enough—to reflect in her set for the Broadway production. Landesman explains how other theatre groups might design the play:

> The environment has to be unbelievably depressing, but in such a way that the audience sees it, but Thelma and Jessie don't. . . . Also, it should only become depressing over time to people watching it. . . . [I tinted the set with] "yucko" colors with nothing bright to relieve the eye. . . . The other trick was to show how kitschy and bad their taste was, and how poor their cultural environment was, without making it comic. I used lots of trashy pieces, but all of them were very familiar, things you might find in Woolworth's. . . . And nothing popped out as being overwhelmingly hideous.[17]

Landesman's choices were clearly at odds with Norman's intent and would eventually affect the critical response to '*night, Mother*.

Although New York critics are notorious for overlooking design achievements, most of the reviewers at least mentioned Landesman's set, a production element that differed substantially from Norman's conception of the play. *Variety* said, "The lower-middle-class living room and kitchen are Polaroid accurate."[18] Norman's script never mentions the Cates' class status. If anything, given her aim at universality, Norman would probably prefer a general middle-class ambiance.

Howard Kissel, in *Women's Wear Daily*, came closest to characterizing Norman's intended nondescription by calling the set one of those "characterless boxes carved out by giant cookie cutters after WWII." John Beaufort, in the *Christian Science Monitor*, gave the set the "Good Housekeeping Seal of Approval," an implicitly condescending reference to what are traditionally considered women's values.[19]

Each of these publications, of course, is geared toward the interests and ideology of its particular constituency and, as a result, takes a somewhat different perspective on the productions it reviews. *Variety* is the mouthpiece of the entertainment industry; *Women's Wear Daily* is centered in the garment industry; The *Christian Science Monitor*'s ideology is explicitly clarified through its denominational affiliation. The *New York Times* remains the arbiter of sophisticated, cultured, monied tastes and values.

Frank Rich, in the *New York Times*, tried to place Norman in the context of American values that would help stake a claim for the play's transcendent appeal. In an article about the visual arts' influence on set design, Rich noted the stylistic similarities to painter Edward Hopper in *'night, Mother*'s set design.[20] Landesman created a false proscenium arch with black borders that narrowed the stage opening and somewhat forced the spectator's perspective into the living room/kitchen set. Rich wrote that the set is "framed in black to give us Hopper's perspective of looking through a window at night."[21]

Rich also pointed out that both the publicity poster and the *Playbill* cover used for *'night, Mother*'s program borrow from Hopper's *Solitude*. The painting is of a long country road, drawn in perspective, with a solitary house among trees along its side. *'night, Mother*'s *Playbill* cover is a photograph shot from the same perspective as the painting: a country road surrounded by trees, which partially hide a bungalow-style house. The perspective's vanishing point sends the viewer's eye through the trees to a bright spot on the horizon where the sun, it appears, would be setting. The scene is domestic, but also lonely: The *Playbill* cover evokes a feeling of suburban isolation similar to Hopper's solitary, rural scene. This allusion to a key figure in American art helped Rich to contextualize *'night, Mother* as serious, transcendent drama.

Within this domestic scene, the male reviewers' responses to Jessie and Thelma are significant in relation to their ambivalence about the gender subtext and their comparison of the play to canonical standards. Thelma Cates is variously called the "fuddled mother," "scatterbrained but decent," "not too bright," a "fussy, silly woman with a frumpy wardrobe and an insatiable sweet tooth," and a "lonely flibbertigibbet of a vacant mother."[22] Robert Asahina, in the quarterly literary journal *The Hudson Review,* wrote sarcastically and condescendingly, "Thelma is not so quietly deranged . . . prattling on inanely about hot chocolate, knitting, television and a host of lowbrow concerns with which Norman has burdened her in order to let the audience know that this is a drama about Real People."[23]

Robert Brustein, on the other hand, championing the play as an authentic American drama, calls Thelma "salty, shrewd, good natured" and sees her as an affirmative life force.[24] Brustein is alone among the male critics in this positive view of Thelma. Feminist writer Trudy Scott takes Brustein's view even farther by focusing her review on Thelma as the play's dramatic agent: "Jessie dispassionately lists her reasons for not wanting to live, revealing herself as an emotionally dead character. Thus, the compelling and propelling viewpoint of the drama falls to Thelma. . . . [T]he remainder of *'night, Mother* charts the progress of Thelma's dilemma."[25]

Scott frames her discussion of the play within the mother/daughter conflict, and she privileges the mother's perspective: "Norman's portrayal of a woman's capacity to give, to sustain, to fight for a child's life and, ultimately, to accept the voluntary withdrawal of that life is painful and precise. . . . Rarely do playwrights attempt serious explorations of the experiences of older women."[26]

Marsha Norman's 'night, Mother
Kathy Bates as Jessie and Anne Pitoniak as Thelma in the 1983 Broadway production.
(Copyright 1983 Martha Swope)

Most critics tend to see Thelma's desperate attempts to keep her daughter alive as "absurd suggestions,"[27] and place Jessie's choice at the center of the dramatic action.

In a clear example of reception filtered through gender biases, the male critics' responses to Jessie were based almost uniformly on her physical appearance onstage, which substantially altered their reception of the play. They collapsed performer Kathy Bates' appearance into the character's and proceeded to construct their own list of reasons for why Jessie decided to commit suicide. First among these, according to critics, is her weight. Although the fatal, tragic flaw in Norman's text is epilepsy, the production's received flaw, which provides the cause of Jessie's ultimate demise, is fat.

Typically, John Simon, in *New York Magazine,* was most blatant in his word choice. He called Jessie "fat, unattractive, and epileptic." Other reviewers followed in kind, describing Jessie—although they were responding to Bates' performance and her body—as an "overweight young woman with sallow skin," "a good looking, though overweight woman, sloppily dressed," "pudgy and plain," "heavy set, slow moving and morose," and "overweight and homely."[28] The male critics unanimously saw Jessie as a loser. She has lost her husband; her son is a juvenile delinquent; she is epileptic, and groggy with self-hatred. Her salient characteristic in performance, however, is not her personal history, but her weight. Even a woman writing in *Ms. Magazine* condemned Jessie as "dumpy from over-eating."[29] These critics correlated what they saw onstage to the play's motivating action so emphatically that Jessie's appearance became more significant than Norman's actual dramatic device.

Jessie's appearance is never mentioned in Norman's script. In fact, the dialogue seems to indicate that if anything, Jessie is thin. Thelma tells her daughter, "You never liked eating at all, did you? Any of it. What have you been living on all these years, toothpaste?" (p. 36). Norman had Kathy Bates in mind for the role of Jessie while she was writing, but there is no evidence that weight was a factor when Norman constructed the character nor that she wanted to cast Bates because of her body size. If she had been thinking in terms of Bates' weight, Norman probably would have deleted Thelma's reference to Jessie's ability to live on toothpaste.

Jessie's weight is not an issue in Norman's play as written, but eating as a ritual exchange in the shared history between mother and daughter is prevalent in the script. As Lynda Hart has pointed out, Jessie's desire for nourishment is now spent. She can no longer find the right food; even the elaborate preparation of hot chocolate in *'night, Mother* is useless, since Jessie has lost her taste for the treat. Hart says that "Jessie's lack of appetite denies the whole mother/daughter history" of love as nurturance.[30] Based on this feminist textual analysis of Norman's script, it is even more ironic that Jessie is condemned in performance for gluttony.

A character's appearance is used frequently in dramatic literature as a psychological barometer. The evil of Shakespeare's Richard III, for instance, is presented in direct relation to his misshapen appearance, and, of course, Cyrano's nose is a prime example of appearance molding character. But these physical qualities are intrinsic to the dramatic text, a predetermined element in the play's reception. My point here is to indicate that spectators' expectations of a character's appearance must correlate with the performer's appearance, or other inferences are drawn based on culturally dictated readings of the body they see in space.[31]

This gender bias in relation to character and performers' appearance has a direct bearing on a play's categorization as tragedy or melodrama.[32] Writing on the dominant press reception to Norman's play, dramaturge Collette Brooks noticed that critics frequently compared *'night, Mother* to plays prototypical of American tragedy, such as *Death of a Salesman*. Brooks agreed that "For all intents and purposes, *'night, Mother* was written in 1949 by Arthur Miller,"[33] and dismissed Norman's play from a feminist perspective because of its similarity to the male standard. Other critics felt compelled to grapple with the play's difference from the canon.

As critics hold marginalized texts like *'night, Mother* beside canonized texts like *Death of a Salesman*, the history of literary selection is thrown into relief against an ideological background of cultural power. Discussing recent feminist critiques of literary canon-formation, Christine Froula observes, "The critique of patriarchal/canonical authority assumes that literary authority is a mode of social authority and that literary value is inseparable from ideology."[34] From a revisionist perspective, cultural authorities have determined the canon's selection and then mystified its terms, so that this reified body of work seems to have always been in place. The invisibility of both its constructors and the origins of its construction render the canon peculiarly (but purposefully) remote from question or attack.

Barbara Herrnstein Smith emphasizes that the canon was originally formed according to standards of value and evaluation that have since been mystified and obscured, leaving their byproduct—the traditional canon—as an apparently empirical measurement against which all ensuing literary work is compared. But, as Smith points out, "All value is radically contingent, being neither an inherent property of objects nor an arbitrary projection of subjects, but, rather, the product of the dynamics of an economic system."[35] The mystification of the literary economic (or cultural) system in which canon-formation works obscures what Smith calls the "personal economy"—a subject's needs, interests, and resources—on which the larger system is based. Cultural authority and power constructs the ideal reader and critic from a group of similar subjects, for whom the canon meets its personal contingencies of value. The value systems of other, less powerful or authoritative subjects are then characterized as "pathological."[36]

The cultural power invested in a canon allows it to perpetuate the dictums of the ideology it represents. Annette Kolodny points out that canonization projects and protects the construction of the canon: "The fact of canonization puts any work beyond questions of establishing its merit and, instead, invites students to offer only increasingly more ingenious readings and interpretations, the purpose of which is to validate the greatness already imputed by canonization."[37] How, then, is a woman's novel or play to be compared to this self-perpetuating list of male novels and plays, which expands its ranks only for those works that already resemble its historical members?

'*night, Mother* does bear a distinct resemblance to *Death of a Salesman,* Miller's classic American domestic drama, which won the Pulitzer in 1949. In some ways, both Jessie Cates and Willy Loman have been denied the promises of the mythic American Dream and both resort to suicide as a final effort to shape their lives. Willy Loman, however, is a father, and his death leaves at least a financial legacy to his wife and sons. Jessie's death leaves no similar legacy to her mother and in effect wipes out even the heritage of regeneration Thelma might have left at her own death.

Death of a Salesman was revived on Broadway almost exactly a year after '*night, Mother* opened. From a body image perspective, it is interesting to note how critics responded to the physical appearance of the male performers in the virtuosic Willy Loman role. Lee J. Cobb set the standard in the original 1949 performance. Cobb was a big man, but reviewers do not refer to him as overweight or unattractive. Instead, they recall his massive size as a mark of authority.

Douglas Watts remembered Cobb's Willy as a "large, lumbering victim." Comparing Dustin Hoffman to Cobb in the 1984 revival, Frank Rich noted, "Mr. Hoffman's Willy is a total break with the mountainous Lee J. Cobb image. He's a trim, immaculately outfitted go-getter in a three-piece suit." Edwin Wilson, in the *Wall Street Journal,* wrote, "Most Willy's . . . have been large in stature. . . . Seeing a smaller man like Mr. Hoffman in the part, one realizes the values that come from size. Willy's wife and young sons look up to him, and this is easier to understand in a larger man."[38]

Since Hoffman could not gain authority from his size, the conception of the character was changed to accommodate the actor and Loman garnered his authority elsewhere. In Miller's play, the actor and the character are not locked into a transcendent, absolute correlation. Writer John Beaufort noted that "Mr. Miller reportedly has restored the word 'shrimp' and certain other allusions that designated Willy's stature. The changed emphasis creates an unmistakably new perspective."[39] In the *Salesman* revival, the character was collapsed into the appearance of the male star. In '*night, Mother,* the performer's appearance was collapsed into the reception of the character. Since the culture is not as prescriptive about how men should look in certain social or performance roles, Willy Loman cannot be considered a failure because he is short or heavyset. The man matters more than the body. This is the opposite of the reception to Kathy Bates in the role of Jessie.

For *'night, Mother* to be a tragedy according to the dominant culture's criteria, Jessie should have been played by a performer with the body size and appearance of Farrah Fawcett. The death by choice of an unsuccessful, homely, overweight woman is considered melodrama because its implications do not resonate enough to be considered tragedy by the generic male spectator.

The analogy to *Death of a Salesman* is also apt in terms of *'night, Mother*'s genre categorization. Paul Lauter, writing on the evolution of literary standards, notes that canons were originally formed to keep high art separate from the popular culture of the lower classes. Lauter says, "The literary canon is, in short, a means by which culture validates social power."[40] Like canons, genre categories are also expedient ways of ranking drama or literature according to what is actually a social hierarchy.

Arthur Miller's plays are generally classified as domestic drama, in that they deal with family issues in which father/son relationships are privileged. *'night, Mother* can also be categorized as domestic drama, but the classification assumes different connotations when the writer is a woman and the mother/daughter conflict is foregrounded. Reviewers walked a fine line between wanting to applaud *'night, Mother* for its "moral inquiry" and trivializing its "domestic cliché."[41] In the change from male writer to female and father/son focus to mother/daughter, domestic drama is reduced to kitchen drama, which is considered specific rather than universal, and melodramatic rather than tragic.

Domesticity and family assume different meanings when received in the context of plays by women. While Miller can write about the family and be canonized, Norman's attempt to tackle similar issues is seen as evidence of the preoccupations of her gender class. Howard Kissel, for example, dismissed the play by comparing it to other "shockers" like *Sorry, Wrong Number*.[42] *Sorry, Wrong Number* is about a bedridden woman who overhears her own murder being plotted and tries to get someone to believe her story before the murder finally takes place. The comparison is somewhat revealing, since it indicates that Kissel categorized the play in a genre known for female hysteria and paranoia. Another reviewer deprecated *'night, Mother* as a "suspense melodrama."[43]

David Richards called *'night, Mother* "resolutely domestic" and compared it to *K2*, Patrick Meyers' two-(male)-character play in which a pair of climbers are trapped on a mountainside.[44] Meyers uses a situation of entrapment to allow his characters wide-ranging philosophical speculation. Norman's characters are trapped in the quotidian detail of home and hearth. Jessie and Thelma's preoccupations are philosophical and existential, but because their debate rages in the context of a home and because they are women, their reception is qualitatively different.

Defined as the ability to speak to the generic spectator, universality is the criterion critics applied when deciding whether *'night, Mother* deserved a place in the canon's legions. As Staiger notes, "Claims for universality are disguises for achieving uniformity, for surpressing through the power of canonic discourse optional value systems. Such a cultural 'consensus' fears an asserted 'barbarism' and a collapse into the grotesque and monstrous, because it recognizes the potential loss of its hegemony. It is a politics of power."[45] Under the rubric of universality, critics determined whether or not *'night, Mother* had the potential to subvert the cultural hegemony of the male canon. If the play could be perceived as universal by the generic male spectator, the threat of what was seen as its particularized female perspective could be neutralized. Some critics decided that *'night, Mother* failed this test, while others argued either that it passed or that the play did not attempt universality.

Variety, the industry barometer of economic success, called *'night, Mother* a "non-box office subject" that "lacks universal application. . . . There's pity but no terror, no purgative release for the audience. The heroine's action, as the author no doubt intended, remains a private, isolated instance of human failure. The audience isn't a partner."[46] Norman's play fails to be universal because it does not quite meet the criteria of Aristotle's *Poetics,* and does not address or relieve the fears of the spectators to whom *Variety* would have it speak. Watts, the *Daily News* reviewer, wrote that "the troubling aspect of the play is that Jessie is not a truly tragic figure. Her self containment as she busily sets things in order about the house suggests one dedicated to her awful purpose, true, but also suggests a congenitally deranged woman."[47] By suggesting Jessie's problems are hereditary and therefore individual, Watts denied the play's universal appeal. The *Newsday* reviewer approved of what he perceived as Norman's limits in *'night, Mother:* "There is no awkward stretch for imagery or universality. . . . [The play] doesn't develop to reveal a deeper truth."[48] Ironically, considering Norman's stated intent, this critic applauds her for avoiding universality.

Robert Brustein, however, Norman's initial champion, insisted that *'night, Mother* did pass the universality test. He returned to Aristotle to justify his belief in the play, writing that *'night, Mother* is "*chastely* classical [emphasis mine] in its observance of the unities," particularly time, which is measured synchronously onstage and in the audience. Brustein said this "helps explain the enduring strength and validity of the *Poetics*. . . . Nothing reinforces one's faith in the power and importance of the theatre more than the emergence of an authentic, universal playwright—not a woman playwright, mind you, not a regional playwright, not an ethnic playwright, but one who speaks to the concerns and experiences of all humankind."[49] Clearly, Brustein perceives Norman as an authentic, universal playwright.

Women Playwrights and the Feminist Canon

Brustein attempted to obscure Norman's gender under an Aristotelian mantle of respectability. Other writers refused to accept her as generic and made her gender an issue. Some way had to be found to contextualize the playwright that would avoid threatening the male dramatic bastion. Critic Robert Asahina, who disliked the play and wondered at the Pulitzer award, wrote, "I suppose the logic was to honor the playwright, not the play."[50]

This emphasis on the person over the play appears in feminist criticism as well as in mainstream contexts. In the politically disparate feminist press, two documents regarding *'night, Mother* and Marsha Norman are pertinent: an interview with Norman in *Ms. Magazine* and two opposing reviews in *Women & Performance Journal.*

Trudy Scott's positive review of *'night, Mother,* quoted earlier, ran directly before my own negative review in the same issue. My review is, in a sense, a response to the mainstream press reception to Norman's play, and stands as a critique of the context into which it tried to insert Norman and her work. I saw the play as coopted into a scheme of male dramatic and ideological values, and noted that women are getting the Pulitzer Prize for plays that "depict women killing themselves or living totally immobilized in their backwoods, suburban homes. . . . It's ironic; or is it? When so-called feminist plays like *'night, Mother* and *Crimes of the Heart* are cheerfully honored by the . . . coveted prize, there's a not-so-subtle message underlying the Pulitzer awards. It's a form of anti-feminist backlash."[51]

My response was colored by a mistrust of the institutional approval Norman's play received. The review went on to question whether the play is at all feminist: "The premise alone defies feminist categorizing: If feminist plays are defined as those that show women in the painful, difficult process of becoming full human beings, how can a play in which suicide is assumed from the first moments be a thorough consideration of women?"[52]

I privileged the daughter's dilemma, with which I felt it was impossible to empathize, and saw the mother as a one-note character with objectives that are exercises in futility. In a surge of cultural feminism, I failed to find a universal application for the play, although my implied spectators were women. By shifting the axis of categorization for universality to women, my review implied that Norman's play does indeed fit the requirements of the male canon and does not belong in a canon of any kind of feminist plays.

I now think that *'night, Mother* is typical of liberal and cultural feminist drama that is, as Case remarks, "animated by the absent male."[53] All the intimacies shared by Jessie and Thelma somehow relate to the father, son, and brother, whose impact on the narrative is integral to every revelation and action the two women undertake. Like most traditional American dramas, *'night, Mother*'s focus on individual suffering and the play's unwillingness to discuss Jessie's dilemma in terms of a wider social context make it weak as a political statement and inadequate from a materialist feminist perspective.

The lack of further feminist press response available on *'night, Mother* is partly because Broadway prices generally keep these productions inaccessible to those outside a comfortable income bracket and therefore might not be of interest to many feminist press readers. (The play opened at ticket prices of $27.50 top on weeknights, and $29.00 on weekends.)

In addition, the feminist press has been slow to develop a feminist critique of performance. When they do cover theatre by women, feminist reviewers seem caught between applauding the woman's efforts and critiquing the work against a standard that is yet to be defined in the balance between ideology and art. Since the feminist canon is nascent at best, particularly in theatre, the feminist press tends to shy from the work and to concentrate instead on the woman. *Ms. Magazine*'s feature on Norman is a good example.

Ms. Magazine's editorial viewpoint generally subscribes to liberal feminist ideology in that it frequently features women who are successful by the dominant culture's standards. When it strays from its liberal feminist stance, the magazine leans toward a cultural feminist critique, highlighting women's essentially female attributes. Both tendencies are apparent in the Norman interview.

The *Ms.* profile "Playwright Marsha Norman: An Optimist Writes About Suicide, Confinement, and Despair" stresses Norman's feminine abilities. She is a good listener ("I listen better than any other thing") and she has an intuitive knack for "speaking the generally unspoken."[54] The interviewer is careful to keep Norman accessible to the readership; she is compared to literary women like Tillie Olsen and Toni Morrison, who are credited with "giving voice to those who generally go unheard."[55]

The interview clarifies that although Norman sees herself as a role model for young women, she is careful to distance herself from feminism as a movement ("I don't join or show up at meetings").[56] Yet Norman clearly knows that because her story about a mother and daughter has garnered a great deal of attention on Broadway, it is a victory for herself and for other women. She admits, "The theatre says, Who lives today? Whose stories matter?"[57] The interview foregrounds mother/daughter relationships. Norman speaks at length about the daughter's need for autonomy from the mother and stresses that their relationship is material for drama as much as the more familiar father/son relationship.

The *Ms.* feature, however, generally places Norman outside the theatre context. She is inscribed as a woman first and as a playwright only secondarily. Even the graphic layout of the article helps support the writer's contextualization of Norman, and would undoubtedly influence the reader's reception. The photograph of Norman that runs on the first page of the feature is dark and arty. Her face is placed against a black background, outside of any specific locale or setting.[58] The feature includes no mention of either women's theatre or other women playwrights. It ends as a picture of a woman capitalizing on her ability to listen, to relate to others, and to translate women's unique experience.

This position is the basis of cultural feminism, in that it valorizes, rather than deconstructs, sexual difference. Gussow picks up on these cultural feminist ideals and persistently ties Norman to the context of her domestic environment in his *New York Times Sunday Magazine* cover story. In contrast to the *Ms.* article, however, he also scrutinizes Norman's position in theatre in relation to the male-dominated canon of good drama. Gussow places her at the "crest of a wave of adventurous young women playwrights—a proliferation that is the most encouraging and auspicious aspect of the current American theatre."[59]

Again, the supporting graphic material that surrounds Gussow's text offers clues to his perspective. Norman is featured on the cover of the magazine section. The photo is a full body shot, in which Norman, with her arms folded across her chest, stands to the right of a few rows of empty theatre seats in what is obviously a plush Broadway house. Norman looks serious and businesslike; she is not smiling.

On the first page of Gussow's story, a photo of Norman is placed above the headline, "Women Playwrights: New Voices in the Theatre." The photo displays Norman in her work environment. Her word processor is to the left with a cup of coffee beside it, and a telephone is obvious in the background. In the foreground of the photo, below the word processor, is Norman's knitting. She faces front, unsmiling, with her hands resting on the table top positioned like hands in dishwashing advertisements. Her fingers are long and feminine, and her wedding ring is on her left hand.

The remainder of the article is illustrated with photos that generalize this contextualization to the other women mentioned. The playwrights are pictured either alone, out of any context, or in empty theatre auditoriums. Production photographs are relegated to domestic space—Pitoniak and Bates in the kitchen, the cast of *Crimes of the Heart* in the kitchen celebrating a birthday, and the three characters of Tina Howe's *Painting Churches* in the family home. Although many of the women Gussow proceeds to mention have written nondomestic plays, the kitchen and hearth are what the *Times* chooses to highlight.

While it is obvious that Gussow would like to elevate Norman's play into the canon of good American drama, he is frustrated by the problem of her gender, which he foregrounds throughout the article. Unintentionally or not, Gussow undermines Norman's stature by insistently highlighting her feminine domesticity:

Shortly before *'night, Mother* opened on Broadway, after spending a long evening making script revisions with her director, Tom Moore, she returned to her Manhattan apartment and typed the changes into her computer. It was 2:30 in the morning by the time she was satisfied with the result, and as the printer clattered out a clean copy of the play, Miss Norman sat back and took up her knitting, adding inches to her new red sweater. The juxtaposition of the technological and the homespun is a quintessential picture of this artist at work.[60]

Although Norman has become successful in what Gussow defines as a man's world, she has not lost her femininity; she still knits, and her values remain homespun. Technology is her tool, but her knitting needles, clattering along with the printer, are equally representative of her new voice.

Gussow feels *'night, Mother* is qualified for inscription into the male canon, since "the audience has shared a catharsis of grief and pain" and the play is as "tough-minded as it is sensitive."[61] Norman qualifies for male privilege, but she continues to be feminine—sensitive and emotional. Norman and her sisterhood of young women playwrights are marked by their difference from men when aspiring to the same dramatic ends.

Gussow quotes Jon Jory, producing director at the Actors Theatre of Louisville—where Norman's work first caught public attention—who says, "The characters in [women's] plays very often seem more emotionally affecting to the audience than characters men have been writing about. . . . Women are creating characters you can love."[62] Gussow's portrayal of Norman continues along this theme.

Unlike the *Ms.* article, which foregrounded Norman's intuitive female abilities, Gussow links her to female places and spheres, emphasizing her home life with her husband and family. He describes her as an upper-middle class, cultured intellectual: "She and her husband, Dann Byck Jr., often play Schubert in their living room in private piano-clarinet duets. . . . Sitting at her dining room table surrounded by the objects of her life . . . a conversation with her roams freely from Kierkegaard to Aristotle, from Flaubert to Doris Lessing."[63] The roaming conversation, however, is always personal: "She speaks about her fears."

Not surprisingly, Norman's appearance is much more important to Gussow's feature than to the *Ms.* interview. He writes that her "dark view of life comes not from a Samuel Beckett, but from an affable, determined, and *petite* [emphasis mine] young woman who looks more like a graduate student than a serious playwright wrestling with profound emotions."[64] Space can be made for her in the male canon of mountainous men, since she will never be tall enough to tower over the old figures. Norman herself admits, "I am convinced that the fact that I am 5 foot 4 is a real factor in the way I see the world. . . . Eighty percent of the people on the planet are taller than I am. . . . I am wandering around in this land of giants."[65]

The size analogy is clear throughout Gussow's article. The women he discusses in addition to Norman are described as a small but growing minority, climbing up the beanstalk of traditional American drama. Lumping them together solely by gender, he likens playwrights who are essentially dissimilar when analyzed according to ideological concerns and theatrical style. Norman is rendered the prototype of his group profile, and Broadway theatre and Pulitzer prizes are the standardbearers to which he assumes all women playwrights aspire.

By failing to acknowledge that some women playwrights do write from a more polemical, feminist ideological stance than Marsha Norman, and that some write to challenge the form and content of the dramatic canon, Gussow neatly side-steps any reference to the history of feminist theatre or to the issue of a two-gender audience. Norman aids and abets him by remarking, "Now we can write plays and not have people put them in a little box labelled 'women's theatre.' "[66]

Feminist theatre women were invited to respond to Gussow's interpretation of the gender issue in a special section of *Performing Arts Journal*. The women writing in *PAJ* unanimously reproached Gussow for inserting Norman and others like her at the head of what he described as a homogeneous, new phenomenon. Collette Brooks, former associate artistic director of Interart Theatre, noted that the writers Gussow featured "all share certain socio-economic affinities. . . . [T]hrough pieces such as his, the *Times* sustains reputations it largely served to create in the first place."[67] In its position of power to mold spectator response and delineate a horizon of expectations for theatre-goers, the *Times* creates stars of its own choosing, who serve the paper's—and its readers'—ideological interests. Brooks went on to say: "By canonizing these works, effectively suppressing alternative visions, we are at once crippling an art form and leaving our psychic landscape strewn with testaments to the extraordinary limitations that this culture has placed upon human possibility."[68]

In his rush to add a woman to the male list of good American drama, Gussow missed the possibility of a shift in the gender of the spectator that will fundamentally disrupt the construction of the canon. *'night, Mother* ultimately did become part of the canon—the play is often produced in regional theatres around the country, and has been included in many anthologies published since 1983. Norman's play can be considered for canonical membership because Norman is still writing for male spectators under the guise of universality. Staiger writes, "If a [play] is claimed to be universal, what the proponents of such a possiblity are implying is that such a [play] speaks in the same way to everyone. Not only does this claim wipe out historical, cultural, and social difference, but it denies sexual difference, treating all individuals as uniformly constituted."[69]

By conferring the mantle of universality on Marsha Norman, and giving her the microphone as the new voice of American theatre, Gussow denied the sexual difference of both playwrights and spectators. Director Roberta Sklar wrote in the *PAJ* response, "Historically, the audience has been called upon to receive the theatre within the generic category of Man. Now we are called upon to receive it within the term Woman, as the gender sensibility of the audience is being re-defined."[70]

Sklar's cultural feminist assertion is debatable, in that a new, feminist canon constructed for female spectators presents the same danger of universalizing for exclusionary subject positions as the generic category of "Man" has done throughout theatre history. Fitting a woman's play into any canon—male or female—implies that it is acquiescent to the ideology perpetuated by that canon. Canons, by implication, exclude not only worthy plays but worthy spectators on the basis of their ideological perspectives. In feminist critical analysis, the gender of the spectator is being reconsidered and reassigned, but the reinstallation of another monolithic subject position from which to view performance should be avoided. A useful by-product of the deconstruction of traditional canons will be the dismembering of the generic spectator whom the dramatic canons once addressed.

Wresting authority away from the powerful, controlling voices in cultural discourse is an on-going project in feminist criticism. Christine Froula succinctly summarizes the feminist critique of canon-formation:

> We can, through strategies of rereading that expose the deeper structures of authority, and through interplay with texts of a different stamp, pursue a kind of collective psychoanalysis, tranforming "bogeys" that hide invisible power into investments both visible and alterable. In doing so, we approach traditional texts not as the mystifying (and self-limiting) "best" that has been thought and said in the world, but as a *visible* past against which we can . . . imagine a different future.[71]

Studying texts like Marsha Norman's *'night, Mother* against the context of traditional texts forces an awareness of the ideological nature of cultural discourse. As women playwrights continue to assert their voices in the traditional male forum, gender will remain an issue with which to reckon.

3

Ideology in Performance:
Looking through the Male Gaze

One of the basic assumptions of feminist criticism is that all representation is inherently ideological. Since dominant cultural meanings both constitute and are reconstituted by representation, deconstructing performance from a feminist perspective entails uncovering the ideological determinants within which performance works. Ideology defines a way of thinking, a particular set of worldviews that works as its own hermeneutics. No one is without ideology; people are raised with and cultivate certain ways of thinking and seeing that help them make sense of their culture.[1] Ideology is based on assumptions about how the culture operates and what it means.

Ideology circulates as a prevailing term in performance from its creation to its reception. Herb Blau charges, "Everything in the structural reality of theatre practice is ideological. . . . As an ideological act in its own right, any performance involves questions of property, ownership, authority, force, and what may be the source of ideology—according to Nietzsche—the will to power."[2] By canonizing certain texts and their meanings, and mystifying the origins of their authority, dominant cultural ideology appears in representation as naturalized and seemingly nonideological. Feminist criticism aims to dismantle this pervasive myth in theatre practice. Blau adds, "There is an ideology of perception which in turn affects the ideology of performance."[3] In other words, the whole structural reality of the performance exchange between producers, performers, and spectators is ideologically marked.

The issue of subject-formation is an integral part of any discussion of spectatorship in performance, since representation implicitly constructs a particular viewing subject to receive its ideological meanings. And subject-formation is itself an ideological enterprise. Dominant psychoanalytic readings of subject-formation, such as Freud's and Lacan's, for example, are explicitly ideological, as they trace this process across paths that distinctly diverge for male and female children. Freud called the process of a child's realization of

des Kindes

difference from his [*sic*] mother, which causes him to shift his alliance from mother to father and subsequently develop a subconscious, libido, and ego, the Oedipus complex. Feminist psychoanalysts have pointed out the obvious gender-bias in Freud's work, in that the female's process of subject-formation is not at all adequately theorized.[4]

Lacan's approach to subject-formation has become a useful theoretical point of departure for feminist film theory, and will inform the following discussion of spectatorship in avant-garde theatre practice. Briefly, in Lacanian theory, the child's moment of individuation occurs during the "mirror phase," and is tied to language acquisition. Freud's pre- and post-Oedipal phases become Lacan's Imaginary and Symbolic realms. The Imaginary belongs to the mother, and the child exists with her there prior to language. The child begins to leave this prelinguistic realm when he experiences the mirror phase, in which he sees himself for the first time as separate from the mother.

Lacan's mirror phase yields two important psychological conditions. First, the child realizes he has a penis and his mother does not. Second, he sees in the mirror a more perfect self, a kind of ego ideal. Afraid his alliance with the mother will cause him to be castrated as he believes she has been, the child rejects the Imaginary and enters the Symbolic realm of language, in which the father dominates.

The moment of recognition in the mirror phase occurs at the same time as the entry into language. The child enters the world of grammar, sequence, self, and Other—according to Lacan, a world in which he can now recognize difference. The loss of the mother, implied by her difference from the phallic model the child achieves with his entry into language, leaves a legacy of desire, which the male child goes on to resolve in heterosexual relations. Feminists revising Lacan's work have dubbed the Symbolic realm the "Law of the Father." By extending Lacan's theory, they suggest that the dominant culture is centered on such male epistemology—or phallologocentrism—in which the phallus is the ultimate signifier.[5]

Many artists working in postmodern performance have instituted a partial critique of subjectivity. They consider identity unstable and refracted, and the psyche as not quite the coherent, unified site of individuation that modernism once claimed and that traditional psychoanalysis once posed.[6] In the contemporary American theatrical avant-garde, postmodernists such as Richard Foreman, Robert Wilson, and Elizabeth LeCompte have questioned the assumptions behind conventional theatre terms such as character and narrative, which once grounded modernist conceptions of the subject.

Their performance work illustrates the widely held belief that character can no longer act as a stable referent, and that narrative can no longer be assumed to be a coherent, linear system that delivers a single, authoritative meaning. The postmodern performance texts are deconstructed into metacommentaries on the issue of textuality, so that the critique of the performance apparatus, which once reified character and narrative, becomes part of the subject of the performance.

Since much of the postmodern work places the entire representational apparatus into crisis, one might expect to find an equally radical deconstruction of the gender-biases built into the history and form of theatre in the work as well. But despite their aesthetic radicalism, the American postmodernists have for the most part disregarded or disclaimed the ideological implications of their work, and left intact the gender dichotomies of the cultural status quo maintained by traditional theatre.[7]

Ideology, however, continues to circulate as a meaningful term in contemporary avant-garde performance. Even as they purportedly depose the reign of narrative, many of the postmodernists continue to deliver meanings with unexamined gender-biases—the story of gender difference remains undeconstructed. Foreman, for example, attacks the conventional expectations of performing and viewing, but fails to disrupt the gender assumptions of the representational apparatus he otherwise deconstructs. Foreman's work illustrates a rich vein of postmodern aesthetics, whose radical commitment to new forms is undermined by its maintenance of gender dichotomies. And although his statements against ideology are articulate and persuasive, Foreman's personal ideology is a decipherable subtext in the conservative gender meanings inherent in his work.

Political Theatre versus Formalism

When Foreman began his Ontological-Hysteric Theatre in the late 1960s, other experimental theatres were also organizing in New York City. Ensembles such as the Performance Group, the Open Theatre, and the Living Theatre were using performance techniques to affect a change in public consciousness and ideological perceptions. With the surge of social awareness prompted by reactions to the Viet Nam War, the civil rights struggle, and the nascent feminist movement, performance increasingly became a crucible for social experiments.

Against a background of social radicalism, theatre practitioners endeavored to use their art to persuade people to change their consciousness. Some groups abandoned conventional theatre hierarchies to work collectively, and broke down what they saw as artificially imposed barriers between performers and spectators. Richard Schechner's Performance Group, for example, returned to the model of theatre as ritual, and in his environmental stagings encouraged spectators to participate in the performances on physical, emotional, intellectual, and sometimes sexual levels. The aim was to join in the collective unconscious, articulated in the visceral, present moment of the performance space.[8]

During the same era, Foreman, too, was preoccupied with the nature of human consciousness. But his more formalist concerns were diametrically opposed, both in method and goal, to those of the socially and politically oriented groups. At a profound level, Foreman's reason for wanting to alter the specta-tor's consciousness was individualistic—in an age of collectivism—and aes-thetic, and had nothing to do with social change.

Foreman saw consciousness as a purely perceptual mechanism that filters the world through the senses. He felt that habit teaches people to shut down their senses, cutting them off from realizing their greatest perceptual potential.[9] To free people to expand their perceptions, Foreman constructed a rigorous attack on habitual ways of seeing the world and seeing art. Rather than using performance as a forum for the contemplation of political issues or as a way to resolve moral dilemmas prompted by cultural upheaval, Foreman focused on form and structure. He believed in resisting moral dichotomies, and located his work within what he considered people's essentially ambiguous moral state.

Foreman, in fact, saw a conservative tendency in art that tries to clear up this ambiguity. Like Brecht, Foreman considered traditional theatre bourgeois, because it offers catharsis by presenting clear resolutions to moral issues. But where Brecht sought political contemplation from his spectators, Foreman in-sisted they immerse themselves only in the perceptual ambiguities derived from the wealth of sensory input he constructed.

For Foreman, the spectators' theatre experience can only concern the pro-cess that is constructed in front of them at the eternally present moment: the reality of the stage picture assembled in time and space, tableau by tableau. His work appeals to immediate perceptions, which he assumes can be purely aes-thetic, and can occur in forms and structures that are themselves pure, unencum-bered by ideology. Foreman says he aims to "subject the audience to a kind of perceptual massage that will allow us to free ourselves from the need for the security of ideological prisons of one sort or another."[10] Foreman believes ideology obstructs the spectator's ability to perceive. But what would percep-tions mean without ideology? Perceptual stimuli, it seems, need to be organized by some interpretive mechanism, in which ideology, by necessity, plays a large part.

Foreman, however, insists his representations are ideologically void. He calls the work of political performance groups "social theatre" in which specta-tors are led to see—"like dumb animals are led"[11]—propositions that the author has constructed. This social theatre is not a real theatre, in Foreman's strict phenomenological sense. His theatre manipulates objects in time and space to which he assigns no meaning other than the perceptual value equally distributed in his scenography. By suggesting that ideology can be detached from percep-tion, Foreman implies that there is a pure, universal way of looking. Under scrutiny, however, it becomes evident that the way of looking at performance Foreman's work demands is entirely specific. The male gaze, with the ideologi-cally weighted gender markings it carries, is clearly operative in his work.[12]

Because Foreman's work does assume a particular way of looking, his representations are not free from ideological reference. The assumptions of his worldview are most evident in the way he uses women performers in his work. By detailing two of Foreman's aesthetic concerns—the equivalence of objects in the perceptual field and the deconstruction of habitual narrative pleasure in representation—and applying them to his use of women as icons, Foreman's ideological assumptions become apparent.

Phenomenology and Visual Pleasure

Foreman takes a phenomenological approach to the stage space and the objects he manipulates within it. His work is influenced by Gertrude Stein, whose "present moment" landscape plays stripped phenomena to their essences to counter the overarticulation of images she perceived in literature and theatre.[13] The metaphorical, associative value of, for instance, a rose, is stripped of meaning to become "a rose is a rose is a rose." Wrenched out of any context, it becomes a phenomenon without associations that impose interpretive meaning. Kate Davy writes that Foreman, too, "began with a strict phenomenological approach, the goal of which consists of the simple practice of an understated seeing of that which reveals itself *in* what is seen. . . . The premise is that modern society has become so conditioned to understanding the world in terms of sophisticated hypotheses that individuals have all but lost the ability to discern what constitutes the fundamental character of a being."[14]

To this end, Foreman constructs his scenography to render the ordinary extraordinary. Potatoes, in *Rhoda in Potatoland* (1976), for example, become larger than life. Clocks, such as the grandfather clock in *Sophia = (Wisdom) Part 3: The Cliffs* (1973), become animate objects that enter the playing space. Once all objects are enlarged to human scale, there is no longer a hierarchy available on which humans and objects can be ranked. The potatoes and the clock assume human proportions and, conversely, the humans assume the perceptual valence of the objects. The live performers in Foreman's work lose their privileged place and become objects equal in perceptual weight to any other prop in the stage picture. The performance's reality becomes simply a web of perceptual relationships.

The essence of things is further revealed by disrupting the spectator's equilibrium through the intentionally uncomfortable process of perceiving the production. Lights shine directly in the spectators' eyes, making it difficult to see the playing area. Loud noises startle the spectators out of passive contemplation, jolting them back into full awareness. The texts constantly comment on Foreman's process of creating them, calling attention to the arbitrary construction of words themselves. Snatches of familiar music are used to seduce the spectator into a feeling of ease, then are abruptly curtailed.

Foreman says this kind of artistic experience *"must* be an ordeal to be undergone. The rhythms *must* be in a certain way different and uncongenial. Uncongenial elements are then redeemed by a clarity in the moment-to-moment, smallest unit of progression."[15] Clarity is achieved when the spectator sees the world "as it is," stripped of association and meaning other than perceptual relations. Foreman writes, "This new art is not EXTRACTED from the flux of life, and is therefore in no sense a mirror or representation—but a parallel phenomenon to life itself."[16]

One can argue, however, that any extended series of events happening in a space as tightly controlled and carefully constructed as Foreman's theatre is indeed a representation. Whether the events on stage represent what he calls the "flickerings" of his consciousness,[17] an aesthetic idea, or a narrative construct, they are arranged to be seen as a heightened form of reality. The performers are behaving in a particular way during a period of time for a particular reason. Entering the liminal theatre space, they represent something; they are not simply presenting themselves. They remain framed by the representational apparatus.[18] In fact, among all the theatre conventions Foreman discarded or attacked, his allegiance to the strict proscenium arrangement, with its convenient frame and distanced relationship between performers and spectators, is the most crucial element in explicating the meanings constructed by his tableaux for the pleasure of the male gaze.[19]

Even though his preference for picture-frame staging is clearly bound by the representational apparatus, Foreman would avoid the issue of representation by calling his productions "life." The crux of phenomenology, on which Foreman draws, is the certainty that the world exists only insofar as it empirically registers on one's consciousness. Looking for a sure, scientific system based on the tangible, immanent appearance of things, Foreman reduces any perceivable stimulus to what he sees as its phenomenological essence. As the *auteur*, he is then free to manipulate these phenomena into a web of relationships that illustrates how they appear in his consciousness. In his first manifesto, Foreman writes, "Acting against materials (the table, the floor, the other actor's body) is establishing this new language that doesn't *read* but 'illustrates.'"[20] He implies that things can simply be seen (that is, perceived) without being meaningful or filtered through an intellectual or ideological system.

What this new language and those phenomenological essences illustrate, however, is an ideological perspective. Phenomenology is a science of subjectivity that places man (the generic is used intentionally) at the center of the universe. Foreman borrows significant tenets of phenomenology to theorize his work. For example, as an empirical system, it refuses to consider the human subject as a product of his or her history or era.[21] The science instead suggests that phenomena can be illustrated as they are, as opposed to being constructed through the ideology of the perceiving subject. In other words, the assumption at the heart of phenomenology is that there is a universal way of looking, that any perceivable object has a stable, universal essence that can be read the same way by any individual.

Phenomenology does not allow for the consideration of individual subjects, each shaped by a different set of historical and cultural circumstances—including the variables of gender, sex, class, race, and sexual preference—that influence how they see what they see. Applied to theatre or literature as a critical method, a phenomenological perspective implies that there are stable texts with immanent meanings that can consistently, rightfully be grasped.

Similarly, Foreman assumes the spectator will read his productions as he means them to be perceived by suspending his or her ideological perspective, worldview, and "essential illustrations" to embrace Foreman's. The spectator is not supposed to read the work—that is, to filter it through his or her own sensibility—but is asked instead to "blast"[22] into Foreman's world and perceive his constructs without evaluation.

The iconography in Foreman's productions, however, does not merely illustrate phenomena, but constructs a specific version of perceptual relationships for the gaze of a particular spectator. Foreman's ideological assumptions can best be examined by exploring his notion of theatrical displeasure.

Foreman writes that for man to be aware of his essential imbalance— "(man: imbalance of inner and outer)"[23]—he must never be lulled into a false sense of order or into perceiving the world as a coherent whole. In his second manifesto, he chides,

> But man wants usually to be able to believe that, just like the animal, he is at home in the world. That nature is his proper realm. So to point-out that man is NOT at home—
> Well, man can sometimes deal with that intellectually as the "message"
> So a realistic (which means comforting-style) work can tell the story of shipwreck, and sentiments of shipwreck can be expressed
> Because man can handle that emotionally by looking at it as ONE EXPERIENCE out of many . . . and so his conscious thinking makes him feel O.K. even in the face of a momentarily disturbing STORY about REAL PEOPLE.[24]

Foreman's style is antithetical to the kind of storytelling that allows the spectator to feel an illusory at-oneness. As he rejects the notion of catharsis, Foreman also rejects traditional linear narrative as a form that inspires a false sense of unity and coherence. Foreman was greatly influenced by Brecht, whose plays are a series of short episodes heralded by placards that break the narrative flow. Each moment in Foreman's plays is a discrete unit of information, and they do not necessarily add up to a meaningful whole.

In the landscape plays his texts resemble, the story is static; it does not follow a conventional plot or build in intensity toward a single, authoritative meaning. Foreman's texts, in fact, resemble what Frederic Jameson has called the schizophrenic breakdown of language, which "reorients the subject or speaker to a more literalizing attention to [its] words."[25] In Jameson's description, "As meaning is lost, the materiality of words becomes obsessive. . . . [A] signifier that has lost its signified has thereby been transformed into an image."[26] Words in Foreman's texts become material signifiers without signifieds, and are turned into a literal image of themselves as words.

This process occurs in Foreman's productions both aurally and visually. Performers pronounce sentences that hang in the air as nonsequiturs, and Foreman uses isolated words as scenographic elements strung up randomly in their obsessive materiality around the performance space. The written text has the same weight as all the other theatrical elements. It is incomplete, it does not offer the authority of a final ending, and it frustrates spectators' habitual expectations of narrative resolution found in traditional theatre. All this leads to a kind of boredom and displeasure, intentionally provoked so that the spectator has to work to overcome it perceptually.

The idea of pleasure in representation has frequently been suspect. Brecht begins his "A Short Organum for the Theatre" by saying, "The 'theatre's' broadest function was to give pleasure. It is the noblest function that we have found for 'theatre.'" He later writes, "Nothing needs less justification than pleasure."[27] Brecht, however, relates pleasure to history. He places it in a social context and suggests that our definition of pleasure should change over time and adapt to the current age.

Feminist film theorists have debated the gender-specific meaning of pleasure in the viewing experience. By analyzing the cinematic apparatus through a psychoanalytic interpretive strategy, critics such as E. Ann Kaplan, Mary Ann Doane, and Laura Mulvey suggest that film offers visual pleasure by objectifying the women in the narrative for the active male protagonist, with whom the male spectator is meant to identify. Women are also fetishized as objects to be looked at, thereby decreasing the threat of their sexual lack.[28] These feminist readings of film spectatorship emphasize that classical cinema constructs the spectator as male, leaving female spectators few—and unsavory—options for how to position themselves within the cinematic experience.

In "Visual Pleasure and Narrative Cinema," Laura Mulvey draws an analogy between psychoanalytic processes and those at work in film. Mulvey traces the psychological principles based on sexual difference in the workings of the cinematic apparataus. She notes that the pleasurable expectations of narrative cinema rely on the scopophilic instinct, which Freud defined as looking at another person as an erotic object. To activate the scopophilic drive, narrative cinema invites the male spectator to identify with the narrative's hero as the kind of ego ideal he saw in the mirror phase. The filmic hero becomes the spectator's ego ideal.

By associating his look with the hero's, and vicariously pursuing the woman in the narrative as the object of his desire, the mirror phase is duplicated for the spectator in cinema.[29] The woman is reduced to the Other—she who lacks the phallus. Simultaneously, cinema abates the threat of the castrated woman through fetishistic mechanisms that reduce her to a passive, acted-upon entity.

Mulvey concludes that the gaze, pleasurably directed by the cinematic apparatus, is in fact male, and that cinematic representations are constructed for male spectators. She writes, "The fascination of film is reinforced by pre-existing patterns of fascination already at work within the individual subject and the social formations that have molded him."[30] Filmic representations, by replicating the process of sexual differentiation, reproduce gender roles in which men are active subjects and women are passive victims—not subjects at all. Classical cinema reaffirms the gender positionings taught by the dominant culture. Mulvey insists that to break these patterns of fascination, it is necessary to "break with the normal pleasurable expectations in order to conceive a new language of desi.e."[31]

Recall that the Lacanian model positions women in the realm of the Imaginary, excluded from the Symbolic. In the sensuous realm, language is outside. Left passive in a narrative articulated by men who control its linguistic, social, political, and psychological power, women become objects pursued for the fulfillment of male desire. If male desire is the underlying principle driving narrative, then to disrupt the cinematic and narrative patterns that rob women of their subjectivity, women's desire must somehow find its place in representation.[32] Many feminist film critics have called for the abolition of visual pleasure in narrative cinema as one way to begin an alternative cinematic practice.[33]

Mulvey writes that by avoiding narrative forms that invite male identification and female passivity, male visual pleasure can be circumvented. The voyeuristic/scopophilic gaze can be broken down and critical distance can be imposed to break the "sleeping," fantasy state of the passive spectator. Just as Brecht argued that theatrical pleasure mystifies and perpetuates a hierarchy of social class, Mulvey argues that visual pleasure reifies relations of gender and sexuality. Here, Mulvey's ideas align with Brecht's alienation theory and, to a certain extent, with Foreman's aesthetics.[34]

In some ways, Foreman's construction of images cannot be parallel to that of the cinematic apparatus because he cannot control the spectator's gaze as carefully. Mulvey notes that the gaze is tightly controlled in cinema through the possibility of shifting its emphasis and direction with camera angles and editing. She writes: "It is the place of the look that defines cinema, the possibility of varying it and exposing it. This is what makes cinema quite different in its voyeuristic potential from say, striptease, theatre, shows, etc. Going far beyond highlighting a women's to-be-looked-at-ness, cinema builds the way she is to be looked at into the spectacle itself."[35]

Foreman's scenography, however, is intended to force the spectator's eye to scan the stage picture and in some respects to control the gaze by playing with focus. Davy argues, "He assumes that the spectator is continually scanning the visual field subliminally, and it is this kind of 'wide-angled' vision he is aiming for. He does not want the eye to become fixed on one point to the exclusion of others."[36] Foreman equalizes the elements of the visual field by using oversized props and a great deal of scenic color and detail. And he stretches strings across the stage to form geometrical patterns that pull the spectator's eye around the space.

Foreman also uses a kind of seduction to thwart the spectator's expectation of visual pleasure. Davy describes this effect in his work:

> A similar effect [to the enticement of musical numbers and their subsequent abrupt end] is achieved through visual imagery insofar as Foreman is successful in exploiting sexual impulses and prurient or voyeuristic tendencies. In *PAIN(T)* (1974), for example, numerous tableaux consisted of [Kate] Manheim and her sister, Nora, naked and in positions that were sexually implicit, if not explicit. At the same time, through techniques of "hiding and revealing," Foreman made it extremely difficult for the spectator to see the two women. Hence, with his new production style, Foreman worked to place the spectator in a kind of rapidly alternating "pull and push" situation, where at one moment the spectator can sense himself being seduced, or pulled into the emotional and intellectual realm of the play, and in the next moment he feels himself being pushed back or away from it.[37]

Foreman, then, does control the spectator's gaze to some extent. The female nude is constructed for the male spectator's gaze as a seductive image that Foreman can withhold, obscure, or offer at will. By assuming the seductiveness of female nudity and mounting illustrations of his own "relation to the problematic question of eroticism,"[38] Foreman offers this de-equalized stage picture as a challenge to be overcome. To achieve his aim of equalizing all the objects in the performance space, the seduction of the naked woman must be resisted. She must become an object no more important or interesting than the others. Foreman flatly states, "The aim is to discover how to live with lucidity and detachment amidst the powerful allure of this naked body. The ideal is not to be ruffled by it, but to create stage excitement that neutralizes its powerful tendency to pull focus."[39]

While he attempts to debunk traditional notions of theatrical pleasure, Foreman's idea of psychological pleasure remains intact. The pleasure that he alternately offers and denies is the same as that of traditional narrative theatre and film—women as erotic objects. Whether he obscures the object of desire by blinding the spectator with bright lights, allows the female nude to be available for male voyeurism, or blatantly fetishizes her with gigantic phalluses, the female nude is valued over the other objects in the stage picture as an erotic object. She is never reduced to an essence or phenomenon. Instead, her construction testifies to the conservative ideology to which this avant-garde artist subscribes.

Women as Ideology: Foreman's Early Work

The more specific analysis of the iconography in Foreman's early work that follows is contingent upon several points. First, this research necessitated the use of photographs and slides of Foreman productions from 1973 to 1977.[40] Although experiencing Foreman's plays in time and space is important to their total effect, the intent here is to look at recurrent images in the work. These images will be examined as ideological motifs that construct women as icons and afford a kind of psychological pleasure that Foreman seeks elsewhere to suppress.

Secondly, the intent here is not necessarily to condemn the work for trading in the currency of female sexuality, but to show that the preponderance of female nudity implies ideological assumptions that Foreman elsewhere denies. The power relationships inherent in the woman-as-icon imagery unbalances the stage picture in a manner different from Foreman's other scenic devices. The following productions are representative of the kinds of female images that appear in Foreman's early work, which are clearly constructed for a male gaze.

In these four productions, it is impossible to find textual justification for Foreman's stage pictures, and in fact, irrelevant to look for it. The text of *Sophia = (Wisdom) Part 3: The Cliffs* (1973), for example, is not a traditional narrative that might explain, in the course of relating its story, why Rhoda (Kate Manheim) should be naked. Foreman's texts are present in his productions for their objective, material value, rather than for their sense or interpretive meaning.

As the central character, Manheim appears nude quite frequently. The most salient images in the piece—for this analysis—are Manheim sitting nude on a bench, surrounded by one or two women and three men, all of whom are clothed; Manheim completely nude, with cotton balls stuck on her body, a man holding her hands over her eyes while another man stands beside them holding a larger-than-life foot; Manheim in a blanket, underneath which she is nude; and the recurring image of Manheim, again nude, methodically rolling on the floor with a fully clothed man who pins down her arms while they roll. There is no aggression implied in their encounter, but because the man is clothed, he is seen as more powerful than Rhoda.

The pace of *Sophia* was slower than the works that followed, and consisted of more static tableaux. As a result, the nude woman does not appear to be used here as an alternately hidden and revealed seducing agent. She seems instead to be gratuitously nude, perhaps to pull the focus and to challenge the spectator to perceive other objects in the visual field. Rhoda/Manheim appears vulnerable. Her body is barely covered by the blanket. Sitting on the bench, she pulls her limbs tightly into her body. Her eyes are covered and she is unable to see. She is pinned down by a man. She is constructed to be looked at, to be acted upon and reacted to in a manner in which the other performers are not. Her nudity strips her, in a sense, to an essence that marks her more than the other performers. Her femaleness is flaunted, limiting her to a sex class that has historically been at the mercy of male ideology.

John Berger, in *Ways of Seeing,* makes an analogy between oil painting and capitalist ideology that might be apt here:

> Oil painting did to appearances what capital did to social relations. It reduced everything to the equality of objects. Everything became exchangeable because everything became a commodity. All reality was mechanically measured by its materiality. The soul . . . was saved in a category apart. A painting could speak to the soul—by way of what it referred to, but never by the way it envisaged. Oil painting conveyed a vision of total exteriority.[41]

Foreman's work in *Sophia* functions in much the same way with regard to women. The objects in the performance space are there to be manipulated for the spectator (Foreman/male) as commodities, theoretically equal, but totally exterior. Ironically, reducing a woman to an exterior leaves her only with her sex; and her sex is an irreducible sign. A naked female body is laden with connotation, the most prevalent of which is sex object. In Foreman's productions, female sexuality becomes a commodity to be traded between Foreman and the male spectators.[42]

Foreman's attitude toward women as commodities is illustrated by an anecdote Kate Davy (*Richard Foreman and the Ontological-Hysteric Theatre*) tells about *PAIN(T)* (1974). The proscenium arch for the play was decorated with nineteenth-century French pornographic postcards. Foreman made similar postcards of Kate Manheim and her sister, Nora, the two women prominent in the production. After performances, Foreman would offer to sell the postcards for a certain price. If anyone accepted his offer, Foreman would raise the price higher and higher until the postcards became prohibitively expensive and, as Davy says, "inaccessible" or "unconsumable."[43]

Foreman constructs images of women as enticing products that he assumes male spectators will very much want to consume, either visually or through monetary exchange. To foil the spectators' pleasurable expectations, he shines lights in their eyes so that the seductive images are visually obscured, or outprices the postcards that bear the image of the nude female performers. Whether the product is accessible or not, Foreman still has constructed women as commodities. When the spectator is willing to exchange for them, Foreman makes it quite clear that they are not for sale.

Foreman has in a sense secured the women and their images as the objects of his own desire. They are his property, and while he displays them to male spectators in a game of hide and seek, he frustrates the system of male exchange in which women are commodities who are assigned value only through their purchase on the visual economy. Foreman thwarts visual pleasure in principle, but it remains in his productions in fact.

Foreman is the extratheatrical protagonist in the narrative of male desire which underlies his work. During these early performances, he would sit at a console in front of the playing space, running the lights and the sound. By controlling the speed of the taped sound track that often held performers' cues, he was able to manipulate the rate and flow of images, which effected the *a* perceptual difficulty and discomfort he wanted the spectator to undergo. He was the active male who controlled the production and was able to secure his desire.

Foreman says he was dealing explicitly with issues of eroticism in *PAIN(T)*, attempting the "boldest manifestation of erotic impulses I could face."[44] He sees eroticism as a distraction that disrupts other activities, and wanted, in this production, to explore the Western dichotomy between the demands of the body and those of the intellect.

The production's dominant theme is painting. Within the stage frames that Foreman constructs, women are the object of the painterly male gaze. The portable perspective grid used as a prop as well as a metaphor in *PAIN(T)* is always close to the front of the visual field. Through it, the spectator can see, at one point, a nude woman standing on a low platform, hands on hips, legs spread with one knee slightly bent, positioned directly behind a potted plant. The plant stands on a pedestal. The female body is treated as a kind of still life, an object to be arranged and captured like a bowl of fruit or an arrangement of ferns.

Manheim and her sister are often paired in *PAIN(T)* and their stances and attitudes parallel each other. At one moment, the women rest their feet on the low fence used to frame the playing space. Their arms are raised at the back of their heads to hold up their hair in a coy pose while they look out at the spectators. A man in a dunce's hat rests his hands on the fence and looks at their legs. In another image, the two women strike poses at parallel places in the stage picture. Nude except for brief underpants, knee-high socks, and tie-shoes, the women stand in profile, one leg slightly behind the other, right arm bent perpendicular to the body and the left arm at right angles to the shoulder. The same man looks at the fence while the women look out at the spectators.

The subject of *PAIN(T)* is the relationship between watching and being watched. In another pose, the women, nude now except for socks and shoes, appear close enough to embrace. They touch each other's faces. To their right (from the spectator's point of view), two men stand at a kind of high bar, watching. In a similar image, the same two men parallel each other, holding white cloths to their mouths while the nude woman from the still life looks across a low fence at Manheim, who is seminude. In another image, the still life woman, still nude, watches Manheim and her sister roll around on a bed set far in the rear of the space, where their interaction can just dimly be perceived. A close-up photograph of this image shows Kate and Nora Manheim, again semi-nude, lying with their heads at opposite ends of the bed and their legs inter-twined.

John Berger proposes that women sometimes interiorize the knowledge that they are being watched, so that their presence becomes a complex combina-tion of "surveyor" and "surveyed." He writes, "Women watch themselves being looked at. . . . The surveyor of woman in herself is male: the surveyed female. Thus she turns herself into an object—and most particularly an object of vision—a sight."[45] Berger's analysis begins to define the seductive look of women who are constructed to be looked at—for example, women in pornography (as we will see in chapter 4)—and here, Manheim and her sister. Their look implies knowledge of another look—the gaze of the male. The woman's image is constructed so specifically to fulfill male desire that his gaze is implicit in her own. The projection of male desire she wears completely denies her own subjec-tivity.[46]

In *PAIN(T)*, the women performers seem aware of the sexual allure of their poses, and as such, are projections of male desire. Davy says, "[Kate] Manheim is continuously aware of the process of performing while she is onstage"[47]:

> "I watch the audience very carefully and lots of times I try to figure out what people are thinking, especially people I know." When there is no one out there that she knows, she sometimes wonders, "Who am I doing this for?" and then, "I will single out someone who looks interesting and fantasize that I'm doing it for that person." The presence of spectators is important for Manheim.[48]

The performer's gaze is directed outward, while she is continually aware of the gaze directed at her. Manheim's passivity is implied in her description; she becomes both surveyor and surveyed.[49]

The attitude of the nude male performer in *PAIN(T)* is very different. He is completely revealed, his body position is straightforward instead of seductive, and he wears a hat. In one image, a lowered chandelier is shined directly onto his penis. The nude male performer who appears now and then in Foreman's work is qualitatively different from the nude female as a sign with denotative or connotative potential.

Because of the gender-specific nature of representation, a nude male is still identifiable as the active protagonist of the narrative at hand. Fully displaying the penis in representation, instead of objectifying the male, seems to concretize the realization of the mirror phase. A nude male onstage makes women's lack—

particularly when the nude female shares the representational space—more pronounced. As feminist attempts to eroticize or objectify the male body in pornography for women have shown (efforts detailed in chapter 4) the simple gender reversal does not work.

Michelle Barrett cautions, "Representation *does* bear some relation to something which we can know previously existed. . . . [It] is linked to historically constituted, real relations."[50] The male body does not signify the history of commodification that the female body represents, and in a representational exchange set up for male visual pleasure, the nude male is not the object of the exchange.[51] A male body cannot be objectified in same the way a woman's can be, especially when the spectator is contructed as male, as he is in Foreman's work.

Similar images of naked women appear in *Rhoda in Potatoland* (1976). Manheim once again appears naked except for shoes and socks, a peculiar state of undress that recurs in Foreman's work, which more than anything seems to increase Manheim's vulnerability. In one image, she sits on a bed tilted out toward the spectators. In another, Rhoda, now wearing a dark bra and transparent underwear as well as socks and shoes, is in the space with another woman in similar underclothes. Rhoda, slightly crouched over in profile, has one hand on the curve of a gigantic potato that fills the frame of a window at the rear of the stage. The other woman crouches behind Rhoda, with her hand on Rhoda's buttock in a position that echoes Rhoda's hand on the potato. While these images can be described formally in terms of the repetition of shapes in Foreman's stage picture,[52] from an ideological perspective he is reducing women's bodies to a plane equivalent with potatoes.

Within the same stage picture, another woman, fully clothed, sits forward of the pair in the stage space, holding an oversized coin that reads "ONLY BEING A TOURIST." Foreman is willing to parody the psychological aspects— such as voyeurism—operating in his work. But in the postmodern context, as Jameson points out, parody turns into pastiche, the imitation of "dead styles," since the stylistic innovation and individuation available for parody in modernism is no longer possible. Jameson describes pastiche as follows: "Pastiche is . . . a neutral practice of such mimicry, without parody's ulterior motive, without the satirical impulse, without laughter, without that still latent feeling that there exists something *natural* compared to which what is being imitated is rather comic."[53] Voyeurism is "naturalized" in representation constructed for the male spectator. But calling attention to it in the postmodern context does not make it comic, so much as reifies it and allows it to continue operating as a referent.

In *Book of Splendors* (1977), Foreman's use of woman-as-icon takes its most Lacanian turn. The stage picture includes many women naked except for boots or shoes and socks, or wearing short shirts and wide suspenders that barely cover their breasts. A nude man reappears in this production, plastered against the plexiglass cage that encloses him. (The male nude is usually segregated in Foreman's productions, when he appears.)

The man this time is completely nude, leaning against part of the narrow box with one hand pressed against the glass at his side, the other pressed against the glass above his head. Although his position in the cage would seem to frame him as an object to be looked at, the position of his body makes it appear that he is looking out of the box into the rest of the scene. His position, and the connotations of his gender, once again work to thwart his objectification.

Elements of bondage and dominance and phallic images are prevalent in *Book of Splendors*. Rhoda is naked except for the high black boots she wears. She is blindfolded, then tied up with a long, thick piece of ridged black tubing. The phallus makes its most concrete appearance here as a long, curved, hard piece of material that Rhoda holds arched up from her vagina. The male performers also carry phalluses in *Book of Splendors,* but theirs are straight and shorter, about half the size of Rhoda's.

Rhoda's phallus is a clear illustration of fetishism. According to Freudian psychoanalytic theory, women are threatening to men because they lack a penis, which compels men to fear losing their own. Fetishism equalizes this threat by imbuing women with metaphorical phalluses. In *Book of Splendors*, Foreman both fetishizes Rhoda and constructs an image in which the phallus is presented as the supreme signifier. As Rhoda holds the phallus to her vagina, a male performer wearing a black hood stands behind her, tilting her head back. Another hooded male performer kneels in front and slightly to the right of her (from the spectator's point of view), holding an open book above his head at the level of her vagina. The man behind her holds a funnel at her breast, from which a piece of white cloth "pours" like milk over the book, down onto the crouched man.

Read from a Lacanian perspective, the image is a return to the pre-Oedipal, Imaginary phase. Rhoda still has a phallus—she becomes the phallic mother. The men are hooded, unable to see and therefore not yet ready for the mirror phase, in which they recognize their own penis and their mother's lack. The mother's milk feeds the male child, who holds the book, the Symbolic realm of language and the Law of the Father. The child will eventually separate from the mother into the male realm. This image epitomizes Foreman's use of women in his work. They are strictly relegated to the Imaginary (and imaged), pre-Symbolic realm.

Images such as this one fill in the gaps in Foreman's written texts. His scripts might be fragmentary and open-ended, but his performance texts, carefully constructed with visual images, close on the inscription of women within gendered, heterosexual relations. As the production's *auteur,* Foreman is in some ways the ultimate, most authoritative spectator. He is the final author/

father of the performance text, and clearly shapes its meanings for his own narrative and visual pleasure.

Foreman's theatre is in a sense strictly therapy. Even Foreman admits he is illustrating his own traumas. Davy cautions, "Foreman works solely to please himself rather than a prospective audience,"[54] and Foreman agrees, "The work is all extremely personal. I'm doing it for myself. And then offering it to anybody else that might be encouraged by it, a little bit."[55] Those who might be encouraged by Foreman's work are the male spectators for whom the performance is in fact constructed.

Davy characterizes Foreman's plays as belonging to the " 'entity writing' category," in which "entity is linked to being or the human mind which is *internal* and has no identity—any sense of audience is absent."[56] But even in the process of simply allowing words to appear on the page—which is how Foreman describes his writing process—the language created through Foreman's identity is still gender-specific. As feminist revisions of Lacan have shown, language and words are formed through a psychological process that is ideologically marked and gender-biased. The one identity Foreman clearly maintains is his maleness. And as a scenographer, Foreman chooses iconography for which he himself as spectator—and by extension, male spectators—is clearly implied.

The problem with Foreman's theory of aesthetic rigor and his goal of altering consciousness by changing perceptual patterns is that it presupposes a spectator who is willing to be changed by the work in such a way. A spectator with different, but equally strong, ideological commitments might resist the formal manipulations of the work; she might read into Foreman's pictures in a way that belies his intent.

Foreman attempts to deconstruct the signs he chooses to their phenomenological essence, but for a feminist spectator observing his use of women he cannot go far enough. A woman is never "a woman is a woman is a woman," particularly when she is part of a representational frame. An image of a woman cannot merely denote, as might the essential signs Foreman attempts to construct. Placing women in a representation always connotes an underlying ideology and presents a narrative driven by male desire that effectively denies women's subjectivity.

Even as he tries to empty his work of anything but pure phenomena, Foreman reveals his operative ideological assumptions. He consistently elevates women to the level of myth, which Roland Barthes defines in part as "a type of social *usage* which is added to pure matter. . . . Myth is a type of speech chosen by history: it cannot possibly evolve from the 'nature' of things."[57] Foreman's construction of women is not natural or meaningless; it reflects the discourse of women's objectification in the history of representation.

Foreman has created a theatre from and for his likeness, which is itself a meaningful act. A feminist spectator is obviously unforeseen in his work, because she refuses to approach the work with the desired attitude. She is unwilling to leave her ideology outside the theatre and look at the work through the male gaze. She can only perceive it through a feminist filter that belies Foreman's claims of nonideology.

4

The Dynamics of Desire: Sexuality and Gender in Pornography and Performance

The role sexuality plays in performance and in the visual representation of women as sexual subjects or objects is an issue intensely debated within the feminist critical community. With its overt imaging of sexuality in an economic context constructed for and controlled by men, pornography has become the focus of this debate. This focus has prompted the creation of two opposing positions on the function of pornography within the culture. One position is represented by feminists who are prosex and who support the cultural production of sexual fantasies—for some groups, often in the form of lesbian pornography and the creation of performance-like, sadomasochistic rituals. The opposing view is articulated by antipornography feminists who argue for legislation against pornographic images of women, contending that pornography effuses sexual violence against women in the society at large.[1]

Alice Echols, in her critique of their analysis, writes that antiporn feminists have gone as far as legislating against imagination in the form of fantasy which "they claim is dangerous because it entails the substitution of an illusion for the 'social-sexual reality' of another person. In rejecting as so much 'male-identified mind-body dualism' the belief that fantasy is the repository of our ambivalent and conflictual feelings, [antiporn] feminists have developed a highly mechanistic, behaviorist analysis that conflates fantasy with reality and pornography with violence."[2] The insidious alliance between antipornography feminists and conservatives in the New Right—who have launched a moral crusade against both pornography and alternative sexual lifestyles—makes lucid analysis of the representation of sexuality crucial.

The feminist antiporn movement has its antecedents in American feminism of the 1970s, which shifted its focus away from sexuality to a notion of sexual difference that reified gender.[3] Unifying women around the commonalities provided by gender required a concomitant disarming of the perceived threat lesbian sexuality posed to the cohesiveness of the movement, highlighting, as it would, women's differences in their choice of sexual preference. Sue-Ellen Case believes that this shift marginalized lesbians by recasting lesbianism in political terms and desexualizing the lesbian lifestyle with the suffix "-feminist."[4]

The lesbian prosex position vis-à-vis pornography and sexual fantasy is in some respects an effort to recuperate the lesbian position within feminism. Lesbians have a lot at stake in the antipornography debate, because despite feminist efforts to reduce it to female friendship, or to diffuse it across a lesbian continuum, lesbianism is still defined by a choice of sexuality.[5] The antisex morality of the antiporn movement threatens to render lesbians not only marginal to feminism, but totally invisible.

If sexuality is censored, if fantasies are legislated against, if the feminist movement is allowed to dictate or implicitly condones governmental legislation of the "proper" expression and representation of sexuality, the free expression of self and sexuality will slip into a totalitarian framework. The fact of lesbian sexuality as sexual expression and representation makes the lesbian perspective crucial to an understanding of the politics of pornography.

This chapter will briefly review the opposing positions on the pornography debate, applying their principles to various forms of performance and the visual representation of women's sexuality. From performance art and erotica, through lesbian performance and lesbian pornography, a range of materials will illustrate the influence of both traditional and feminist theories of gender and sexuality on the representation of women within the culture.

Lack of Illusions:
The Antipornography Debate and Cultural Feminist Performance

The model antipornography law drafted by Andrea Dworkin and Catherine MacKinnon defines pornography as "the graphic sexually explicit subordination of women through pictures and/or words."[6] The law goes on to enumerate the various conditions under which the representation of women is considered pornographic, focusing on sexual objectification as the primary determining factor. In an accompanying statement, Dworkin clarifies the issue of subordination in terms of an imbalance of power: "Subordination is a social-political dynamic consisting of several parts. The first is that there is a hierarchy. There's somebody on the top and somebody on the bottom. . . . The second . . . is objectification. The third . . . is submission. . . . The fourth is violence."[7]

For Dworkin, the insertion of power into social, political, and sexual situations automatically establishes a hierarchy that leads to violence against women. Feminists who embrace this position as an argument against pornography are often allied theoretically and politically with cultural feminism.[8] Cultural feminists tend to valorize what they see as innate, biologically based differences between men and women. Women as the life source, for example, and men as destructive warmongers are distinctions commonly drawn by cultural feminists. Since the feminist antiporn campaign is based on an analysis that sees male sexuality as inherently aggressive and violent, the cultural feminist stance offers a theoretical framework for this view.

Because male sexuality is problematic within the stereotyped, polarized version of the sex/gender system that distinguishes this analysis, much cultural feminist performance art attempts to evade the issue of sexuality and desire by privileging spirituality. Theoretically locating their performances in a natural, spiritual realm is an attempt to eradicate the dominance/submission paradigm that underlies representation.[9] However, as some critics argue, this focus on spirituality also tends to remove the possibilities for potential resistance, that is, for representing women with power.[10] If power adheres in sexuality, and cultural feminists assume power leads to violence against women, it becomes politically and artistically necessary to attempt to disengage representation from desire.

This desexualizing is particularly important to heterosexual cultural feminist performance artists, who view the disarming of desire as one of the first steps toward the "feminization" of the male. In cultural feminist performance art, and in cultural feminist theatre, which is discussed in chapter 5, the body is idealized as a spiritual vessel, and sexuality is reduced to reproductivity, often symbolized by women's contextualization in nature.

Performance artists such as Leslie Labowitz and Hannah Wilke maintain this personal, spiritual, biologistic approach to politics and representations of the body. Since their work focuses on a reification of sexual difference, they opt not to examine differences among women based on race, class, and sexual preference. Instead, they propose unifying, essential female connections that will forge the globe in spiritual peace. In *Sproutime* (1980), for example, Labowitz invites spectators into a greenhouse setting, where she is "nude and softly lit,"[11] watering her sprouts. Performance art historian Moira Roth, who is sympathetic to the retreat into nature and spirituality, says, "Certainly she is expressing not only her own need, but one increasingly shared by others, both men and women, for psychic and spiritual nourishment in such a painful moment in history."[12] Feeding the spirit, however, disregards the pervasiveness of external gender codes and markings that operate on and within the body's communication of meaning.

Wilke also privileges women's biological, natural capabilities over an examination of the cultural construction of gender differences in her performance art. Like most cultural feminists, Wilke universalizes her images of women's bodies, ignoring the specificity of the historical moment with statements like "Women are the same everywhere in the world."[13] Her claim that women are "biologically superior. I can have a baby, you can't" indicates her prescriptions for the ideal expression and fulfillment of womanhood. Wilke believes: "To be the artist as well as the model for her own ideas, whether sexually positive or negative, she [the artist] must also resist the coercion of a fascist feminism, which devolves on traditional politics and hierarchies in feminist guise rather than self-realization with respect to the physical superiority of women as the life source."[14]

While Wilke's assertion sounds like a mystical, spiritual charge, at base this touted superiority of women translates into procreation. Implied in this analysis is the maintenance of traditional family structures and gender roles. No attempt is made to deconstruct the biological/essentialist view of women. There is no critique of the cultural construction of sexuality or gender implied in Wilke's manifesto.

Roth and Lucy Lippard trace the origins of this tradition in feminist performance art to the practice of consciousness-raising, the predominant cultural form of the early women's movement.[15] The autobiographical nature of feminist performance work in the 1970s was in line with feminist politics based on sharing personal experience and on searching for commonalities among women. Since women share basic biology, the nude female body became the literal and metaphorical site in performance art for women's unification.

The prevalence of nudity in the work reflected the movement's concern with attitudes toward women's bodies. Nudity in performance also paralleled the impetus in women's fiction and poetry to provide a forum for women's newly heard voices, by attempting to symbolically reclaim women's subjectivity through the body. The body art concept also stemmed from the cultural feminist impulse to expose women's innate differences from men, and to signify a departure from the more violent tradition of male performance art that preceded the feminist work.[16]

Female nudity continues to be a frequent image in cultural feminist performance art. Many performers insist that the female body, stripped to its "essential femaleness," communicates a universal meaning recognizable by all women. They see the nude female body as somehow outside the system of representation that objectifies women, free of the culture's imposed constructs and constrictions. Yet Lippard points out that performers like Wilke and Carolee Schneeman, who frequently performed nude, had beautiful bodies that implicitly legitimized their exposure in the performance space according to the dominant culture's standards. Although they purportedly displayed their bodies to signify unity among women, in the genderized terms of the performance space their bodies became accountable to male-defined standards for acceptable display.

Another performance artist, Rachel Rosenthal, exposed her body in *Bonsoir, Dr. Schon!* (1980) only to point out its flaws, which she could not reconcile with her more flattering attributes. Rosenthal says she was embarrassed to the point of fainting by performing nude, yet she submitted to a self-devised humiliation session in which her "'bad points' are demonstrated to the audience by female assistants and marked with red tape, rubber bats, spiders, and snakes."[17]

Wilke, Labowitz, and other artists attempt to use nudity in performance to create female subjectivity, but they are caught in the gender-polarized terms and objectifying strictures of the performance apparatus. Rather than stripping the performer of her socially constructed gender role, her nudity relegates her to subservient status as "woman." From a materialist feminist perspective, the female body is not reducible to a sign free of connotation. Women always bear the mark and meaning of their sex, which inscribes them within a cultural hierarchy.[18]

Cultural feminist performance artists such as Labowitz and Wilke avoid sexual referents that would force a confrontation with desire and sexuality by grounding their work in nature and the body, which is displayed and reified as the site of gender difference. These performance artists attempt to evade the power hierarchy that cultural feminists find explicit in representations of women by separating images of the female nude from sexual desire.

Sexuality, however, is a tangible currency in the representational exchange. Sexuality is at base the expression of affectional preference, while gender is based on sex-class. But sexuality, in Western culture, is as rigidly constructed and prescribed as gender. While it is crucial not to conflate sexuality with gender, expressions of sexuality further illustrate the operation of gender codes and constructs in the representation of the female body.

Because heterosexuality—the pattern of linking oppositional gender classes into sexual partnership—is naturalized by dominant ideology, it is not seen as a material choice, and is therefore compulsory.[19] Recasting sexuality as a choice—for instance shifting a woman's desire from men to other women—also affects how she sees herself as a woman. Once heterosexuality is no longer compulsory, femininity also becomes suspect as a "natural" construct. The choice of lesbian sexuality is in some ways a rejection of the female, as that gender class has been culturally constructed.

Sexual role-playing, then, has implications for gender play; the way people perform their sexuality influences how they wear their gender.[20] If desire is the subtext of narrative, sexuality and gender are equally motivating forces behind representation. A body displayed in representation that belongs to the female gender class is assumed to be heterosexual, since male desire organizes the representational system. Disrupting the assumption of heterosexuality, and replacing male desire with lesbian desire, for example, offers radical new readings of the meanings produced by representation.

Just as the sex/gender system is a cultural construction mandated to serve sociopolitical ends, desire is also constructed out of cultural contexts. As Gayle Rubin notes, "Desires are not preexisting biological entities, but rather, . . . they are constituted in the course of historically specific social practices."[21] Desire and sexuality, as cultural constructs, also influence gender formation. Rubin adds, "Gender affects the operation of the sexual system, and the sexual system has had gender-specific manifestations. But although sex and gender are related, they are not the same thing, and they form the basis of two distinct arenas of social practice."[22]

Visual representations of women illustrate the overlaps and distinctions between sexuality and gender, and chart the operation of desire in relaying meanings between images and viewers. The magazine *Eidos*, for example, bills itself as "erotic entertainment for women."[23] The title refers to the basic ideas by which members of a culture organize and interpret their experience. In the context of pornography and erotica, the editors are laying claim to a new organization and interpretation of sexual experience. *Eidos'* content will reinterpret the relationship between gender and sexual desire by aiming its erotic content at heterosexual women readers, instead of men. It reverses the traditional gender roles the pornography industry reinforces by portraying men as sexual objects and women as the viewers.

Eidos' editors attempt to address the sexual objectification of women in pornography by reversals that would objectify the male for women's visual pleasure. Women are depicted in nature, and the images of naked men are meant to feminize men by placing them in parallel positions. Women's sexuality is portrayed as gentle, emotional, and nonaggressive. The images of men propose that, immersed in nature and spirituality, men can be taught to give up their aggressive, violent sexuality and become feminized as artistic nudes. In a manner similar to cultural feminist performance art, *Eidos* implies that stripping people to their nude bodies will also strip away the layered cultural constructions of both sexuality and gender.

The editors' implication, however, is misguided. The representation of bodies is always ideologically marked; it always connotes gender, which carries with it the meanings inscribed by the dominant culture.[24] Simply switching gender roles, and gender values, continues to bind representation to the system of sexual difference that gives it shape. As E. Ann Kaplan points out, female desire is not at all as powerful as male desire in representation.[25] Reorganizing this binary opposition so that the weaker term is placed in the theoretically powerful position does nothing to deconstruct the dichotomy. It simply exchanges the placement of the terms.

Eidos assumes the same purist, vaguely self-righteous pose that characterizes cultural feminist performance art. Sexuality and desire are disarmed, their power dynamics purportedly erased by the inscription of both male and female gender into a natural, dispassionate, spiritual space. There is no fantasy implied in the magazine's scenarios, and few interactions are represented. The images are cerebral, rather than erotic, more a comment on the editors' careful avoidance of what the culture considers pornographic than the production of a different kind of sexual excitement. The images do not really work as a new pornography.

Erotica such as *Eidos* tries to generate "politically correct" sexual images by portraying the body as a spiritual vessel and by simply reversing male gender positioning. In contrast, performance artist Karen Finley works to disrupt traditional pornography by obstructing the exchange of meaning between image and spectator, and by locating the body as the source of excrement and detritus.

Finley became a controversial performer on the downtown Manhattan art scene in 1986. She had been performing her unique brand of performance art on the European performance scene for quite some time, but was brought to the attention of New York audiences when *Village Voice* writer C. Carr began to call special attention to her pending local appearances that spring. Carr's beat is the offbeat, as it were. Since her tastes run toward feminist, lesbian, and other gender-bending performers, she was clearly intrigued by Finley, and featured her upcoming downtown performances in a kind of hot tips preview section.

Several weeks after Finley began to present (very) late-night performances at venues such as The Kitchen, the *Voice* ran Carr's cover story "Unspeakable Practices, Unnatural Acts: The Taboo Art of Karen Finley."[26] Carr's style for the Finley story was somewhat incendiary, although no more so than other, even more sensational cover stories the *Voice* had run on topics such as gay male back-room sex clubs like the defunct Mineshaft. Finley, however, is a woman, and the fact that the paper featured a cover photograph of her performing with one of her breasts exposed—and its nipple erect—prompted an outpouring of angry response from readers and other *Voice* writers that filled the paper's letters pages and opinion columns for several weeks.

Finley has worked as a hustler in strip joints in Chicago and San Francisco, and now reverses the power relations inherent in stripper/spectator positionings in her performances. The element of sadomasochism present in the stripper's relationship with the spectator is complex and subtle, as power circulates between the two positions. The stripper is essentially inaccessible. She is positioned as an elusive object of desire, guarded by the representational frame, who can be seen, sometimes touched, but not *had* within the terms of the exchange. In this context, she is in some ways the sadist in a relationship built on male masochism. Yet male spectators can certainly fantasize themselves in positions of power, which would reverse this relationship.[27] The framework for the exchange is economic. Spectators pay to see the image of the stripper as commodity; they buy control over the gaze. Whether they position themselves as sadists or masochists, their power lies in controlling the illusion that the stripper is performing for them.

Finley, however, refuses to give male spectators their money's worth. Rather than offering her body as a sadistically inaccessible commodity, an idea for male spectators to consume in a masochistic exchange, Finley offers herself as already consumed. She appears as refuse from an exchange of sexual power that is completely self-contained. What remains of the body and sexuality has already been digested, processed, and regurgitated as splintered, violent images and incoherent words, to be meaningfully reassembled only by spectators with stomachs strong enough for such consumption.

In her foulmouthed and often physically foul performances, Finley subverts traditional gender expectations by presenting what Carr calls "a frightening and rare presence—an unsocialized woman."[28] Although Finley bases her work in the body, her content is not the biologically ordained capabilities idealized in cultural feminist performance art. She focuses on the circulation of sexual power assumed by a woman who will not be socialized as sexually submissive according to her assigned gender role. Much of Finley's uncontrolled, stream-of-consciousness verbiage spews from shifting personae marked only by gender: "Finley often appropriates the male point of view and male desire in her language. Or some woman character starts fucking whoever [*sic*] up the ass, magically acquiring the power of men. Her work returns again and again to oral or anal sex, usually associating them with power."[29]

By changing gender roles in her performance, assuming nameless personae who describe random sexual encounters with partners across a gender spectrum, Finley's sexuality seems autoerotic. Because she appropriates the male perspective while maintaining the female gender, all sexuality appears to be about power, and about the body's capacity for expressing its base urges and desires.

Finley does not characterize her work as pornography, but Carr qualifies her relationship to it: "Whatever might spew from the wound in the psyche Finley describes is the language of pornography. But she renders the pornography impotent. In this id-speak, shitting, vomiting, and fucking are all equal. Desire attaches to disgust."[30] Finley performs in gender-mixed clubs, but thwarts heterosexual male spectators' desire by basing her narratives in grotesque perversion. In performances called "I Like to Smell the Gas Passed from Your Ass," "I'm an Ass Man," and "Yams Up My Granny's Ass"—in which Finley dumps a can of yams over her naked buttocks and lets it drip into her boots—she subverts pornography's representation of desire with images that confound mainstream sexuality by shifting the typical balance of power.[31] Her aggressive denial of the power dynamics of legitimate sexuality—that is, heterosexuality, in which men are powerful and women are passive—angers male spectators, who often throw lit cigarettes at her.

Finley refuses to participate in the rules of representation by objectifying herself. In performance, objectification implies an active male spectator who is invited to identify with the narrative's hero in his search for the fulfillment of his desire.[32] Finley does not offer herself as a passive object. She forces men to be passive in the face of her rage, and she desecrates herself as the object of their desire, thereby mocking their sexuality. Her refusal to play the game leaves the male spectator nowhere to place himself in relation to her performance. He can no longer maintain the position of the sexual subject who views the performer as a sexual object.

Finley's work revises the power balance in traditional pornography, because her body is subordinate only to her own will. She changes the axis of the power exchange by claiming sexual power for herself to wield. Cultural feminists assume sexual power forms a hierarchy that leads to violence against the women who cling to its lowest rungs, but such a hierarchy develops only when there are sexual subjects and objects available to rank and trade. Finley has taken her body off this representational commodities market by refusing to appear as a consumable object.

Karen Finley breaks from cultural feminist performance art traditions that evade issues of sexuality and power. She clearly is not speaking for global feminism, but she is still publicly performing issues that are ultimately personal. She describes her art as the expression of personal pain and rage, of emotions she cannot resolve intellectually. She performs in a trance, unrehearsed. Analysis seems to be missing from her primordial ooze. Although sexuality and gender are shattered and meaningless in her narratives, what remains is a quivering mass of unnameable, ruptured flesh—the human waste of sexuality, gender, and performance. The shock value in Finley's work foregrounds cultural constructions in a negative, brutal way that eventually forces spectators to look away.

Like the Mephistophelian scientist in David Cronenberg's remake of *The Fly* (1986), Finley can only transport herself to lower and lower, more debased forms of life. There is not much potential for radical change in Finley's work because—like cultural feminists determined to define themselves in opposition to men—she is still caught within the representational system to which she refers. Although male spectators are challenged and confronted in Finley's work, her aims are achieved by abusing herself under representational terms that remain operative from the male point of view. Finley perverts the stripper's position, but remains defined by its traditional history. Because she is mired in the corporeality of her own flesh as it has been abused in the system of representation, she never takes flight into sexual and gender fantasies of liberation.

Fantasy as Liberation: Lesbian Performance and Sexuality

The structure of desire, by necessity, differs across sexual preference. Pornographic narratives or any kind of performance for sexual partners of the same sex construct a different relationship between performers and spectators on the basis of gender roles. In lesbian performance, the representation of desire is often startling because of this difference. Lesbian sexuality is given voice and imaged in theatre, where heterosexual male desire has historically reigned in the form of the male gaze.

The kind of lesbian performance discussed below must be distinguished as one variety of lesbian theatre. Performances at the WOW Cafe take their cues from work which took place in club settings in Manhattan's East Village from 1982 to 1984.[33] The club performances were characterized by a mix of styles and conventions, ranging from stand-up comedy to camp genre parodies, all marked by a distinct lack of polish with regard to script construction, acting, directing, and scenic values. Although many of these lesbian performance pieces are now being presented in more conventional theatre settings, they are antithetical in both form and style to lesbian theatre which remains in the well-made play tradition, of which the work of the late playwright Jane Chambers is perhaps the most well-known example.

In the lesbian performance context, playing with fantasies of sexual and gender roles offers the potential for changing gender-coded structures of power. Power is not inherently male; a woman who assumes a dominant role is only malelike if the culture considers power as a solely male attribute. Creating a stage motivated by different kinds of desire allows experimentation with style, roles, costume, gender, and power, and offers alternative cultural meanings. Lesbian performance foregrounds the subversion of the dominant culture's gender-polarized images of sexual power in the context of lesbian desire. Lesbian performers, writers, and directors often parody dominant cultural images of gender to deconstruct gender-specific conduct and codes.

Lesbian performance in Manhattan's East Village is housed primarily at the WOW Cafe, which now occupies a floor in a nearly-abandoned warehouse building on East 4th Street, across from LaMama. When the Cafe opened in 1982, it offered a place for mostly lesbian women to meet, to drink coffee or buy beer from an impromptu kitchen, and to be entertained by informal performances. For a time, lesbian performers based at WOW also performed at other East Village performance clubs, which made for a theatre experience not unlike a progressive dinner for their audiences. On any given weekend night, spectators could see an 8:00 P.M. show at WOW and travel en masse to the 11:00 P.M. show at Club Chandalier or 8BC. There, farther into the remotest reaches of the lower East Side, spectators could watch WOW performers work in a different space, for an audience somewhat more mixed across gender roles and sexual preferences.

Performances at WOW are now offered at 8:00 P.M. and 11:00 P.M., drawing their audiences by word of mouth from the established East Village lesbian community. In a sense, as Lois Weaver, one of the WOW founders, recently remarked, it is a "community built around a theatre." Or, as WOW member

Alina Troyano countered, it is "theatre of necessity." Troyano originally came to WOW "looking for girls."[34] The Cafe's social setting is as important as the entertainment it offers. The social element lends the performance pieces an aura of "community theatre," which helps to structure its meanings. There are many "in-jokes" in WOW Cafe performances, which might be lost in different venues.

Expanding the boundaries of gender roles is a given both in the performances and the WOW space, in which the spectators, as well as the performers, wear costumes that push at the constructs of gender-specific codes. Since most of the spectators at WOW are lesbians, the performers' manipulation of traditional sexual and gender roles is mirrored in the audience. Often, women known in the community to be more "masculine" in manner and style will arrive to see performances dressed in "feminine" costumes—or vice versa. This inversion is mirrored in performance, where for the spectator, part of the fun is frequently seeing someone she knows assume her opposite "butch" or "femme" role on stage. To be "femme" is an option for lesbians that falls at one end of a gender role continuum that offers "butch" as an option at the other end.

The contradictory use of butch/femme in lesbian performance assumes the underlying pervasiveness of this opposition within a culture and a representational system that supports its operation. But if the lesbian subject position is seen as a refusal of this culturally constructed opposition—that is, as a refusal of strictly dichotomized choices—the layering of gender stereotypes onto the lesbian performer fundamentally shifts their meanings.[35]

Attention to gender costuming is key to *Chit Chat with Carmelita* (1984), an ongoing lesbian performance structured as a talk show. Hostess Carmelita Tropicana (Alina Troyano) is a lesbian performer dressed in female drag (that is, as a very feminine woman. Femininity, in the lesbian context, is foregrounded as drag, the assumption of an "unnatural" gender role), as are many of her invited guests. These performers foreground the gender role of women in heterosexual society and within the lesbian community by exaggerating the gestures and costuming of the feminine woman as "femme." The concern with costuming in the construction of character and personae in *Chit Chat* is important and elaborate, as if to acknowledge that people's carefully constructed "looks" have much to do with the way they are gender coded. The gender-specific costumes, however, assume new meanings through the performers' sexual and gender role-play.

In *Chit Chat*, Carmelita appears in a long, red, flowered evening gown, wearing a feather boa and heavy makeup. Carmelita is a Carmen Miranda "send-up," a persona with a thick Cuban accent constructed by a performer whose actual ethnicity is also Cuban. Thus, Troyano parodies both her ethnic and her gender role. The "femme" costume on Carmelita Tropicana is a comment on both itself and the performer. Carmelita appropriates the exaggerated feminine apparel for lesbian theatre. The audience shrieks their approval at her appearance and, with catcalls and applause, participates in the parody of sexual meanings.

At another point in the piece, Carmelita appears dressed in a tuxedo as the Spanish-speaking pop singer Julio Iglesias to sing love songs about women. This double lesbian drag show foregrounds the notion of gender as drag,[36] and parodies the camp tradition of male homosexual female impersonation. Carmelita's impersonation of Iglesias also appropriates the popular romantic music tradition—another bastion of strict gender role education—to express lesbian sexuality.

The structure of the piece parodies typical talk show formats. Carmelita sings several off-key melodies, including a flourishing rendition of Debbie Boone's "You Light Up My Life," offers a Cuban/Japanese cooking lesson in which she hacks up a chicken with a meat cleaver, and interviews various guests. Tammy Whynot, Lois Weaver's character from the Split Britches Company's production *Upwardly Mobile Home*, appears as one of the guests. Whynot is also a "send-up" of the femme role. Weaver wears her dyed, platinum-blonde hair bouffant-style, paints her face with heavy but tasteful makeup, and decorates herself with rhinestone jewelry and satin dresses. The effect is meant as commentary: Exaggerating stereotypes in the lesbian context foregrounds gender as an unnatural construction. Still, Weaver's and Troyano's impersonations of female gender are affectionate and empathetic.

In an improvised exchange, Carmelita interviews Tammy Whynot about her new book, and Weaver reads a poem called "When Mama Was Away" that satirizes the working mother's dilemma. Weaver arrives at Club Chandalier already in character, and maintains the Tammy Whynot persona throughout the evening as she mingles with the audience. Five or six *Chit Chat* guests are lesbians from the community with whom most of the audience are personally acquainted. Several performance artists attend, playing their trademark performance personae. This intertextuality helps to create the representation's shared meanings.

The people who really understand the articulated and implied nuances of *Chit Chat*, however, are lesbians. Lesbian sexuality is overtly acknowledged in the piece, from Carmelita's feminine flirting, to director Holly Hughes' Super-8 "dykeumentary" of lesbian couples being knocked down by ocean waves on Provincetown beaches, to a segment called "Tattle Tale," in which several "famous" lesbian couples are interviewed à la *The Newlywed Game* about their sex lives. Lesbian desire is also an undercurrent that heightens the exchange, acknowledged implicitly between spectators and performers.

Lesbian desire is always assumed in WOW Cafe performances. Lesbianism automatically becomes the axis of categorization, so that when lesbian content is infused into a popular cultural format, the form and its conventions are foregrounded, not the lesbianism. Despite the director's intentions, in a film like Donna Dietch's *Desert Hearts* (1986), it is the lesbianism of the two main characters that is shocking, given the viewing expectations of a general audience. Since lesbianism is assumed in WOW performances, the genderized conventions of popular forms become startling instead.

The WOW Cafe performers always assume lesbianism as a fluid base from which to fantasize and explore changing gender roles. For example, lesbianism as a neutral category, apart from a polarized gender continuum, appears in *Heart of the Scorpion* (1984), a parody of Harlequin Romances written, directed, and performed by Alice Forrester. In the typical melodramatic, unrequited love format, Annabelle, selflessly working as a governess for a young girl, is snubbed by her would-be lover, Ran. In the performance, both Annabelle and Ran are played by Forrester. Since there is no attempt to play the vocal range or body language of the male character, the couple is represented as lesbian. As Kate Davy points out, "Making all of the couples women not only parodies the Harlequin Romance formula, but heterosexual relationships as well, in so far as they are grounded in polarities of sexual difference. . . . Although, clearly, the production is devised primarily for entertainment, the intent to undermine the social and sexual values of the romance genre is evident."[37]

Sexuality is often directly represented in lesbian performance, both as content and as style. In *Heart of the Scorpion,* the foregrounding of lesbian romance in the parody subverts traditional expectations of the genre. In *An Evening of Disgusting Songs and Pukey Images* (1985), a coproduction by Spiderwoman Theatre and Split Britches, lesbian sexuality is integral to the production's content and style.

Spiderwoman Theatre is one of the oldest working feminist theatre troupes in the United States. The groups' three principal performers are sisters Muriel and Gloria Miguel and Lisa Mayo, Cuna-Rappahannock Indians who were raised in Brooklyn, New York. Spiderwoman's productions are both grounded in and parody the sisters' ethnicity. The name of the troupe refers to a Hopi household god known as the goddess of creation, who taught her people to weave.

From this mythic inspiration, Spiderwoman developed a technique called "story-weaving," in which they intertwine stories with words and movement.[38] They borrow freely from ritual traditions, storytelling, Native American myths, and slapstick comedy. Their aggressively nonlinear performance texts are an amalgamation of styles and contents, all presented with feminist intent.

Split Britches is in some senses an offshoot of Spiderwoman Theatre— Peggy Shaw and Lois Weaver, two of Split Britches' three performers, met while performing with Spiderwoman and eventually left the group to work together. Deborah Margolin is the third member of the Split Britches company, but did not perform in *Pukey Images.*

The narrative in this production is nonlinear and incoherent, but Shaw and Weaver conduct a subtextual seduction that clearly represents lesbian sexuality. Even though *Pukey Images* was presented at Theatre for the New City—a bit out of the WOW context but part of the East Village neighborhood—most audience members know Shaw as the more butch and Weaver as the more femme in one of the community's most visible lesbian relationships.[39] In *Pukey Images,* however, Shaw and Weaver shift back and forth on a continuum between butch and femme roles.

The other performers wear Spiderwoman's trademark bright colors and eclectic Native American fabrics and feathers. Shaw and Weaver wear dark pants, leather vests with no shirts, and sometimes bowler hats, evoking a kind of *Chicago*-style, steamy Bob Fosse look. Through most of the performance, they dance around each other, but the sexual tension between them permeates the stage regardless of other events. They seduce each other by trading charged sexual power in which desire is the only shared meaning.[40]

Split Britches' productions are known for their often eclectic combinations of fastidious attention to realistic detail with bizarre flights of surrealistic fancy. In their signature piece, *Split Britches* (1983), the stultifying daily routine of three rural women is captured by repetitive dialogue and long pauses, then suddenly interrupted by bursts of energy and narrative color. The narrative is based on the experiences of women from Weaver's family in the Blue Ridge Mountains of Virginia. Although much of her work as a director and performer could be called semi-autobiographical, Weaver says she sees performance as a chance for people to put their fantasies on stage. Split Britches' performances usually create eccentric characters that grow from all three performers' desire to perform the less visible parts of themselves.

In *Upwardly Mobile Home* (1985), for example, Weaver again plays the bleached-blonde Tammy Whynot, a would-be country western singer, reflecting her own geographic and cultural origins; Shaw plays a lesbian mother, a role she plays at home, but which is distanced in performance by the addition of an Eastern European accent; and Deborah Margolin plays the aggressive, hard-sell manager of their performing act, playing off her own Jewish ethnicity.

The trio is living in poverty in a van parked below the Brooklyn Bridge, acting as a support system for their friend Lost Petal, who is participating in a bridge-sitting contest. If Lost Petal wins the contest, she will win a mobile home and share it with the others. Since the three visible characters are unemployed performers forever dreaming up ways to attract agents and backers, the narrative is set in a theatrical context.

The basic, simple plot of *Upwardly Mobile Home* is disrupted by surreal, imaginative monologues that break the fourth wall and linear narrative conventions the play establishes. For instance, without dropping her Eastern European character, Shaw directly addresses the spectators, asking them if their seats are

Spiderwoman Theatre's *An Evening of Disgusting Songs and Pukey Images*
Lisa Mayo, Muriel Miguel, Peggy Shaw, Naja Beje, Lois Weaver, Pam Verge, and Gloria Miguel
in the original 1978 production in Florence.
(Photo by Antonio Sferlazzo/Françoise Lucchese)

The Split Britches Company's *Split Britches*
Lois Weaver (foreground), Deborah Margolin, and Peggy Shaw (standing)
in the 1983 signature production.
(Photo by Eva Weiss)

The Split Britches Company's *Upwardly Mobile Home*
Left to right: Lois Weaver, Peggy Shaw, and Deborah Margolin in the
1985 production.
(Photo by Eva Weiss)

comfortable, and if they are getting what they paid for. She makes the audience aware that it is separate from her fantasy, disrupting the normal theatre convention that requires suspension of disbelief.

This willingness on the part of lesbian playwrights and performers to locate their work in theatre conventions, rather than in the illusionless documentation of most cultural feminist performance art, allows for the use of fantasy to imagine different realities. Gender roles, for example, are reimagined along an expanded continuum. Sexuality and desire, as opposed to being banished as taboos, are continually present as subtext in these performances. The presence of lesbian desire, in fact, helps to refashion the manner in which gender and sexual roles are played in both performance and reality. Basing their work in the conventions of theatre also allows these performers to comment on and manipulate the traditional gender-coded performance apparatus.

Lesbian performances at WOW generally take themselves much less seriously than most cultural feminist performances. Self-parody in terms of gender, race, ethnic identity, and class provides a starting point for redefining all demarcations of gender, race, ethnic identity, and class. In one of *Upwardly Mobile Home*'s more absurdist moments, Margolin engineers the trio's audition for a Jewish agent. Wearing a Supremes-style dress that encloses them in an elasticized embrace, Shaw, Weaver, and Margolin sing "I Like to Be in America" from *West Side Story* in Yiddish. Only Margolin is at all comfortable with the translation, but the fact that Shaw and Weaver stumble over the lyrics and the accent foregrounds the parody. The dress alludes to the construction of black female performers as cultural commodities, while the translation into Yiddish comments ironically on the idealism of all immigrant aspirants to the American dream. By drawing from a grab bag of personae mixed across gender, race, ethnic identity, and class, and performing them without attempting to layer impersonations on top of their already specific characterizations, the Split Britches performers redirect spectators' attitudes toward differences among women.

In lesbian performance, performers' bodies are not displayed nude, but in the costumes of their cultural constructs, which the performances subvert through pointed comedy. The body is frequently presented in WOW productions in various stages of undress. Pornography echoes through the performances in the sense that sexuality is always present and referred to—just as it is in "real life"—but it is made inaccessible to the spectator by its placement within the representational frame.

Since this sexuality is often costumed in butch/femme artifacts of traditional gender roles, some performances at WOW have been criticized as "politically incorrect." These charges generally come from cultural feminists disturbed by the butch presence in WOW performances, which they see as validating male images and values. By reading the signs of "butchness" too literally as male, these spectators miss the critique that grounds the work. Detached from the male representational context, the signs of male gender are assigned new meanings. After all, a lesbian performer dressed "like a man" is still a *not* a man. The power connotations of her costume take on fundamentally different values because it is worn in the context of lesbian sexuality.

Reassigning Gendered Meanings: The Case of Lesbian Pornography

Print pornography is the most direct, available representation of sexuality in this culture, and in a sense, exemplifies the construction of shared meanings between images and viewers. Mass market heterosexual pornography, for example, can be seen as a basic paradigm of male desire driving representations of women. Much print pornography assumes the same relationship between image and reader implied between strippers and spectators in striptease performances. There are performative connotations to the representation of the female body in heterosexual male print pornography, which is constructed for the satisfaction of male desire. Therefore, alternative pornography, such as women's erotica or lesbian pornography, can illustrate how desire can be differently represented, in print and in performance.

From a cultural feminist point of view, pornographic imagery is woman-hating regardless of whose desire it represents. Lesbians, for instance, get "bad press" in the pornography debate, for reasons that revolve around both sexuality and gender. In the late 1970s, a group of lesbians called Samois advertised its preference for sadomasochistic practice. The small, San Francisco-based group's crusade to increase the visibility of s/m as an option for the expression of lesbian sexuality prompted heated debate in feminist circles, most notably at a 1982 Barnard Conference on sexuality.[41] Because s/m lesbians traffic in power roles, which are assumed to be gender marked, antiporn feminists assume their sexuality is male or male-identified. This assumption conflates sexuality with gender.

Power is inherent in sexual and gender role play, since the gender system is polarized along a continuum on which men are seen as the dominant extreme and women as the passive, submissive other. As Echols cautions, "We should acknowledge the possibility that power inheres in sexuality rather than assume that power simply withers away in egalitarian relationships."[42] Sadomasochism makes textual what is subtextual in many sexual relationships. Both as a paradigm of the culture's construction of gender, and as a sexual choice, s/m can be seen as a literalization of the power status inherent in the dichotomized male/female roles. First Amendment issues aside, perhaps lesbian s/m offers an opportunity to explore the nature of power and sexuality apart from strict gender dichotomies.

The Barnard debacle and the resulting lengthy, angry dialogues in the feminist press prompted the publication of lesbian pornographic magazines that spell out in images and words some lesbians' alternatives to "politically correct" feminist sexuality. In a visual space meant at least theoretically to be free of male subordination and objectification of women, these magazines offer representations of one kind of sexuality based in lesbian desire. By imaging and performing fantasies in which power becomes a neutral quality available to women, their editors suggest that the nature of sexuality and gender can be explored and perhaps fundamentally changed.

As in lesbian performance, lesbian pornography evinces a willingness to experiment with sexual and gender roles. The lesbian porn magazine *On Our Backs,* for instance, is billed as "Entertainment for the Adventurous Lesbian,"[43] which places sexuality in the context of fantasy, imagination, and experimentation. On the cover of the Spring 1985 issue, two women are photographed against a white wall, wearing outrageous, punk-style outfits—leopard-design, skintight pants, leather jackets, studded belts and bracelets, and high heels. One of the women has a tiny dildo attached to her belt. The image introduces *On Our Backs'* iconography, which is aggressive, but irreverent.

Lesbian pornography presents sexual fantasies constructed through costumes and locations, many of which echo scenarios in traditional male pornography. There is some direct appropriation of male forms in lesbian pornography, but they acquire new meanings when they are used to communicate desire for readers of a different gender and sexual orientation. An *On Our Backs* photo spread called "Rock 'n' Roll Ramona," for example, resembles a similar spread in the June 1985 issue of *Hustler,* which is called "Slash: A Different Drummer."[44] Both scenarios contextualize their images in performance terms by implicitly or explicitly referring to the conventions of striptease.

The *Hustler* scenario sets Slash in a performance context. She is alone on stage with a drum set, which she never plays. She uses the drum sticks merely to point to her vagina, substituting for the missing (but implied) phallus. Slash's costume borrows the iconography of prostitution, and contextualizes her within s/m imagery. She wears a studded collar around her neck, studded leather bracelets on both wrists, and a leather corset with thin shoulder straps, the bodice underlining her erect nipples. The corset is attached to two garters that hold up black, fishnet stockings, worn with high-heeled silver sandals.

Throughout the scenario, thick cigar smoke appears to be drifting into the frame from an offstage source, implying that male spectators are watching the performance in a cabaret setting. The performative nature of the spread associates it with striptease, in that Slash is constructed as the elusive object of male desire. In one of the photographs, Slash smokes a cigarette with one hand, holding her drum sticks in the other. The iconography is almost butch; her look is a kind of dare. This implication of sadism is part of the turn-on for the male spectator. Her power is implied only as part of her objectification, and remains controlled by the male gaze.

Stripper Seph Weene, in an article written for the "Sex Issue" of the feminist journal *Heresies,* analyzes striptease with descriptions analogous to *Hustler*'s contextualization of Slash:

> I suddenly realized that what was at issue between us performers [strippers] and the audience was power. The men came, some of them, to suffer; their attitude was "She is making me horny, but I'll never have her." To them, the show was exquisite frustration, the sexy woman on stage, a tormentor. The other group of men came to pull imaginary strings; they saw themselves as masters. . . . In other words, some of the men fantasized themselves as passive, others as dominant.[45]

Power is clearly at issue in the striptease context of Slash's performance in *Hustler*. Through her objectification in the representational frame, she is inaccessible. Her inaccessibility makes her taunts and temptations sadistic, but control remains with the male spectator, who can choose how much power to give her and how to position himself.

In *On Our Backs*' featured photo spread "Rock 'n' Roll Ramona" (p. 22), much of the iconography used in *Hustler* is recontextualized for lesbian readers. Ramona's costume echoes Slash's—she wears a dark corset that highlights her erect nipples, a garter belt, high heels, stockings, black gloves, and a studded leather wrist band. The spread begins with photographs of Ramona in a performance context; they document an actual performance in a real setting.

The text beside the photographs informs the reader that Ramona performs in Baybrick's (a now-defunct lesbian bar in San Francisco) Burlesque for Women dance show. Ramona makes her living by stripping for lesbians. In contrast to the wordless spread in *Hustler,* Ramona's interview with "Fanny Fatale" accompanies her photos. While Slash is inaccessible and sadistic, the *On Our Backs* interview text describes Ramona's sexual exploits with women who come to see her show.

The interview is focused on her sexuality in the context of her life as a performer, and highlights an interest in butch/femme sexual role-play. Ramona reports, "I get these beautiful feminine women after me, and they say, 'Ramona, I don't know about you. You're not feminine and you're not masculine. You're like a mountain—that's why I want to climb you!'" (p. 26) Ramona invites a blurring of gender distinctions that characterizes lesbian sexuality.

Performers in heterosexual striptease are trapped by their gender roles and the assumption of their heterosexuality (although, ironically, many strippers in heterosexual clubs are lesbians).[46] The artifacts of gender as shifting, less clearly readable values is part of the arousal in lesbian striptease. This shifting of gender terms is also highlighted by Ramona's interviewer, Fanny Fatale, who happens to be a stripper herself (and is also the editor of *On Our Backs*). Fatale points to the loosening of gender strictures as the qualitative difference between stripping for men and stripping for lesbians: "The dancers loved performing for the all-female audiences because they had more freedom of expression. They were not limited to ultra-feminine acts only. They could be butch and dress in masculine attire."[47] As a result of the butch/femme play, the power valences shift, and become available to both performer and spectator. The female spectator is allowed to enjoy the power of her desire, which is shared by the performer.

S/m sex often uses role-playing and constructed scenarios, both to explore the implications of blurred sexual and gender roles such as Ramona's "mountain," and to act out strict gender extremes. Antiporn feminists abhor the element of fantasy in s/m and disapprove of role-playing in the context of sexuality. Robin Ruth Linden, in her introduction to a collection of essays called *Against Sadomasochism,* insists that "Sadomasochistic roles and practices attempt to replicate the phenomenology of oppression through role-playing."[48] She contends that s/m attempts an "eroticization of power and powerlessness . . . achieved through enacting fantasies involving variations on polarized roles. . . . Ritualized 'scenes' are arranged around specific activities in which sexual partners have a mutual interest."[49] Linden's cultural feminist critique fails to consider the positive ramifications of role appropriation and experimentation. The lesbian s/m pornographic costumes and scenes in *On Our Backs* are actually genderless. They have been assigned connotations by the contexts in which the culture has inserted them. Inserting them in different contexts disrupts their traditional meanings.

Toward a New Articulation of Gender and Sexuality

Under the dictates of the antipornography debate, desire has come to be seen as a male trap that automatically objectifies and oppresses women. To investigate sexual and gender roles in representation, however, where desire is an influencing factor, it is important to acknowledge that desire is not necessarily a fixed, male-owned commodity, but can be exchanged, with a much different meaning, between women. When the locus of desire changes, the demonstration of sexuality and gender roles also changes.

The political differences that separate feminists around the pornography debate translate into aesthetic differences between cultural feminist and lesbian performance art. Antipornography activists and cultural feminists are caught in a restrictive, literal interpretation of desire as male that limits their ability to see the potentialities of representation. By avoiding the representation of sexuality and desire for the safety of nature and spirituality, thereby limiting women to the capabilities biology outlines, cultural feminist performance artists prescribe a world chiseled in unchangeable gender differences, in which passion is expressed as a gentle, affectionate embrace.

Yet ironically, these artists cannot escape the infections of representation.

They contradict their aims when they locate so much of their work in the nude female body, yet insist that men (and women) blind themselves to desire and sexuality. With techniques that are essentially documentary, since they fear illusions, cultural feminist performance art fails to take flight into the freeing fantasies that lesbian performance imagines.

Determined not to be objectified by the illusions that have perpetuated women's oppression under representation, and determined to disinfect themselves from the harm done by the representation of male fantasies in both performance and pornography, cultural feminists situate most of their work in real settings, real time, and real bodies. Lesbian performers, detached from any concrete consideration of male sexuality, since it is not at all important to their work, are willing to experiment with male forms, including fantasy. Lesbian artists sift through popular culture, conventional theatre forms, and even pornography, to see what they hold that might be salvaged for use.

As lesbian performance and lesbian pornography make clear, albeit in different ways, it is unnecessary to abandon everything once considered malelike for a world of nature and spirituality considered ultimately femalelike. Power, sexuality, and desire have historical connotations assigned by the dominant culture for reasons of social, economic, and cultural expediency that have restricted women's abilities to express themselves and their sexuality within this culture. But power, sexuality, and desire can be recuperated from the strictly male domain, and can assume distinctly different meanings placed in different sexual and gender contexts.

Putting imagination and fantasy back into play allows for a limitless revisioning of a reality that has been hampered by strict gender and sexual roles. The representation of lesbian desire allows a rearticulation of gender and sexuality in the meaningful exchange between spectator and performer.

5

Cultural Feminism
and the Feminine Aesthetic

Cultural feminist performance art, as we have seen in chapter 4, posits the female body as a radical site of opposition to male models. Many of these artists use nudity as an attempt to fulfill *l'écriture féminine*'s proposal that women can articulate their subjectivity by writing with their bodies. Carolee Schneeman, for instance, in *Up To and Including Her Limits* (1975), which she performs nude, reads from a long scroll she removes from her vagina as a kind of feminine writing drawn from Lacanian lack.[1] While their performances are meant as what Schneeman calls a gift "of my body to other women: giving our bodies back to ourselves,"[2] these performers fail to see that the female body is still a sign which, when placed in representation, participates in a male-oriented signifying practice.

There is some disagreement among feminists, however, about such a critique of representation. The apparatus-based theory, influenced by Brechtian aesthetics, is prevalent in materialist feminism, and is discussed in detail in chapter 6. Cultural feminist theatre criticism and practice, on the contrary, tends to retain the theatre-as-mirror analogy as the locus of its theory. These critics and artists propose that if women's hands hold the mirror up to nature, as it were, to reflect women spectators in its glass, the gender inequities in theatre practice may be reversed.

Continuing to think within the binary opposition of sexual difference, they assume that subverting male-dominated theatre practice with a woman-identified model will allow women to look to theatre for accurate reflections of their experience. Their effort is to define what cultural feminism poses as a feminine aesthetic, which reflects sexual difference in both form and content.

The question of feminist aesthetics is somewhat debatable because of the prescriptive implications of "an aesthetic"—many practitioners fail to address the normativizing implications of aesthetic criteria, feminist or not. Aesthetic criteria, as we have seen, are the basis of canon-formation, and canons are by definition exclusionary. Yet the importance of defining models for feminist artistic practice has persisted as an issue. The feminist debate over aesthetics is in some ways a response to realism as the dominating form of modern American theatre.

Realism is prescriptive in that it reifies the dominant culture's inscription of traditional power relations between genders and classes. Its form masks the ideology of the author, whose position is mystified by the seemingly transparent text. Catherine Belsey suggests that in conventional readings of realist texts, the reader is identified as the subject position from which the text is made intelligible. Belsey says that "classical realism interpellates subjects in certain ways" and that "certain ranges of meaning . . . are 'obvious' within the currently dominant ideology, and certain subject-positions are equally 'obviously' the positions from which these meanings are apparent."[3] Belsey characterizes classical realism as "narrative which leads to 'closure,' and a 'hierarchy of discourses' which establishes the 'truth' of the story."[4] The crisis that propels the realist plot is resolved when the elements that create the textual disturbance are reinstated within a culturally defined system of order at the narrative's end. Since it is embedded in oppressive representational strategies, realism has come under general attack from feminist critics and theatre makers.

The Limitations of Realism

The nature of realism as a conservative force that reproduces and reinforces dominant cultural relations has been suspect at other moments in theatre history. Both Bertolt Brecht and Antonin Artaud intended to uncover the political and aesthetic myths of realism by, on one hand, distancing spectators from the theatre's lulling narrative and, on the other hand, by total physical immersion in a theatre experience of sensual gestures free of narrative authority.

The feminist stance vis-à-vis realism takes different forms, influenced by the different feminist ideologies. Liberal feminists, and women who argue against the need for establishing new dramatic forms, find nothing to fault in the traditional well-made play and the psychological acting practices that give it voice. Rosemary Curb writes that since liberal feminism "accepts the basic social structure and does not call for a radical transformation of consciousness," when "women's theatre groups and playwrights of this generation represent women's struggle, they most often choose realism as their theatrical mode."[5] Some liberal feminists argue that it is necessary to master the old forms prior to diverging from them, an argument that implicitly legitimizes the view of theatre history as necessarily continuous and based on accepted canonical standards.[6]

The female playwright retains authority over the narrative in the liberal feminist interpretation. Her responsibility becomes imaging her female characters in a positive way within the traditional dramatic structure. Since the realist narrative pattern is deemed appropriate to women's expression, liberal feminists see the genesis of gender inequities in theatre—both onstage and backstage—in the lack of positive female role models.

Cultural feminist theatre makers' argument against traditional dramatic forms is in many ways historically indebted to the American experimental theatre movement of the 1960s and early 1970s, which challenged the politics and aesthetics of fourth-wall realism. The Open Theatre, the Living Theatre, and the Performance Group, among others, imported European techniques from Brecht, Artaud, and Grotowski to undermine traditional theatre aesthetics and the ideology it expounded. Clamoring over the fourth wall into the laps of their spectators, they challenged the distinction between performers and spectators so rigidly imposed in traditional theatre, and dislodged the reign of realism with a more expressionistic style that relied on symbol and myth to convey its meanings.[7]

Their attack on realism, however, failed to address the traditional form's strict gender codings as an issue in the construction of meaning and in performance production. Many contemporary feminist theatre makers, such as Megan Terry and Roberta Sklar, left the experimental theatres to form their own groups when their invisibility in the male forums was articulated by the American women's liberation movement. These women carried away some of the basic tenets of experimental theatre—the revised relation between spectator and performer and the shift away from traditional plots into nonlinear, expressionistic narratives—and brought them into feminist theatre.[8]

By rejecting both realism and the genderized posturings of the male-dominated experimental theatre groups, the new feminist theatre meant to create "woman-identified" productions.[9] This work, created by women for women, focused on women's experience and their connections to each other through gender and sex. Identifying with each other as women was meant as an antidote to their oppression under patriarchy.

In theatre, woman-identification demanded the creation of forms that would break from the historically male tradition. Cultural feminist theatre groups such as the Women's Experimental Theatre and At the Foot of the Mountain made their plays nonlinear, wrote them collectively, allowed them to end without the authority of narrative closure, and used direct address and a documentary style. They intended to subvert realism's relentless plotting toward the white, middle-class, male privilege the history of dramatic texts maintained.

Consciousness-raising became the process by which women shared their experiences in the new wave of American feminism. Consciousness-raising groups formed networks of support for women and allowed a protected forum for sharing aspects of their lives that had historically been silenced. The intent was to discover commonality and to derive strength from the assertion of their universal experiences as women under patriarchy.

Cultural feminist theatre adopted consciousness-raising's modus operandi as its form. The basics of consciousness-raising's methodology, in fact, continue to structure cultural feminist theatre, as communal testifying to common experience and unequivocal support among women remain prevalent among its techniques.

In the 1980s, however, the consciousness-raising model runs into obstacles best articulated by the identity politics that have somewhat unsettled cultural feminism's claims for commonality. Identity politics describe the current tendency in feminism to valorize cultural and ethnic differences. Black women were among the first to insist on their differences from the white, middle-class feminist model, and were soon followed by Hispanic women, other women of color, and Jewish women.[10] Racism has become a bone of contention in the women's movement, as racial and ethnic minorities stake out their differences from the dominating white feminist voice.

Some of these claims, however, read as a kind of cultural nationalism that remains compatible with cultural feminism. Universalisms sometimes continue to be posed, but from racially or ethnically oriented points of view. Deborah Rosenfelt and Judith Newton, for example, point out that some criticism by women of color "posits a universalized 'the Black Woman' or '*La Chicana*'": "Some of this work explores—often quite usefully—the textual integration of myth, folklore and oral tradition, but it tends not to interpret the political implications of this contemporary recuperation of traditional materials or to consider in any depth the changes in social fabric which demarcate the time of origin from the moment of adaptation."[11] This work, however, is crucial in order to approach a materialist formulation of differences among women prompted by history, race, ethnicity, and class.

Cultural feminist theatre, as a predominantly white women's project, is aware of the surge of identity politics, but continues to insist that our commonalities as women override our racial and class differences. Alice Echols submits that cultural feminists "believe that the degree of dissidence within the women's movement demonstrates, not the diversity of the movement, but the extent to which patriarchy has defiled the mother-daughter bond and, by extension, all relationships between women. They further make feminism synonymous with female bonding and contend that the rehabilitation of the mother-daughter relationship is central to feminism."[12] The focus on mother/daughter relationships is the primary content of cultural feminist theatre, and crucial to its formulation of a feminine aesthetic.

Woman-Identification and the Female Body

Rather than investigating the representational apparatus' psychological and material implications for spectatorship and authorship, critics and practitioners who theorize the feminine aesthetic retain the theatre-as-mirror analogy and inquire into the form and content of theatre production. Cultural feminist theatre critics such as Josette Feral, Linda Walsh Jenkins, and Rosemary Curb tend, like their French counterparts, to locate the body as the site of women's differences from men, and to valorize those differences as politically and aesthetically desirable.[13]

Hélène Cixous, whose theatre manifesto "Aller à la Mer" has much to offer a cultural feminist aesthetic, describes the female stage as a "stage/scene without event. No need for plot or action; a single gesture is enough, but one that can transform the world."[14] Cixous' intent is to undermine the oppressions of male language through the body and gesture. But in most cultural feminist theatre practice and criticism, the female voice, rather than the body, is privileged for its different way of speaking/telling female stories.

This emphasis on the voice theorizes women's expression without considering the larger implications of representation as narrative, in which the actual physical body onstage tells as much of a story as the written text. The female body as a performance text with particular genderized meanings is rarely considered in cultural feminist theatre. Instead, the female body becomes equated with the female voice.

Feral, for example, looks for the characteristics of a feminine voice in performance. She assumes that by replacing male language with its opposite—a supposedly contiguous, fluid, irrational, body-centered, fragmentary, nonlinear, open female language—"a vast picture of the world is presented, this time from a feminine point of view."[15]

Jenkins, too, in her investigation of women's drama, looks for plays that are "replete with female signs" and "contributions to drama that are authentically female."[16] Jenkins proposes that there is an arc of recognition available to female spectators that will usher them into the dramatic forum from which they historically have been exiled, once authentic femaleness has been fully represented. Defining what she calls a female "biogrammar"—another metaphor for writing the body—Jenkins says, "Authentic writing comes out of what a writer's body has actually known, however fictionalized: That's the source of her dream landscapes and that's what has been recording her life. The experiences the body has known on the basis of gender provide one of the richest resources for authenticity in personal voice."[17] Jenkins' postulation of "authenticity" is questionable from a materialist feminist perspective, since it does not take into account the cultural construction of gender, but instead considers it an immutable, inherent quality. By drawing a correlation between the arc of recognition and the authentic female voice, Jenkins implies that on the basis of their gender alone women spectators and performers will be able to share a commonly meaningful theatre experience.

Her position echoes Annette Kolodny's suggestion that a unique female literary tradition embodies female structures of signification, "symbolic systems that constitute female experience in women's writings."[18] The implication is that male interpretive strategies and signification will be ill-equipped to decipher the meanings apparent to women. Similarly, Curb defines "woman-conscious" drama as "all drama by and about women that is characterized by multiple interior reflections of women's lives and perceptions. . . . Woman-conscious theatre presents a multi-dimensional unravelling of women's collective imagination in a psychic replay of myth and history."[19] Curb presumes that women have a collective, transhistorical imagination that can be reflected in their drama and elevated into myth.

The impulse to reclaim women's history and myths situates cultural feminist theatre as a forum for rending "the invisible visible, the silent noisy, the motionless active," and as an institution of "useful myths and countermyths."[20] But it fails to allow room for what historian Linda Gordon, from whom I have been quoting, calls "more ambivalent analyses of the past."[21] The need to reclaim women's history and to portray women's collective struggles against the patriarchal backdrop on which women have been victimized leads to a flattening of women's experience. No room for questioning, doubt, or debate appears in this forum, which is constructed as perniciously monolithic.

The Women's Experimental Theatre's (WET) production *The Daughter's Cycle Trilogy* (1977–1980), written by Clare Coss, Sondra Segal, and Roberta Sklar, is a rich example of cultural feminist ideology and performance practice. The trilogy is WET's rewriting of the House of Atreus myth from a feminist perspective. The text begins by posing a basic question that resituates the narrative: "What happened to the women?" By theoretically positioning women as the myth's subjects, WET retells the tale as a paradigm of women's position in the nuclear family.[22]

Each of the three parts of *The Daughter's Cycle* relates directly to the family, and at least indirectly to the classic Greek story. Part I, *Daughters* (1977), begins from the premise that "Every woman is a daughter,"[23] and goes on to reclaim the mother/daughter relationship from the patriarchy. The piece begins and ends with the recitation of each performer's matrilineage, which stands as testimony to their revision of family connections and history from a female perspective.

The script refers to the playing space as a sphere, and its terrain as the daughter's mind: "A collage of verbal, physical, and vocal imagery emblemizes the environment in which the mother/daughter relationship is created. The images and rhythms blend to project the terrain of the daughter's mind—sound traces, elusive imagery, fragments of song, ancient memories" (p. 34). A kind of dreamworld is projected in which the icons of the mother/daughter relationship are imaged. These icons are resolutely domestic. In one scene, a skein of yarn is used to measure the distance between mother and daughter. In another, sounds and physical images of washing and drying dishes are used as background for "writing the contract," in which the daughter accepts her culturally ordained role that is her mother's legacy (pp. 38–46).

Coss, Segal, and Sklar note that "women have historically been relegated to the domestic sphere": "We have chosen not to turn away from that sphere but to look into it as thoroughly as we are psychically willing and able to do. . . . We bring the setting of the plays into the domestic sphere where so much of what happens between women happens—the kitchen, the shared bedroom, the dining table. It is a deep entry into the familial experience."[24] The repetition of sex-role-related gestures is described in *Daughters,* the iconography of which recalls the struggle for separation and intimacy that characterizes the mother/daughter relationship. In one recurrent image, the mother rests her hands on the daughter's shoulders, and they both "look out" (p. 31).

The intentionally maintained distinction between public and private spheres is further emphasized by the women's descriptions of their husbands and fathers as outside this domestic scene, circulating within the public economic and social arenas. No attempt is made to critique women's culturally determined domesticity. On the contrary, the mother's position as family nurturer, and therefore primary support, is glorified as part of her reclamation.

The mother is contextualized with images of primary elements. In Curb's interpretation of the play, "The mundane becomes sacred as daughters see mothers performing ritual mysteries":[25] "My mother works with fire and water and knives and air and earth. My mother works with mysteries that cannot be explained. And I as a woman have my hands in fire and water and knives and air and earth. And I as a woman have my hands inside my mother" (p. 45). The repetition of this imagery, both physically and vocally, inscribes the performers into a primal scene in which their femaleness is evoked in its relation to nature.

Daughters' performance style often calls for direct address. The spectators are implicated both as witnesses to and participants in women's inscription in this domestic scene. As Curb describes, referring to other cultural feminist texts, "The spectator/reader becomes a present participant in an historic event recreated as the flow of a ritual in which we all play all the parts."[26] The chorus of performers positioned as daughters in WET's text addresses the spectator. The "you" of the text implies a universal "we" who will recognize its female symbolism and identify with its uniquely female experience.

The rhetorical questions that structure the text assume the spectator is a woman: "How are you seeing this play? —as a mother? —as a daughter? Is it possible to see it as both?" (p. 44). "Can you talk about your mother without crying?" (p. 27). Feral believes these rhetorical questions, so prevalent in female texts, are indices to the female form:

> Women . . . also explore their unconscious and their relations to the Other, in the conviction that there they will find answers to the many questions they ask themselves. This process is the source of the continual questioning, the constant appeal in women's writing addressed to the Other, to the Other within themselves, their inner, repressed selves, but also to the Other outside of themselves, their doubles, as we all are for one another.[27]

Female doubleness is a recuperation of the Other positioned in male theory as she who lacks. In this rewriting of the female body, the Other becomes an image of Woman's self, we who can always find the Other in each other, as a mirror image peering back and offering the gift of self-definition.

WET's founders say they are looking for new theatre techniques that will be adequate to describe their anthropological research into women's lives: "In our firm belief that women have a separate experience, we have been engaged in developing research forms and presentational forms as well as content that articulate the female experience."[28] There are Brechtian elements in *Daughters'* production style. The scenes are episodic and very brief, punctuated by blackouts. Each scene is named and decribes another part of the fable of women's prescribed role in patriarchy. The chorus sometimes manipulates the lighting devices, and frequently quotes or echoes the mother/daughter characters in the third person. In "Home," the third segment, "The chorus, seated at one side, witnesses and describes the action of the mother/daughter totem, and directs the focus of the audience to the ritual nature of this enactment. 'This is what happened to me'" (p. 29).

Far from breaking spectator pleasure into critical distance in the Brechtian manner, however, the text calls for attention to the ritual nature of its exchange and implies that the spectator will concur that the events described have happened to all women. The text breaks with the mystifying conventions of fourth-wall realism, but constructs in its place ritual systems that demand a similar suspension of disbelief.

Since cultural feminist ideology is based in female biology, giving birth is posed as the common ritual and as a metaphor for women's creativity. In *Daughters,* the act of giving birth is related in poetic language that leads the spectator through the physical experience of bearing a child. The birth scene is "an invitation to the sensuality and the wonder of the birth story" (p. 6), which the performers relate as they "advance towards the audience with a held urgency" (p. 7). The birth metaphor is emblematic of the mother/daughter bond, but its glorification of motherhood also implies that a woman's self-fulfillment can best be attained by fulfilling her biological capabilities.

The birth ritual, and the ritual of the performance text, requires common beliefs, common faith, common ways of seeing. A certain acquiescence is required, a certain willingness to accompany the performers on their mother/daughter journey and to identify with it as archetypal. The fact that *Daughters* is based on workshops in which "hundreds of other women" discussed "their experience and their role within the family"[29] seems to lend it empirical credentials. As theatre anthropologists, WET has established "facts" about women that their dramatic presentation authorizes.

Electra Speaks (1980), the third part of the *Trilogy*, focuses on the struggle against male dominance embodied by the father, the son, and the phallologocentric language that traps women in dominant discourse. The piece ends with Electra leaving the metaphorical house of Atreus, but does not go on to propose what her voice will sound like or what her body will express outside its discourse.

Not coincidentally, WET is unable to envision female expression that is not somehow tied to the male-dominated, nuclear family paradigm against which it is defined. Sexual difference is so deeply embedded in the terms of its debate that Electra must remain in the nuclear family's neighborhood to continue to exist at all. WET's next major work was *Woman's Body and Other Natural Resources* (1980–1985), a trilogy based on women's relationship to food, which once again located its investigation within family relationships.

The three plays, *Food, Foodtalk,* and *Feast or Famine,* used the same research methods as the *Daughters* trilogy to explore "women's profound relationship to food" on a personal and global scale.[30] After *Feast or Famine* was performed at the Women's Interart Center in New York in 1985, Segal and Sklar began to reassess the demand for their work.

In the "increasingly conservative 1980s," they feel feminism "no longer seems to be a conscious, pressing part of a mass movement": "The Women's Experimental Theatre is not currently active. The decline of economic and audience support tells us this is not the time. We have decided, however, not to formally close up shop. We want to remain open to the rumblings of a distant thunder—that of an old, or new, feminist need."[31] The lack of economic support for feminist projects might indeed be blamed on the strictures of a conservative administration. But declining audience support perhaps stems from other problems. Because 1980s feminism is slowly, painfully coming to terms with the differences among women located in race and class, the universal model of womanhood to which WET subscribes might now be perceived as inadequate or outmoded in its transcendent formulation.

After all, the spectator identifying with WET's heroic protagonists is constructed according to sexual difference. Her subjectivity is articulated only in oppositional terms, and only to the extent that she can legitimate the claims for commonality proposed by the female performers. The centrality of the mother/daughter relationship is a device for establishing this commonality and smoothing over the differences between women.

The father/son relationship that continues to structure the signification systems of dominant American drama has been replaced by its opposite. The genders of the performers and spectators have been switched from male to female, but they are still working through a representational situation defined by (absent/present) men. The universality of the female position can only be defined against the universality of the male. The traditional white, middle-class, male transcendent spectator has been replaced with a generally white, middle-class, female transcendent spectator positioned as "the daughter." An Asian woman tells the story of her mother in *Daughters,* but her story's placement is meant to highlight women's commonality, not their differences.

This problem is further illustrated by two works in progress presented by At the Foot of the Mountain (ATFM) theatre for the Women and Theatre Program Conference held in Chicago in August 1987. Then-ATFM artistic director Phyllis Jane Rose, who had been with the group since its inception in 1974, prefaced the presentation with remarks that situated ATFM's history within the larger American women's movement. With the prevalence of identity politics as the issue of the 1980s, Rose said ATFM realized they had been a predominantly white, middle-class women's group, and consequently set out to explore their own racism.[32]

As a piece of representation in itself, Rose's opening statement was revealing and hinted at the problems the two plays later clarified. The five-woman ensemble was lined up on chairs facing the spectators. The ensemble was comprised of Rebecca Rice, an African American; Bernadette Hak Eun Cha, born in Korea; Sherry Blakey Banal, Saultaux and Cree, Native North American Bear Clan, Anishabe; Antoinette T. Maher, Irish/Polish American; and Carmen Maria Rosario, Puerto-Rican American. Rose hovered above them during her remarks.

Although the content of her speech referred to the original group's racial and class homogeneity and their intent to change, Rose formally maintained the authoritative role of group director/spokesperson. The "absent presence" of playwright Martha Boesing, another of ATFM's white, middle-class cofounders, also pervaded the group's remarks.[33]

The multi-ethnic performers, under the terms of the apparatus Rose manipulated, were implicitly presented as the solution to the white women's problem. The performances that evening corroborated evidence that the women of color remained inscribed in a representational economy controlled by white women's voices and visions, which referred to the family—and opposition to men—as the scene of women's commonality. Despite their racial and ethnic mix, the ensemble's voices were flattened out into similarity by the production's frame.

ATFM's first piece of the evening was a revisioning of Brecht's *The Exception and the Rule*. The piece, called *Raped*, replaces Brecht's economic, class-based analysis with an investigation of sexual politics that proposes rape as an experience common to all women. The fear of rape, the piece submits, is the single most important factor in women's subjugation. As in WET's *Daughters,* the differences between women are once again elided for an examination of woman-as-victim defined in opposition to inherent male violence.

Rape is treated as a male ritual, a property crime of men against men in which women are victims in the homosocial exchange. The original Brecht text is presented in a melodramatic, broad style, and is interrupted by personal testimonies about rape delivered in direct address. The spectators, as in *Daughters,* are assumed to be women who will identify with the narratives shared.

Since the narratives are all delivered by women of color or of working class status, the stories at first seem to be specific to their cultural contexts. But through the course of the piece, they all begin to sound alike. In a postpresentation discussion, Rose told conference participants that this piece had been in ATFM's repertory since the mid-1970s, and that little of the material had been rewritten. (This production has since been dropped from ATFM's repertory due to performance rights disputes over the Brecht text.) The personal testimonies were drawn from Studs Terkel's book, *Working,* and from the experiences of the original white women's ensemble. The women of color, it appeared, were simply asked to reiterate the testimonies of others and assume their universality.

Rose's explanation—that time had prevented them from inserting new material—seemed lame. Questioned about the lack of a lesbian perspective in the piece, Rose cheerfully proposed that someone find her a lesbian story to interweave with the others. Her response to both issues shifted the responsibility for a truly varied expression of women's experiences away from her control.

Spectators were asked to write their first names on slips of paper and put them in a tambourine during the intermission between the two pieces. The second piece, *The Story of a Mother II,* is much less theatrical than the Brecht adaptation. A revision of a ritual drama originally presented in 1977, it weaves together source material from the multicultural ensemble about their relationships with their mothers. Boesing crafted the writing in collaboration with the performers. The piece begins with a recitation of the ensemble's matrilineage. Its ritualistic narrative style is characterized by storytelling punctuated with percussive musical accompaniment.

The cultural differences between the performers are clear in their narratives, which are moving anecdotes about their mothers' strengths when confronted with supreme adversity, always represented by the dominant patriarchal culture. The interweaving of the narratives, however, under the rubric of *the* story of *a* mother, once again works to collapse the differences between them into a narrative of similarity and universality.

Where the Brecht piece is theatricalized, the tone of *Story of a Mother II* is documentary—that is, assumed as "real"—and reverential. What humor there is in the piece is gentle and poignant. At the conference presentation, it was delivered quietly and with a kind of awe that established a churchlike atmosphere that pervaded the room. After they related their personal narratives, the performers passed among them the tambourine full of the spectators' names and read off the names to invite a prearranged response.

A performer said "The name of the daughter is" and read a name from a slip of paper. The spectator was expected to respond with "The name of the mother is" and to say her mother's name. This ritual proceded until all the slips of paper had been read. To my knowledge, none of the spectators was told the use to which the slips of named paper would be put, and participation in the naming ritual was not presented as optional.

When the naming was completed, the performers asked the spectators to close their eyes and lead them through a visualization exercise in which each woman entered and assumed her mother's body. The reverential tone intensified as this section progressed. When each spectator had purportedly become her mother, she was invited to share her mother's wisdom, prefaced by the words "I always said. . . ." Many of the women in the audience at the conference participated in this section, although the sharing was optional.

The Story of a Mother II's ritual form and its presumptions about audience participation represent the ideological dangers of this cultural feminist form. The sacred atmosphere prompted by the performers' reverential tone naturalizes mother/daughter relationships as the primal link between women. The religious attitude of the ritual suggests a shared system of belief, and excludes spectators who find themselves uncomfortable with the assumption of commonality. Anyone who might have refused to participate in the naming ritual when her name was called would have broken the spell. Refusal to participate was equated with a refusal of faith. The participatory nature of the ritual, therefore, was implicitly coercive.

Focusing on the mother/daughter relationship presumes its centrality to all women and stresses its positive aspects. As some spectators at the conference later pointed out, they were uncomfortable assuming their mother's bodies because their mothers were alcoholic or racist or otherwise inappropriate role models. In the atmosphere of exaltation ATFM established, however, there was no room to explore this ambivalence.

Aside from its political and ideological problems, the ritualistic, participatory form of *The Story of a Mother II* seemed outmoded, a 1960s artifact dusted off in the 1980s context. (In fact, later productions of this piece apparently discarded this part of the format.) The piece seemed reminiscent of an earlier historical moment, of the consciousness-raising days, when we took that necessary first step of acknowledging ourselves as women and the personal nature of our politics. But after a decade of theorizing, practicing, and refining our politics, this reverential stance towards ourselves as women seems simplistic and conservative.

The performers very much resented criticism in the postperformance discussion that suggested their voices were being manipulated through the white women's perspective, as they felt such an analysis denied the strength of their own agency. Rice said the ensemble resisted Boesing's efforts to create a universal image of "mother." The performers felt spectators who complained about the coercive nature of the ritual were implicitly racist. They also denied that the piece implies a universal position for women; ATFM's promotional material, in fact, includes a quote from Carmen Rosario that cautions, "Being a multicultural company doesn't mean that everything we say reflects truths for everyone else in our cultures. We are creating some new paths to collaboration. We're an example for others to create their own."[34]

The conference postperformance discussion, however, was guided by information about the author's and performers' intent. Rose and the performers refused to accept the fact that what spectators see in the representational frame is often very different from what the production's creators intend. The performers disempowered the feminist critical perspective that analyzes the pervasive workings of the representational apparatus and that concentrates on the construction of the spectator.

Rose, who lead the attack on spectators critical of the work, insisted that ATFM had brought the conference "a gift" of their performance. How can a gift be received, except in gratitude? Feminist performances, however, should not be phrased as gifts exchanged between women and therefore beyond critical reproach. Perhaps this model has validity if the performance is clearly defined as a ritual sacrament. But when a performance is presented as representation—regardless of whether or not it is a work in progress, and therefore not "finished"—it becomes available for criticism in terms of its representational frame and the spectator its meanings construct.

Breaking the Female Mirror

In addition to what it revealed about the ideological position of cultural feminist theatre, the heated exchange at this conference highlighted the often antagonistic relationship between feminist practitioners, who want their work to be validated politically and aesthetically, and feminist critics, who want the freedom to study the work from a theoretical perspective.

Although they address the expression of new contents in alternative forms, cultural feminist theatre groups like WET and ATFM fail to deal with the larger issue of women's place in representation and narrative. They assume that in its woman-identified, nonlinear form, their theatre can mirror women's experiences.

Curb frames her discussion of "woman-conscious theatre" in terms of the mirror analogy, asking, "Whom do we see in the mirror of woman-conscious drama? What definitions or boundaries do the seer and the seen share? Does the frame create or define the reflected image?"[35] The assumption is that the reflection of women in women's theatre will be accurate and whole. The cultural feminist theatres reject the mimesis of realism, but they assume there can be a feminist mimesis—that is, that their productions can mirror female content through female forms.

Case and Jeanie Forte write that this "sense of the documentary"—the one-to-one correlation between art and life—"rest[s] on an unchallenged assumption about the way meaning [is] generated. This documentary sense assume[s] a stable system of representation." They go on to argue, however, that representation is a "repressive system . . . enforced by the laws of language, signs, and cultural codes."[36] The cultural feminist theatres free images of women from the constraints of realism, but cannot detach them from the oppressions of the representational apparatus and its ideological encodings. Representation conspires to relate conventional meanings and to lay transcendent, universalizing traps despite experimental forms.

Case argues elsewhere that the traditional mimetic dramatic forms developed from a misogynistic culture that relegated actual historical women to a private, domestic sphere and mythologized them in the public sphere to serve patriarchal needs. From a materialist perspective, Case emphasizes that the division of public and private life in the classical periods from which theatre originated helped to construct a myth of "Woman" that was useful to the male-dominated economy and social structure: "The result of the suppression of actual women in the classical world created the invention of a representation of the gender 'Woman' within the culture. This 'Woman' appeared on the stage, in the myths, and in the plastic arts, representing the patriarchal values attached to the gender of 'Woman' while suppressing the experiences, stories, feelings, and fantasies of actual women."[37]

Women never assumed an active place in theatrical representation, which conspired from its beginnings to detach women as a gender class from their material base and to create them instead as a transcendent myth used to serve the male ideology cultural practices perpetuated. "Woman" was represented simply as a mask carved from male ideology.

Case argues that this form continues to provide the canonic model for Western theatre practice. American realism's "craving for a referent"[38]—that is, its mimetic representations of "the real"—situates the spectator as a subject of coherent identity who can be appealed to through the text's construction to authorize its illusion. If feminism points out that representation does not construct women as subjects, and also views coherent identity as a myth, a feminist mimesis is extremely difficult to theorize.[39] In their desire to present a mirror of "Woman," cultural feminist theatre falls into the representational trap. The Woman they want to redeem is merely the mask carved for women by patriarchy.

Sexuality and desire, as we have seen in chapter 4, are also exiled from full consideration in cultural feminist theatre. Curb fervently believes that "in the widest political and spiritual sense, such theatre is feminist and lesbian. An erotic charge pulses through women's collective self-consciousness. In the mirror of play we see and show sister, mother, daughter, lover, self."[40] However, lesbian desire as active sexuality is rarely imaged. The lack of a lesbian narrative in ATFM's *Raped* or *The Story of a Mother II,* and the absence of an explicitly named lesbian in WET's *Daughters* locates this theatre within the antisexuality stance of cultural feminism, in which lesbianism as a sexual choice has been silenced by a safer, political definition. Instead of actively expressed sexuality, lesbianism circulates in these theatre texts as woman-identification, female bonding, and the primacy of female friendship.[41]

By abdicating the attempt to represent truly sexual female desire, cultural feminist theatre never disrupts the male desire that continues to work as representation's motivating principle. Unless desire is addressed, a woman in representation can never be more than the Woman she is seen to be by the dominant culture—the object of male desire.

"Woman-conscious" cultural feminist theatre presents "an alternative, transubstantiating the grain of patriarchal oppression into the bread which becomes the bodies and selves of women-loving women,"[42] in Curb's evocation. But for all its emphasis on the body, cultural feminist performance practice is predominantly text-bound. The body is curiously lost in practice, perhaps because truly considering the body in space means dealing with the representational apparatus, which the feminine aesthetic is inadequate to handle. Feral, for example, in her rigidly textual analysis of plays by women, can only conclude that "women are divided, multiple beings, whose lack of oneness is expressed in the text by . . . the diversity and simultaneity of voices."[43]

The Artaudian plea for breathing new life into the theatre through the female body-presence is more poetic than practical, since it is impossible to translate theatrically without getting caught in the contradictions of women's place in representation. We are returned continually to the gender markings of the apparatus itself. Brecht's theory and materialist feminist performance analysis suggests that "distantiation" may be the theoretical starting point from which to begin dismantling the representational apparatus. Rather than reifying the differences of women's bodies as an originary source of a primal, female language, the Brechtian/materialist critics conduct a political analysis of the ways in which power relations are structured in the culture and replicated by representation. Only by foregrounding this operation can theatre and performance be used for social change.

6

Materialist Feminism: Apparatus-Based Theory and Practice

I have argued throughout these pages that the address of the traditional representational theatre apparatus constitutes the subjectivity of male spectators and leaves women unarticulated within its discourse. Feminist performance criticism marks out the boundaries of discourse in which women as historical subjects are nonrepresentable.

The female body is imaged within representation only as the site of male desire: "Woman is then the very ground of representation, both object and support of a desire which, intimately bound up with power and history, is the moving force of culture and history."[1] Woman exists as a representation of her own marginality from discourse, as the site of alienation from her own desire. Julia Kristeva, in an often-cited argument, points out:

> A woman cannot "be"; it is something which does not even belong in the order of *being*. It follows that a feminist practice can only be negative, at odds with what already exists. . . . In "woman" I see something that cannot be represented, something above and beyond nomenclatures and ideologies. . . . From this point of view it seems that certain feminist demands revive a kind of naive romanticism, a belief in identity (the reverse of phallocentricism).[2]

Cultural feminist representations of Woman, as we have seen in chapter 5, propose that the female spectator can find a coherent identity in the mirror image they hold up. Cultural feminists fail to see that within the representational apparatus in which they work they are offering a superficial representation of gender identity that remains defined by the ideology of sexual difference, an ideological system that benefits women as social subjects not at all.

Abetted by the theories of femininity proposed by *l'écriture féminine*, cultural feminists continue to work within the modality of sexual difference through their complicity with the representation of Woman as the transcendent, female subject. Teresa de Lauretis, however, cautions: "This femininity is purely a representation, a positionality within the phallic model of desire and significa-

Dress Suits for Hire
Lois Weaver and Peggy Shaw in their 1987 collaboration with playwright
Holly Hughes.
(Photo by Eva Weiss)

tion; it is not a quality or property of women. Which all amounts to saying that woman, *as* subject of desire or of signification, is unrepresentable; or better, that in the phallic order of patriarchal culture and its theory, woman is unrepresentable except as representation."[3] The pressing issue for feminists becomes how to inscribe a representational space for women that will point out the gender enculturation promoted through the representational frame and that will belie the oppressions of the dominant ideology it perpetuates.

In the theory of the technology of gender that de Lauretis develops, *"the construction of gender is both the product and the process of its representation."*[4] Gender is produced by representational processes that inscribe the ideology of gender through both psychoanalytic and material means of production. The materialist feminist project, then, becomes to disrupt the narrative of gender ideology, to denaturalize gender as representation, and to demystify the workings of the genderized representational apparatus itself.

This project necessitates stepping outside the representation of sexual difference. Or, if actually leaving the frame seems a utopian ideal, the project is to reveal the complicity of the representational apparatus in maintaining sexual difference. Strategies of intervention that trace the subject positions sculpted by the lights of the theatrical apparatus, and that allow gender to exceed representational oppressions, are being developed in materialist feminist critical theory and practice. These strategies are informed by the theoretical models provided by film theorists such as de Lauretis.

In theatre practice, textual and performance interventions that undermine the tyranny of male narratives of desire are outlined in texts and productions by Hélène Cixous, Simone Benmussa, and, to a certain extent, Maria Irene Fornes. Theodora Skipitares' performance work with puppets and sculpture also foregrounds the apparatus by absenting live bodies from representation. Spiderwoman Theatre's combination of Native American storytelling with Brechtian technique offers additional examples of materialist feminist performance strategies.

On perhaps an even more radical front, lesbian performances by Split Britches and other WOW Cafe participants break the heterosexual contract that informs representation and the enculturation of gender. The lesbian performance texts formulate what Sue-Ellen Case calls a "strategy of appearances,"[5] in which gender is foregrounded as a performed role. Brechtian techniques structure many of these textual and performance strategies, and may be traced as a legacy from which materialist feminist practice borrows and on which it expands.

Textual Interventions from a Materialist Base

Hélène Cixous' theoretical writing and her theatre texts exist on the borderline between the neo-femininity proposed by *l'écriture féminine* and a more materialist analysis of representational practice. Her play, *Portrait of Dora* (1979), reinterprets the frequently discussed story of Dora, Freud's recalcitrant patient who abruptly terminated her analysis. The play's narrative is fragmentary; its telling shifts contrapuntally between Dora's voice and those of Freud and the major players in what Freud sees as her unresolved Oedipal crisis.

The articulation of Dora's lesbian desire in Cixous' text resists inscription in Freud's male, heterosexual narrative. Although *Portrait of Dora* can be examined as an instance of *l'écriture féminine*'s proposal for writing with the female body, it can also be read as a materialist feminist subversion of representation's presentation of the female body as spectacle.

Sharon Willis reads *Dora* as a staged encounter between psychoanalysis and feminism. The theatre becomes an apt metaphor for this encounter, since the female hysteric positioned as spectacle for the theorizing of the male psychoanalytic gaze can be read analogously with the position of women within representation. Both the psychoanalytic and the theatrical narratives demand that women passively accept their silence within the dominant order and abdicate their desire. Willis suggests that because *Dora* "reframes Freud's text in a way that puts into question the theatrical frame, and the body staged within it, it becomes exemplary of the critical operations of certain feminist performance practice."[6] The reframing in Cixous' text charts Dora's refusal to be mapped into the patriarchal Oedipal discourse.

The effect of reframing—both in Cixous' text and in director Simone Benmussa's staging of it—calls attention to the theatrical apparatus in which the text is embedded. The scrims that divide the playing space into different levels sometimes, although not always, correspond to the play's four levels of time—present, memory, dream, and fantasy, which also work to fracture the narrative.[7] The scrims both conceal events and make them visible, depending on the play of light.[8] Benmussa's and Cixous' insistence on framing as a textual device revealed in both form and content calls "attention to the necessary consequence of any framing."[9] Their insistence on destablizing the narrative point of view systematically undermines the authority of any single narrative position.

Dora's fractured narrative prevents the smooth operation of identification processes that offer the spectator entry into the text in conventional representational practice. Willis points out that the dissociation of body and voice and the text's suggestion of spaces and events that are heard but not seen (such as the click of Freud's lighter) privilege the auditory and prevent the construction of a coherent visual space into which the spectator can be inserted.

The "interference effect" of multiple voices undermines Freud's search for the narrative referent ("Who stands for whom in this story?" he asks, perplexed) as well as the spectator's.[10] In this respect, *Dora* works to materialize Cixous' proposal that placing women in representation will entail "going beyond the confines of the stage, lessening our dependency on the visual and stressing the auditory, learning to attune all our ears."[11] The multiple voices and sound effects that are not imaged visually provide an auditory "space-off" that refers to representations that exceed the conventional frame.[12] These spaces-off resonate technically with the more conventional "voice-over" technique. Voiceovers, however, tend to refer to unseen people, while spaces-off imply a larger, unimaged scene of places and events.

Dora's narrative splits effect the position of the spectator, whom Willis describes as presented with an orchestration of voices that blocks "'normal' narrative development from ignorance and concealment to knowledge and discourse."[13] Dora remains an enigma that exceeds narrative closure. She precipitates "disorder which throws into disarray the conventional cultural and signifying systems."[14] Since she refuses to remove herself as an obstacle to Freud's narrative completion, the classic realist narrative is disrupted and prevented from reinscribing the dominant (old) order.

The separation of body and voice in Cixous' text and the presentation of voice as "an impossible element to stage"[15] disrupts the identification processes by fragmenting any sense of coherent identity and denying the spectator an enunciative point of entry into the text. Willis suggests that "the instability of the text's point of address is a means of insisting on performance *as* address."[16] Dora is *"voiced,* heard as well as seen"; "the body cannot be entirely given over to spectacle when the voice resists consolidation within the frame."[17]

Cixous' text, in its refusal of classical realist narrative conventions in both content and form, is a deconstruction of representational processes that construct male subjectivity as the ideal spectatorial position through psychological identification processes. Dora's desire exceeds the representation that would silence her and disrupts the signifying practice that denies her self-articulation.

Benmussa's *The Singular Life of Albert Nobbs* (1978) also foregrounds narrative and desire in a fashion that denies the spectator's comfortable entry into the text. Albert Nobbs is a woman who effectively trades her female desire to live as a man. She secures a stable economic livelihood as a waiter in a hotel at the cost of completely erasing her sexuality. She becomes prisoner to a gender role chosen from economic need that ultimately steals her soul.

Benmussa directed the premiere productions of both *Albert Nobbs* and *Dora*. Benmussa's text, like Cixous', foregrounds its narrative strategies so that the spectator is forced to be aware of the manipulating authority of the dominating narrative voice. *Albert Nobbs* is based on a short story by George Moore, which in turn is based on a newspaper account of an actual event. Moore enters Benmussa's text as the master narrator. His disembodied voice controls the representation of Albert's life. The story—which Moore shares with Alec, a man of lower class and of Asian descent—both reveals and produces Albert's marginality to dominant discourse. Albert is continually silenced as Moore's voice usurps her own, entering the present level of the play to speak Albert's interior thoughts.

The pattern of storytelling, in fact, is *Albert Nobbs'* predominant mode. Other narratives in the text are consistent efforts to narrativize Albert Nobbs. The hotel staff, Helen Dawes, and the hotel owner, Mrs. Baker, all create their own versions of Albert's life that effectively deny Albert agency. She is able to tell her story only once, to Hubert Page, a housepainter with whom she is forced to share a bed.

Significantly, Albert believes Hubert is a man as she relates the story of adopting her opposite gender role. She is unable to tell her story to another woman—her attempts to reveal herself to Helen and to Kitty McCann, the prostitute, are foiled by the intrusion of men. Telling her story to Hubert, Albert describes her attraction for her employer, Mr. Congreve, which is thwarted by the arrival of his French mistress. When her position in his house becomes untenable, since her desire is denied, Albert assumes Congreve's clothing to enter the workforce as a man. The suppression of her desire through economic necessity excludes her from both male and female discourse. She is "neither man nor woman, just a perhapser."[18]

Hubert Page, however, reveals herself to be a woman as well. She describes her marriage to another woman as the satisfactory fulfillment of her female desire, even while she gains her livelihood as a man. This brief, ambiguous glimpse of Hubert's desire sets Albert on a quest to express her own. But Albert's sexuality has been too sufficiently erased.

Since she has lived most of her adult life in the masculine gender role, she has shunned intimate emotional contact. Her only memory of love or feeling is for her old nurse, a desexualized affection that is an inadequate model for the heterosexual courtship she undertakes with Helen Dawes. Helen taunts Albert for her failure to play the conventional heterosexual role—Helen cannot understand, for example, why Albert does not try to kiss her. Albert knows nothing of these rituals. She can read desire only through the economic necessities of the gender role in which she is imprisoned.

Albert tries to buy a wife, an economic partner for her dream of financial independence. But her efforts are mocked by Helen Dawes' greed and by the heterosexual economy of the hotel staff. Her efforts at partnership defeated, Albert remains alone until her death. Her sexual desire sublimated into financial avarice, Albert hoards her tips, accumulating wealth with which she has nothing to buy. Stacks of money, currency useless to procure her desire, are found in her room when she dies. Her fortune reverts to the state, the ideological apparatus under which she has relinquished her life.

Alternative framings are foregrounded in Benmussa's text through shifts in narrative voice and her manipulation of the representational apparatus. Two ghostly chambermaids pull back the curtains of the proscenium arch to reveal the stage—after George Moore's disembodied voice begins its story in the dark—then pull them closed again at the end of the narrative. The scene presented is marked by two-dimensional set pieces. Albert Nobbs is first revealed as though she is part of the *trompe l'oeil* backdrop of hotel room doors. The effect is a visual metaphor of Albert's two-dimensionality. She is denied both agency and subjectivity by her position in the male narrative and its representation. Her usual position is on the landing of a staircase, neither upstairs, nor down, caught in the discrepancy between her sex and her gender. At her death, Albert seems to simply fade once again into the backdrop, frozen in the task—polishing a pair of men's shoes—that symbolizes her life.

Case remarks, referring to *Albert Nobbs*, "Through the drag role, one can perceive how social constructs are inscribed on the body."[19] Benmussa's text, by narrating and representing an instance of gender impersonation, foregrounds gender as a construct and, as de Lauretis suggests, the nature of gender as representation. Both Albert and Hubert switch gender roles by changing their costumes: Albert dons a cast-off suit of Mr. Congreve's and Hubert takes up her husband's overalls to escape from her life as his wife.

When Albert intends to vacation with Helen Dawes, she buys a new suit and silk ties for her impersonation of a male lover courting his potential fiancée. This costume resonates not only with the masculine gender role, but with lesbians' assumption of "butch" roles as sexual symbols, particularly in the 1920s through the 1950s. The allusion to lesbian desire, however, is subsumed by Albert's position as male, and she is unable to situate her desire via her male—as opposed to lesbian—role.

Hubert, debating whether to return to her old life as a woman, describes the resumption of her female role as putting on women's clothes, but then wonders what story she would tell about her fifteen-year disappearance. Gender is an appearance, but it is always inscribed in a narrative and, as Benmussa's production demonstrates, gender ideology tells a story of male heterosexual desire. Her representation of Albert's assumed role foregrounds, for the spectator, the construction of gender and gendered spectatorial positions in conventional narrative.

Instead of being complicit with this process, Benmussa manipulates the representational apparatus to denaturalize its ideology. There is no escaping George Moore's authoritative reading of Albert's story. He appears as a young boy in the first scene, and Mrs. Baker refers to his fear of Albert when she eulogizes her employee to Hubert Page. Albert is trapped in Moore's narrative. As Elin Diamond points out, in her analysis of the text,

Benmussa's achievement in *Albert Nobbs* is to induce narrativity in the audience while insisting on the coercive effects of a male narrative that (inevitably) refuses or diminishes and distorts the experience of female subjects. Albert's story—or rather Moore and Alec's storytelling—indicts the practice of enacting or telling any woman's story, including those cultural myths and histories that women and men "naturally" consume, inhabit, and perpetuate.[20]

The spectator knows Albert only as the projection of Moore's gaze. To "read" her at all requires the spectator to see her through male narrative strategies. Where Cixous' text decenters the primacy of the gaze in representation by playing with aural, unseen (perhaps "unscene") effects, Benmussa foregrounds the constrictions of the female body literally seen (and "scened") through male constructs.

The Brechtian Legacy

Some of the tenets of materialist practice such as Benmussa's and Cixous'— particularly foregrounding and denaturalizing the representational apparatus— can be traced to the legacy of Bertolt Brecht. Rather than the Artaudian body-presence that informs *l'écriture féminine*'s transposition into a feminine theatre aesthetic, Brecht's theories of alienation and historicization serve as a precedent for materialist feminist theatre practice and criticism. Brecht's "epic theatre" is "a model of how to change not merely the political content of art, but its very productive apparatus."[21]

Brecht's theory is a direct, politically based critique of representational structures that create mythologized subject positions and that mystify social relations. Realist theatre imposes a conservative sense of order by delivering its ideology as normative. The transcendent pose of illusionist theatre makes the society it reflects appear to be incapable of change. Realism naturalizes social relations imposed by dominant ideology and mystifies its own authorship.

Far from suppressing an editorializing, or theorizing, or thinking voice under the mimetic guise of realism, Brecht proposes making the ideological point of view the overarching framework for the theatre experience. Spectators should be led not to accept passively the representational conventions institutionalized before them, but to question the interactions and relationships played out in the representational space.

Rather than succumbing to the seduction of the illusionist text—which fulfills a need as base and transient as consuming a meal (hence, Brecht's term "culinary theatre" to represent such illusionism)—the spectator in epic theatre is given an "exercise in complex seeing" and asked to "think above the stream" rather than to "think in the stream."[22] This critical, reflective position disrupts the process of identification that normally pulls the spectator through the text, subjects him or her to the authority of narrative closure, and offers the relief of catharsis.

Martin Esslin criticizes Brecht by defending psychological processes as the basis of human communication: "In his rejection of identification . . . Brecht comes into conflict with the fundamental concept of psychology that regards the processes of identification as the basic mechanisms by which one human being communicates with another."[23] Brecht, however, feels that embedding these identificatory processes in representation helps to reify oppressive social relations, particularly those of class.

Materialist feminist critics, as discussed in chapter 1, point out that polarized gender behavior is maintained and supported by psychological identification processes. Brecht's theory generally disregards the issue of gender, but a materialist feminist critique can recuperate some of his theories to focus on representation's perpetuation of social relations of gender, race, and sexuality, as well as class.

Instead of emphathizing with the plight of an Aristotelian tragic hero, the epic theatre's spectator is taught "to be astonished at the circumstances under which [the characters] function."[24] Estranging the spectator from the conditions of life outlined by the representation denaturalizes the dominant ideology that benefits from such "natural" social relations. Ideology circulates through a text as a meaning effect which can be deciphered by a spectator freed from the dreamlike state of passive receptivity. If the representational apparatus is ideologically marked, its material aspects must be brought into full view and denaturalized for the spectator's inspection. The mystification of social arrangements is exposed and the spectator is presented with the possibility of change.

Brecht proposes that the artist scrutinize the historical moment like a series of slides under a microscope, then rearrange the images out of their rigid linearity to demonstrate that the course of events can be influenced and changed. His epic theatre is a series of tableaux that frame relationships between people against a social backdrop. It discards linear narrative, presenting instead a series of episodes heralded by titles that unsettle the spectator's expectation of suspense.

This style infiltrates Benmussa's *Albert Nobbs,* in which each short episode is announced by a title such as "Albert's Tale," or "The Flea." This "literarization" of the mise-en-scène is also evident in "The Concert" episode in *Albert Nobbs,* in which an easel is assembled to hold up a two-dimensional drawing of a woman singing and playing the piano. The image is foregrounded as a sign to be read. The "faked" concert breaks the seamless flow of narrative in *Albert Nobbs* by highlighting the artificiality of representation.

Songs, too, are often used in epic theatre as a multimedia technique that demystifies representation. The performers do not fall romantically into song as a heightening of emotion, but clearly break off into a different form of enunciation. The interruption of narrative by song is evident in Holly Hughes' *Lady Dick* (1985), a parody of film noir conventions foregrounded by lesbian representation. In *Lady Dick,* familiar romantic songs intrude on a text motivated by lesbian desire. The popular songs literally sound funny in the homosexual context, a comic effect that helps to estrange their heterosexual content. Split Britches' productions usually include songs, even though none of the three performers can really sing very well. When they sing off-tune or forget lyrics, however, the ragged seams of the spectacle are displayed as rough edges, as impurities that mar the presentation of a realist illusion.

Foregrounding the theatre event as representation means that "the audience can no longer have the illusion of being the unseen spectator at an event which is really taking place."[25] The chambermaids who pull and close the curtains on *Albert Nobbs'* mise-en-scène implicate the spectator as witnesses to the unfolding narrative. "By foregrounding narrative," Diamond believes, "Benmussa exposes the audience's own [desire for] narrativity—our desire for order and closure."[26] The chambermaids' deliberate act foregrounds Albert's story as representation.

Brecht's freeze-framed, demystified narratives quote the social moment as *gestus,* which "demonstrate a custom which leads to conclusions about the entire structure of society in a particular (transient) time."[27] Janelle Reinelt, writing on British feminist theatre, points out that Brecht's *gestus* can be used to illustrate the gender-bias of social arrangements.[28] Rather than a textual illustration, the *gestus* is a visual sign. Since it occurs within the theatrical moment, it prompts consideration of events and relationships drawn out in space. In the Brechtian instance, the social/political relationships between people become textual materials.

Violence acts as a social *gestus* in Maria Irene Fornes' plays. Brutality becomes not only a metaphor, but a visual sign of the power dynamics in the gendered social relations Fornes represents in her plays. The women's attempts to wrest power into their own hands ultimately turns against them, as though women's expression of their desire and agency, in this historical moment, can only be self-destructive.

Conduct of Life (1985), for instance, outlines the oppression wrought by a man against his wife and his child-mistress, whom he brings into the family home as a servant. His wife ultimately kills him to free both herself and the battered mistress, but presses her weapon into the lower-class girl's hand to abdicate responsibility for her act. Fornes illustrates the complicity of women in their mutual oppression, and emphasizes here that gender liberation alone will not serve as an antidote to the inequities of race and class.

The title character of Fornes' *Sarita* (1984) is caught between her conflicting desires for Julio, her violent Latin lover, and Mark, a white man who offers her a ticket out of the oppressions of class and race. Sarita cannot rationally make the leap a liason with Mark requires, and resorts to killing Julio to free herself from her self-destructive desire. Fornes' theme in these plays is the hopeless entrapment of women's desire. Her female characters struggle to fulfill themselves sexually or intellectually but are continually, brutally foiled by the controlling male desire and the legal, social superstructure by which it is legitimated.[29]

In *Mud*, which Fornes directed at Theatre for the New City in New York in 1983, a woman is trapped in the poverty of her cultural history, between two men who are dependent on her for material, emotional, and sexual satisfaction. Lloyd's and Henry's needs keep Mae in an objectified, domesticated position. Her one desire is for knowledge; she wants to learn how to read. Henry begins to teach her, then is crippled mentally and physically by an accident.

After his fall, only Henry's sexuality remains whole. He continues to express his desire through the now distorted posture of his body. His manhood is repulsive to Mae, who is nonetheless subjected to Henry's needs. Unable to learn to read, and now completely objectified by the man who was to grant her entry into discourse, Mae remains outside the register of language. When she decides to leave their home for "something better," Lloyd takes down his shotgun and kills her.[30]

The set is placed on a high mound of mud, which as a scenic device denies any pretensions to realism. The rest of the set is stark and dirty, as are the characters and their clothing. Mae's ironing board and its accompanying, never-diminishing pile of soiled clothes are prominent; there is a table and several chairs, and two doors in the back wall of the shallow set that seem to lead nowhere. The ironing in the play works as a kind of *gestus*—Mae irons constantly, while Henry, before his accident, sits at the table with his books.

The play is broken into brief, episodic scenes in a Brechtian style and, under Fornes' direction, is constructed with visual images that call attention to the constructed nature of the representation. Rather than punctuating the short episodes with blackouts, Fornes slowly dims the stark white light on each scene. In the interims, the performers can be seen dropping their characters, then picking them up again, rather than striving for the continual believability of realism. The characters move into their next positions in the semilight, and the lights fade to black before the next scene is revealed.

Roberta Sklar used a similar Brechtian technique when she directed Jane Chambers' *Last Summer at Bluefish Cove* in Provincetown, Massachusetts, in Summer 1983. Chambers' play is a realist comedy about several lesbian couples who vacation together on a Long Island beach. When a heterosexual woman rents the cottage next door, the inevitable misunderstandings and subterfuge occur, until the heterosexual woman falls in love with the only single member of the lesbian group. A death occurs at the play's end that ruptures this happy union, but Chambers' play follows the basic comic paradigm—a marriage takes place that reinstates the coupled order. *Bluefish Cove* is about romance more than it is about lesbian sexuality, and stories of romance ultimately reinscribe the family.[31]

In many ways, *Bluefish Cove* is about a heterosexual woman who decides to become a lesbian. Most coming-out stories continue to refer to the heterosexual paradigm the "new" lesbian is leaving. The focus is on her decision, on revealing her sexuality to her family, and on her hesitant entry into her new community, rather than on a full consideration of the lifestyle she intends to assume. This locks the coming-out play in an oppositional stance that is defined by the heterosexual world the lesbian wants to leave. In content and form, *Bluefish Cove* never breaks loose from the heterosexual contract that founds representation.

As directed by Sklar, however, several of the play's realist conventions are overturned, which invites the spectators to think more critically about the play's form and content. Performers freeze for several moments at the end of each scene, then move in full light to their positions for the next scene. Once in place, the lights fade on the scene momentarily, then brighten and allow the production to continue. Sondra Segal, Sklar's partner in the Women's Experimental Theatre, plays the romantic lead, and delivers several of her speeches directly to the audience. The direct address also helps break the fourth-wall convention written into the text.

Segal's performance serves as an instance of casting against convention. Spectator expectations for the performers who play romantic leads—even in lesbian plays—require that they be attractive according to accepted cultural standards. This is a rather loaded assumption in a lesbian context, in which standards of beauty are not as strict and not as clearly defined by the dominant culture. But it is a testament to the conservative power of representation that on stage even alternative audiences tend to be influenced by cultural authority and to judge appearance by its standards.

Cultural expectations, as we have seen in the discussion of *'night, Mother* in chapter 2, impact on the spectator's reception of the performance text. By deliberately casting a middle-aged, nonconventionally attractive woman in the Don Juan role in *Bluefish Cove*, Sklar provides a critique of cultural conventions of beauty, sexuality, and age. The choice foregrounds spectators' expectations of romantic leads as youthful, svelte, and conventionally beautiful, and implies that middle-aged women can also be sexual.

Chambers' play is a traditional realist text, and Bonnie Marranca calls Fornes' plays "quotational" realism, "theatre in close-up, freeze-frame."[32] Through overlaying Brechtian foregrounding and alienation techniques on the classical realist narratives, the flow of images and the seduction of the text is broken. The spectator is asked to contemplate the relationships illuminated by Fornes' searing white light and given time to reflect on the social arrangements that order the relationships at Bluefish Cove.

The authority of these narratives and the social order they reinstate are recuperated from the most conservative instances of closure. The texts are opened up and completed only in the spectator's reading of them. As in epic theatre, "In so far as the audience is made to pass judgements on the performance and the actions it embodies, it becomes an expert collaborator in an open-ended practice, rather than the consumer of a finished object."[33] The spectator is invited to find different meanings through his or her reading of the opened text. Brechtian technique in feminist hands can fragment the realist drama into component parts and expose its gender assumptions for critical inspection.

These breaks in the realist text also work toward the historicization that Brecht spelled out as a tenet of epic theatre: "While the theatre of illusion is trying to re-create a spurious present by pretending that the events of the play are actually taking place at the time of each performance, the 'epic' theatre is strictly *historical;* it constantly reminds the audience that they are merely getting a reporting of past events."[34] To most appropriately utilize historicization, Brecht proposes refashioning narratives that are familiar to spectators, so that suspense will no longer play a part in the seduction of the text. Using historical materials allows the estrangement of the familiar.

Theodora Skipitares' performance work frequently reads historical material from a feminist perspective. *Age of Invention* (1983) and *Defenders of the Code* (1987) are rooted in familiar history—the first, of American ingenuity and industry, the second, of genetics. Since the characters in these pieces are represented by puppets or sculptures, a critical distance from the material is established, which allows Skipitares to point out the ironies in the history she describes and to offer her own editorial viewpoint.

Defenders of the Code illustrates Darwin's theories and the implications of modern eugenics with images that make a clear editorial comment on traditional readings of these texts. In one scene, five distinct noses are hung from a rack to illustrate racial differences. The oversized noses eventually develop legs and tap dance. Little white, blond-haired baby dolls are lined up in a scene that illustrates the goals of eugenics. The piece presents the history of scientific myths that have institutionalized the social relations dictated in the canonized works of great men. Skipitares' critique is poignant when the images she constructs are read in counterpoint with the historical texts.

The puppets' operators in *Defenders of the Code* are clearly displayed. The narrators that speak for the puppets stand at the side of the stage, clearly lit, reading the text from music stands. The dissociation of voice and text allows once again for critical distance and comment. A rock band is situated on a high platform to the rear of the stage to accompany the action and to punctuate scene shifts. The spectator is invited to observe each aspect of the representational apparatus, which is foregrounded by Skipitares' clever play with the shapes and light that create her images.

Spiderwoman Theatre uses similar techniques to capitalize on the effects of incongruity and alienation. In their revision of Chekhov's *Three Sisters,* which Spiderwoman calls *The Three Sisters from Here to There* (1982), the male characters are represented by life-sized dolls that the performers manipulate like puppets. When they are not part of the action, the "men" are tossed to the floor with careless disdain, or used as pillows and punching bags. When the

Tuzenbach doll fondles Irina's breasts, or the Kulygin doll commands Masha in a preemptory tone, these actions appear as *gestus* that comment on the structure of gendered relationships.

The Russian sisters' longing for Moscow is translated into the Spider-woman sisters' desire to leave Brooklyn for Manhattan. One of the sisters breaks from the action to tell the spectators how long it takes to get from Brooklyn to Manhattan by subway or car. Spiderwoman breaks up the Chekhov text with topical references, direct address, and films. Musical interludes dispersed through-out the text take liberties with song lyrics to indicate Spiderwoman's political bias and their ironic attitude toward Chekhovian angst. Natasha sings "Don't Rain on My Parade" in the fourth act, and Irina sings "You Made Me Love You" in a campy style to the Baron. The incongruity of these choices fore-grounds the troupe's estrangement of a familiar text hallowed by the theatrical canon.

Denaturalizing historical texts provokes the spectator to contemplate the structure of social relations their mythology perpetuates. The individual solution to both dramatic and social situations is preempted by a focus on people in relation to each other and the dominant ideology that shapes their interactions.

In the "Short Organum," Brecht writes that "the smallest social unit is not the single person but two people."[35] Gayle Rubin also posits the couple as the fundamental social unit, but she emphasizes the necessity of their heterosexuality within the economic structure:

> Lévi-Strauss concludes from a survey of the division of labor by sex that it is not a biological specialization, but must have some other purpose. This purpose, he argues, is to insure the union of men and women by making the smallest viable economic unit contain at least one man and one woman. . . . The division of labor by sex can therefore be seen as a "taboo": a taboo against the sameness of men and women, a taboo dividing the sexes into two mutually exclusive categories, a taboo which exacerbates the biological differences between the sexes and thereby *creates* gender.[36]

Social arrangements mandate compulsory heterosexuality organized by gender polarization to insure the operation of economic and social systems. Rubin goes on to say, "The sexual division of labor is implicated in both aspects of gender—male and female it creates them, and it creates them heterosexual. The suppression of the homosexual component of human sexuality, and by corollary, the oppression of homosexuals, is therefore a product of the same system whose rules and relations oppress women."[37] Brechtian alienation techniques that de-naturalize social arrangements can be fruitfully employed in feminist practice to demystify compulsory heterosexuality and the construction of gender as the founding principle of representation.

In lesbian usage, for instance, the estrangement of male desire and the institution of heterosexuality is often foregrounded by historicizing performance conventions that close on the inscription of heterosexual, genderized social arrangements. Popular genres are historicized, then reinscribed in an alternative lesbian social arrangement. Alice Forrester's *Fear of Laughing* (1985), for example, presented at the WOW Cafe, uses 1950s television as the basis of its parody. Ward and June Cleaver of *Leave It to Beaver* and the father of the ubiquitous *Father Knows Best* are all portrayed by women. Historicizing this familiar cultural material and foregrounding its gender assumptions by casting the production with lesbians makes the ideology of such pieces of Americana readable to the spectator.[38]

In a similar fashion, such historicization also works to defamiliarize the present, as conclusions about current social arrangements can be inferred. The isolated freedom of the individual privileged in liberal humanism is rejected by Brechtian technique. The historicized individual becomes a product of social relations, and the character an "untragic hero" who can be studied within a larger social context.[39] The author, too, is recuperated from the Romantic myth of isolated genius, and is seen as a cultural worker embedded in social relations and history:

> For Brecht . . . the author is primarily a *producer*, analogous to any other maker of a social product. [He opposes,] that is to say, the Romantic notion of the author as *creator*—as the God-like figure who mysteriously conjures his handiwork out of nothing. Such an inspirational, individualist concept of artistic production makes it impossible to conceive of the artist as a worker rooted in a particular history with particular materials at his disposal.[40]

The Brechtian reading, then, offers a revised position for both character and playwright.

Liberal feminist texts, as we have seen, present their characters as individuals struggling alone to attain the freedom capitalism and liberal humanism posit as universally available. Playwrights such as Marsha Norman work within this ethos, theorizing their characters and themselves as individuals who have achieved—or not—their singular success on the dominant culture's terms. Cultural feminists, with their tendency to collective creation, come closer to dispelling the Romantic notion of inspired authorship, but continue to mystify their work as biological organicism.

Materialist feminist theatre makers, on the other hand, are engaged in cultural production in which characters and playwrights are posited in relation to social arrangements, both in the text and vis-à-vis modes of production. These positions are clearly articulated in materialist feminist revisions—influenced by Brecht—of the performer's role in representation.

Performance Texts Articulated in the "Not . . . But"

Brecht's formulation of the alienation effect's application to acting technique is perhaps most pertinent to materialist feminist practice. The Brechtian actor resides in a state of showingness. Rather than being psychologically enmeshed with the character, as the performer is in Stanislavski's technique (which most resembles the spiritual channeling currently popular in New Age metaphysics), the performer continually stands beside the character, illustrating its behavior for the spectator's inspection.

Brecht emphasizes that " 'he who is showing should himself be shown.' "[41] In many WOW Cafe performances and Spiderwoman Theatre productions, lines are frequently dropped or blundered through as memory fails the performers. These mistakes, however, foreground the psychological implications of memorizing lines. What does it mean, after all, to assume a character's speech, and to therefore silence your own? The psychological abdicaton of the performer's identity is undesirable to Brecht, who suggests that the performer should display, rather than become, the character.

The performer "expresses his awareness of being watched" in epic theatre.[42] Diamond proposes these layers of watching as a way to revise Laura Mulvey's reading of the female body's traditional position in representation as constructed for "to-be-looked-at-ness."[43] Diamond substitutes "looking-at-being-looked-at-ness" or even "looking-ness" as a model for Brechtian-influenced feminist theorization of the female body onstage.[44] She expands on Brecht to suggest a triangular relationship between the actor, character, and spectator, one that will also belie Mulvey's demand for an end to visual pleasure:

> The spectator still has the possibility of pleasurable identification. This is effected not through imaginary projection onto an ideal but through a triangular structure of actor/subject-character-spectator. Looking at the character, the spectator is constantly intercepted by the actor/subject, and the latter, heeding no fourth wall, is theoretically free to look back. The difference, then, between this triangle and the familiar Oedipal one is that no one side signifies authority, knowledge, or the law.[45]

The gaze circulates along the triangle, providing three separate subject positions. The one-way nature of the male gaze, owned by a spectator who is obscured in a darkened theatre, specularizes the female body, which is not allowed to gaze back. In Diamond's formulation, the gaze itself is foregrounded— the spectator and actor/subject as character watch each other watching.

Peggy Shaw, for example, in Split Britches' *Upwardly Mobile Home,* addresses the audience through her awareness that they are watching her. She asks spectators if their seats are comfortable and if they are getting what they paid to see. This break in the narrative forces the spectators to confront themselves *as* spectators, participants in the act of looking.

Shaw steps outside the representational frame to look at the spectator look-ing at her, and to comment on the convention of the theatrical gaze. Her story about going to see the fat lady at the circus in *Mobile Home* comments on a feminist position vis-à-vis the gaze. When she entered the fat lady's tent, Shaw says, "She knew I had come to see her being fat. She looked at me and I looked at her."[46] The awareness of looking, freed from the pretense of disguise by the fourth wall, makes the representation of women part of the performance's sub-ject. The performer's awareness of her being-looked-at-ness, and her stance beside her character, implicates her in the act of looking. Since she merely quotes her character in the Brechtian manner, and does not identify with her, the spectator's impulse toward identification is also broken. In Brecht's descrip-tion, "The audience identifies itself with the actor as being an observer and accordingly develops his attitude of observing or looking on."[47]

Positioning the performer as an observer who quotes the character also allows meditation on the actions she has chosen to share with the spectator. The performer's choice of actions will "imply what he [*sic*] is not doing; . . . his acting allows other possibilities to be inferred . . . every gesture signifies a decision; the character remains under observation and is tested. The technical term for this procedure is 'fixing the "not . . . but."' "[48] Purposefully distanced from the representation she is making, the performer embodies a semiotic space in which her presence bears the traces of its difference; her image retains "something of the rough sketching which indicates traces of other movements and features all around the fully-worked out figure."[49] Or, as Diamond defines the "not . . . but," "Each action must contain the trace of the action it represses, thus the meaning of each action contains difference."[50] If the performer is representing gender, the action she chooses will bear the trace of what it is not. The representational apparatus that creates gender can be demystified; the repre-sentation of gender within the "not . . . but" will be a choice made in a critical attitude.

The Lesbian Subject as the "Not . . . But"

The "not . . . but" might point to a materialist practice in which the female body in representation is no longer the object of the male gaze, but part of the discourse of watching that performance promotes. The female body may no longer be a hysterical spectacle, but a term in the new representational debate. As Diamond offers, "The body in historicization stands visibly and palpably separate from the 'role' of the actor as well as the role of the character; it is always insufficient and open."[51] This new representation of the female body is not a closed text that ends in objectification nor is it subjected to inscription in the narrative of compulsory heterosexuality.

In order to rethink representation, de Lauretis proposes that "we must walk out of the male-centered frame of reference in which gender and sexuality are (re)produced by the discourse of male sexuality."[52] She emphasizes that cultural production is "built on male narratives of gender, whether Oedipal or anti-Oedipal, bound by the heterosexual contract." Hence, the "critique of all discourses concerning gender" must rewrite cultural narratives and define the terms of another perspective—"a view from 'elsewhere.' "[53] The lesbian subject position looms as the unarticulated but inferred "elsewhere" in de Lauretis' discourse.

The lesbian subject is "the elsewhere of discourse, the here and now, the blind spots, or the spaces-off, of its representations."[54] The lesbian subject is in a position to denaturalize dominant codes by signifying an existence that belies the entire structure of heterosexual culture and its representations. The lesbian signifies a "blockage in the system of representation" by expressing forbidden contents in forbidden forms.[55] The forbidden content is active female desire independent of men, and the forbidden form is a self-representation that separates gender from a strict correlation with biological sex and compulsory sexuality. The lesbian is a refusor of culturally imposed gender ideology, who confounds representation based on sexual difference and on compulsory heterosexuality.

If gender is representation, then the application of the "not . . . but" can help inscribe a deconstruction of gender within its construction in representation. Lesbian representations of butch/femme appearances point out the possibilities of such a deconstruction. A lesbian assuming a butch or femme role retains traces of difference that mark out her choice. Case describes butch or femme lesbians as "dressed in the clothes of desire"; the roles are "symbols of seduction."[56] The lesbian desire underlying lesbian representations of gender disrupts the system of gender signification.

The drag role requires the performer to quote the accepted conventions of gender behavior. A woman playing a man, or the traditional representation of Woman, is quoting gender ideology, holding it up for critique. By standing outside her gendered character, the performer makes gender available for discussion. When the assumed gender role does not coincide with the performer's biological sex, the fictions of gender are highlighted. When the role does coincide with her biology, as it does when the lesbian plays the femme role, it is noncoincidental to the assumed heterosexuality of the representation of Woman.

In the lesbian context, where the heterosexual assumption has been discarded, gender as representation gets detached from "the real" and becomes as plastic and kitsch as the little man and woman balanced on a wedding cake. Gender becomes a social *gestus,* a gesture that represents ideology circulating in social relations.

The lesbian body, which articulates itself through female desire, stands already outside of gender enculturation. In its refusal of heterosexuality, the lesbian body cannot be narrativized as spectacle. The lesbian is still a representation—as Con Carne tells Garnet McClit in *Lady Dick,* "You're what they watch when there's nothing *buena* on TV"—but she is a sign that disrupts the dominant signifying system. When she assumes a gender role, it becomes part of the material aspects of the representational apparatus, a costume that hangs on a rack of choices.

Joan Nestle, a cofounder of the Lesbian Herstory Archives who became a lesbian in the 1950s, tells a story in the "Sex Issue" of *Heresies* that seems to me to be about gender as representation: "One day many years ago, as I was walking through Central Park, a group of cheerful straight people walked past me and said, 'What shall we feed it?' "[57] They could not read her lesbian self-representation because they could not inscribe her in their heterosexually gendered narrative. With a certain prescience, Nestle remarks, "When [lesbians] broke gender lines in the 1950s, we fell off the biologically charted maps."[58] By transgressing heterosexually divided gender roles, the lesbian confounded the sign system that denotes woman, because the representation of gender *as* representation is based on compulsory heterosexuality.

Garnet McClit, Lady Dick, is perhaps emblematic of the lesbian subject position in representation. Divisions of both gender and biological sex are conflated in her name. The puns on her hermaphroditic appellation run through the play: One character remarks in a kind of Brechtian astonishment, "She's a dick. She can't be!" This is Brechtian defamiliarization at work—implied in the lesbian subject is a "not . . . but" that materializes the gap between sex and gender that lesbian desire can inhabit.

Afterword

Envisioning a space-off of representation—that is, Teresa de Lauretis' "view from elsewhere"—leads inevitably to a kind of utopianism. Where do you actually stand when you step outside of representation, and who stands with you? My text ends with the lesbian subject because I believe that personally, artistically, and spectatorially, hers is closest to the view from elsewhere, and offers the most radical position from which to subvert representation.

As Nestle's mordant anecdote clarifies, and as the East Village lesbian community continues to exemplify, many lesbians "perform" themselves in everyday life as well as in the performance space. If all the world is in fact a stage—that is, if people are continually caught up in representation and ideology, and if we read the ideology of gender only through its representation—lesbians who assert their identity and their right to exist through their self-representations clearly have quite a lot at stake. The danger of representing lesbian sexuality in an era of political intolerance and sexual prudence requires an enormous personal investment from those willing to continue their public, gender-bending masquerades.

A lesbian on the street representing a subversion of gender ideology through a butch or femme role is in some ways the perfect illustration of the Brechtian "not . . . but," foregrounding for her unwitting spectators the in-betweens of nonpolarized gender identity. How this radical meaning can maintain itself in a more formal representational situation might be the continuing question for feminist performance criticism. How can radicalism be maintained in a representational economy that works to neutralize radical meanings?

This question implies a continual consideration of form, content, and context in feminist work. For example, how can the formal experiments with old contents evidenced in the WOW Cafe work truly contribute to cultural change? How radical is the work if it continues to take place in an alternative context in which its spectators are mostly lesbians with a predisposition to the meanings the performances construct? Will the work at WOW, or by Split Britches or

Holly Hughes, be neutralized if it becomes a commodity consumable in a more mainstream economy? Or will it carry its radical meanings to a wider audience?

These questions are not moot. *Dress Suits for Hire,* a collaborative piece by Lois Weaver, Peggy Shaw, and Holly Hughes, is now under negotiation for an off-Broadway run. It will be interesting and important to trace the ramifications of this step up—or into—the mainstream theatre hierarchy. The performers and playwright will happily see their income jump, and the production will be available to a much more diverse audience. Selling a lesbian text to mainstream spectators seems incongruous, but in the best of all possible worlds those spectators will come away from the performance thinking differently about their sexuality and gender assumptions.

Or maybe not. Perhaps the context will prevail, and the desire to consume the glittery Broadway product that hangs like an aura over that excited group of spectators waiting on the ubiquitous TKTS line in Times Square will obscure the meaning of what they see. Perhaps the precedent set, ironically, by the long off-Broadway run of drag-performer Charles Busch's production *Vampire Lesbians of Sodom* will allow the spectators to contextualize a truly lesbian performance piece as just another incidence of harmless transvestism. Or maybe because the production does not fulfill spectators' expectations of traditional, realist drama, they will be angered and alienated for the wrong reasons, and will fail to achieve a more Brechtian state of understanding.

Time, as they say, will tell. But *Dress Suits'* move is exemplary of the issues facing feminist theatre, performance, and criticism. The larger question might be, How does social change really happen through cultural production? Theatre in mainstream American culture is supposed to be an entertaining, consumable commodity. The TKTS line is peopled by spectators who do not expect to choose a production that will challenge their fundamental worldview. How, then, might feminist theatre and feminist performance criticism help to create a propensity for change in those mainstream spectators, a willingness to accept new forms and contents, and to consider the new meanings they create?

There is an attendant issue here. If the objective—idealistic though it might sound—is social change, what is the position of the feminist critic in relation to feminist cultural production? Economics and context once again loom into the picture. Precarious feminist theatre and performance groups need favorable documentation of their work to persuade funding organizations and audiences to continue their support. The feminist critic who writes frankly of a feminist production's problems risks a certain ostracism from the creative community. In the spirit of progress, however, it seems necessary to point out the limitations of even the most well-intentioned feminist work—as I hope I have done here— and to institute a dialogue that resonates beyond the confines of an insular feminist community.

This issue is complex and sensitive, but seems important as the epilogue to this book. In the process of collecting photographs to illustrate of this study, I was chastized by a feminist performance group for not consulting with them while writing. They chided that I must understand how sensitive they are to what is written about them. And I do understand.

But as a critic and a theorist, does my primary responsibility lie in faithfully reporting the authorial intentions of feminist theatre groups and squelching my own response as a feminist spectator? Or does my responsibility lie in attempting to place the work in a larger cultural, theoretical, and ideological context, in which it becomes part of a movement of ideas? Clearly, in this book I have risked alienating myself from people whose efforts I respect by choosing the latter option. My work here is not about the process of creating feminist performance, although creative considerations impinge on the discussion. I have concentrated, rather, on the process of being a feminist spectator, whom I refuse to idealize as always nurturing of feminist work.

Even in the most participatory styles of theatre, a spectator arrives at the work at a different point in its process than those who created it. A critic must approach the work from that point as well. This is the point at which it becomes representation, the organization of meanings communicated between performers and spectators. As I have pointed out here, the process of reception and the entire hermeneutical endeavor will—and should—be different for different spectators. The meanings derived from any one performance will vary endlessly. For a feminist theatre to dictate a proper meaning is as ideologically and politically suspect as any of the mystifications implicitly condoned by the dominant culture's theatre.

But here, again, I bump against a contradiction in my own discourse. Several times, I have pointed out the dangers of pluralism, yet I seem to be arriving at it (although not advocating it) as I write the coda to my text. I do not believe that all feminist critical methodologies or performance practices are equally insightful or efficacious. I have explained my hesitations about liberal and cultural feminist approaches. I maintain that the materialist feminist approach to criticism and spectatorship has the most to offer in the effort toward radical cultural change.

Materialist feminism at least acknowledges the varied responses of spectators mixed across ideologies of gender, sexuality, race, and class. By admitting to this heterogeneity, strategies for how to thwart the white, heterosexual, middle-class male's hegemony as the subject of representation can be formulated. Under materialism, these formulations will not include subsuming spectator differences under some comfortable, homogenous classification. On the contrary, the materialist creative and critical project will be located within those differences, which will inevitably demand new forms and provoke new meanings when they are inscribed in representation.

Notes

Chapter 1

1. See Catherine Belsey, "Constructing the Subject: Deconstructing the Text," in Judith Newton and Deborah Rosenfelt, eds., *Feminist Criticism and Social Change: Sex, Class, and Race in Literature and Culture* (New York: Methuen, 1985) for a discussion of the ideal spectator's position as constructed in realism. The issue of realism and spectatorship is addressed fully in chapter 5.

2. The phrase "resistant reader" was coined with the publication of Judith Fetterley's *The Resisting Reader: A Feminist Approach to American Fiction* (Bloomington: Indiana University Press, 1978).

3. See Teresa de Lauretis, *Alice Doesn't: Feminism, Semiotics, Cinema* (Bloomington: Indiana University Press, 1984), particularly her chapter "Desire in Narrative," pp. 103–57.

4. Linda Gordon, "What's New in Women's History," in Teresa de Lauretis, ed., *Feminist Studies/Critical Studies* (Bloomington: Indiana University Press, 1986), p. 29.

5. See Sue-Ellen Case, "The Personal is Not the Political," *Art & Cinema* Vol. 1, No. 3 (Fall 1987), p. 4, for a relevant discussion of the feminisms in feminist theatre practice.

6. See Annette Kolodny, "Dancing through the Minefield: Some Observations on the Theory, Practice, and Politics of a Feminist Literary Criticism," *Feminist Studies* Vol. 6, No. 1 (Spring 1980), pp. 1–23. Kolodny writes, "Just because we will no longer tolerate the specifically sexist omissions and oversights of earlier critical schools and methods does not mean that, in their stead, we must establish our own 'party line.' . . . Instead, as I see it, our task is to initiate nothing less than a playful pluralism, responsive to the possibilities of multiple critical schools and methods, but captive to none" (p. 19).

7. See Alison Jaggar, *Feminist Politics and Human Nature* (Totowa, N.J.: Rowman & Allanheld, 1983), for her definitions of different feminist epistemologies. See Michelene Wandor, *Carry On, Understudies* (New York: Routledge & Kegan Paul, 1986), for definitions of the feminisms in terms of British feminist theatre. In her chapter "Political Dynamics: The Feminisms," Wandor outlines radical feminism, bourgeois feminism or emancipationism, and socialist feminism as the three major tendencies "as they have emerged in the 1970s" (p. 131). See also my article "Feminists, Lesbians, and Other Women in Theatre: Thoughts on the Politics of Performance," forthcoming in *Themes in Drama* Vol. 11 (1989) for a longer discussion of the way in which delineating the feminisms in theatre clarifies the more obscure appellation "women in theatre." This article was originally presented as a paper at the 1987 Themes in Drama

conference at the University of California/Riverside. An earlier version was published as "The Politics of Feminist Performance," in *Theatre Times* Vol. 5, No. 6 (July/August 1986). Elin Diamond has expressed reservations about my use of the term "cultural" feminism, as she feels, and rightly so, that the culture is "where we all live." For now, however, I continue to maintain that "cultural" feminism is a more precise appellation than "radical" feminism.

8. See Zillah Eisenstein, *The Radical Future of Liberal Feminism* (New York: Longman, 1981), for a study of liberal feminist theory that proposes its potential for radicalism, particularly part 3, "The Contemporary Practice of Liberal Feminism," pp. 175–253.

9. Jaggar, pp. 355–58.

10. See Julie Malnig, "The Women's Project: A Profile," *Women & Performance Journal 1*, Vol. 1, No. 1 (1983), and my "Women's Theatre Program of the ATA: Creating a Feminist Forum," *Women & Performance Journal 3*, Vol. 1, No. 2 (1984). The Women and Theatre Program has in more recent years come significantly closer to a more theoretical—and feminist—stance on the issue of women in theatre.

11. See Francesca Primus, "Women's Theatres around Town: Feminist or Contemporary?" *Back-stage,* December 6, 1985, for interviews with various women working in New York theatre who renounce the feminist label.

12. Case, p. 4.

13. Alice Echols, "The New Feminism of Yin and Yang," in Ann Snitow, Christine Stansell, and Sharon Thompson, eds., *Powers of Desire: The Politics of Sexuality* (New York: Monthly Review Press, 1983), p. 441.

14. Gordon, p. 27.

15. Gayle Rubin, "The Traffic in Women: Notes on the 'Political Economy' of Sex," in Rayna Reiter, ed., *Towards an Anthropology of Women* (New York: Monthly Review Press, 1978), p. 159.

16. Jaggar, pp. 365–66. See also pp. 364–69 for a fuller accounting of radical feminist epistemology.

17. See Adrienne Rich, *Of Woman Born: Motherhood as Experience and Institution* (New York: Bantam Books, 1976).

18. Echols, p. 442.

19. Echols, p. 440.

20. Rosemary Curb, "Re/cognition, Re/presentation, Re/creation in Woman-Conscious Drama: The Seer, the Seen, the Scene, the Obscene," *Theatre Journal* Vol. 37, No. 3 (October 1985), p. 308.

21. Quoted in Dinah Leavitt, *Feminist Theatre Groups* (Jefferson, N.C.: McFarland, 1980), p. 67.

22. Hélène Cixous, "Aller à la Mer," *Modern Drama* Vol. 27, No. 4 (December 1984), p. 547. A strain of utopianism tends to run through *l'écriture féminine*. See, for example, Cixous' manifesto "Laugh of the Medusa," in Elaine Marks and Isabelle de Courtivron, eds., *New French Feminisms* (New York: Schocken Books, 1981), pp. 245–64. See also Toril Moi's chapter, "Hélène Cixous: An Imaginary Utopia," in *Sexual/Textual Politics* (New York: Methuen, 1985), pp. 102–26.

23. Ann Jones, "Writing the Body: Towards an Understanding of *L'écriture féminine*," in *Feminist Criticism and Social Change*, p. 93

24. Case, p. 4.

25. Echols, p. 441.

26. Jones, p. 93.

27. Teresa de Lauretis, "Issues, Terms, Contexts," in *Feminist Studies/Critical Studies*, p. 14.

28. Kendall, "On a Stage of One's Own," *The Women's Review of Books* Vol. 4, No. 10–11 (July/August 1987), pp. 22–23. I, of course, am not the only one to delineate feminist ideologies in this way. The move to specify the work of "women in theatre," or even "feminist theatre," is now gaining wider currency.

29. Rubin, p. 158.

30. Rubin, p. 179. See also Adrienne Rich, "Compulsory Heterosexuality and Lesbian Existence," *Signs* Vol. 5, No. 4 (Summer 1980). Rich, however, proposes a lesbian continuum as a corrective to compulsory heterosexuality that desexualizes lesbian sexuality and is conservative from a materialist point of view.

31. Rubin, p. 183.

32. See also Juliet Mitchell, *Psychoanalysis and Feminism* (New York: Pantheon, 1974); Jean Baker Miller, *Psychoanalysis and Women* (New York: Penguin, 1973); and Nancy Chodorow, *The Reproduction of Mothering: Psychoanalysis and the Sociology of Gender* (Berkeley: University of California Press, 1978).

33. Rubin, p. 194.

34. See also Kaja Silverman, *The Subject of Semiotics* (New York: Oxford University Press, 1983); Jane Gallop, *The Daughter's Seduction: Feminism and Psychoanalysis* (Ithaca: Cornell University Press, 1982); and Jane Gallop, *Reading Lacan* (Ithaca: Cornell University Press, 1985).

35. Rubin, p. 192.

36. Rubin, p. 175.

37. Rubin, p. 174.

38. See Laura Mulvey, "Visual Pleasure and Narrative Cinema," *Screen* Vol. 16, No. 3 (Autumn 1975).

39. See Silverman, *The Subject of Semiotics;* de Lauretis, *Alice Doesn't;* E. Ann Kaplan, *Women & Film: Both Sides of the Camera* (New York: Methuen, 1983), particularly her chapter "Is the Gaze Male?" pp. 23–35; and Mary Ann Doane, *The Desire to Desire: The Woman's Film of the 1940s* (Bloomington: Indiana University Press, 1986).

40. See Belsey for a discussion of these processes as they operate within theatrical classical realism.

41. See de Lauretis, "Desire in Narrative," in *Alice Doesn't*.

42. See Doane's chapter, "The Desire to Desire," in *The Desire to Desire,* pp. 1–37.

43. Michelle Barrett, "Ideology and the Cultural Production of Gender," in *Feminist Criticism and Social Change,* p. 73.

44. See Lillian S. Robinson, *Sex, Class, and Culture* (Bloomington: Indiana University Press, 1978, revised ed., New York: Methuen, 1986), particularly her chapter "Dwelling in Decencies," pp. 3–21, for one of the first attempts to link feminism and Marxism in cultural criticism.

45. Sue-Ellen Case, "Comment," *Theatre Journal* Vol. 38, No. 4 (December 1986), p. i.

46. See my article, "Is the Postmodern Aesthetic Feminist?" in *Art & Cinema* Vol. 1, No. 3 (Fall 1987), for an explication of this issue, which is discussed in detail in chapter 3. See also Sue-Ellen Case and Jeanie Forte, "From Formalism to Feminism," *Theater* Vol. 16, No. 2 (Spring 1985), for a feminist critique of deconstructionist practice in performance.

47. Judith Newton and Deborah Rosenfelt, "Toward a Materialist-Feminist Criticism," in *Feminist Criticism and Social Change*, p. xix.

48. Roszika Parker and Griselda Pollock, *Old Mistresses: Women, Art and Ideology* (New York: Pantheon, 1981), p. 119.

49. Barrett, p. 80.

50. Terry Eagleton, *The Function of Criticism: From the Spectator to Post-Structuralism* (London: New Left Books, 1984), p. 107.

51. Barrett, p. 78.

52. Robinson, p. 18.

Chapter 2

1. The "horizon of expectations" is a term borrowed from reception theory. See Robert Holub *Reception Theory: A Critical Introduction* (New York: Methuen, 1984), particularly pp. 42–44.

2. See Robert von Hallberg, ed., *Canons* (Chicago: University of Chicago Press, 1984); Annette Kolodny, "Dancing through the Minefield: Some Observations on the Theory, Practice and Politics of a Feminist Literary Criticism," *Feminist Studies* Vol. 6, No. 1 (Spring 1980); and Paul Lauter, "Race and Gender in the Shaping of the American Literary Canon: A Case Study from the Twenties," in Judith Newton and Deborah Rosenfelt, eds., *Feminist Criticism and Social Change: Sex, Race and Class in Literature and Culture* (New York: Methuen, 1985) for current discussions of the politics of canon-formation.

3. See Kolodny for a thorough discussion of female significations in literature and their implications for gender-based interpretation.

4. Sue-Ellen Case, "Reviewing Hrotsvit," *Theatre Journal* Vol. 35, No. 4 (December 1983), p. 534.

5. Ibid.

6. Janet Staiger, "The Politics of Film Canons," *Cinema Journal* Vol. 24, No. 3 (Spring 1985), p. 2.

7. Kolodny, p. 19.

8. ART promotional piece, housed at the Lincoln Center Library for the Performing Arts, Billy Rose Theatre Collection.

9. Promotional piece for the Broadway production, housed at the Lincoln Center Library for the Performing Arts, Billy Rose Theatre Collection.

10. This was also the year Alice Walker won the Pulitzer for her novel *The Color Purple*, which made it seem as though feminists were finally carrying off mainstream prizes. But in retrospect, it is clear that Norman's play did not threaten the dominant culture, and that Walker's book struck some sort of nerve that three years later was translated into Steven Spielberg's racist, sexist, comic, and certainly not radical film version.

11. *Variety*, April 22, 1983, p. 2.

12. Elizabeth Wray, in Gayle Austin, ed., "The Woman Playwright Issue," *Performing Arts Journal 21* Vol. 7, No. 3, p. 92.

13. Kathleen Betsko and Rachel Koenig, eds., *Interviews with Contemporary Women Playwrights* (New York: Beech Tree Books, 1987), p. 324.

14. Marsha Norman, *'night, Mother*, Acting Edition (New York: Dramatists Play Service, Inc., 1983), p. 4. All other references will appear in the text.

15. See Mel Gussow, "Women Playwrights: New Voices in the Theater," *New York Times Sunday Magazine*, May 1, 1983, p. 22.

16. Beth Henley, *Crimes of the Heart* (New York: Penguin, 1982), p. 120.

17. Quoted in Susan Lieberman, "'night, Mother," *Theatre Crafts* Vol. 19, No. 5 (May 1985), pp. 22, 46. I do not mean to blame Landesman for this element of the critical reception to *'night, Mother*. A set designer does, and should, maintain some sort of creative autonomy. It is simply interesting to me that Landesman's reading of the text was so wholeheartedly embraced by critics.

18. Humm., *Variety*, April 6, 1983, p. 82.

19. Howard Kissel, *Women's Wear Daily*, April 1, 1983, p. 15; John Beaufort, *Christian Science Monitor*, April 22, 1983, p. 11.

20. Frank Rich, *New York Times*, July 28, 1983.

21. Ibid. When the production moved to the smaller off-Broadway house, another reviewer mentioned that it "allows for more of a sense of audience voyeurism than the wider Broadway stage" (Jack Gilhooley, *Stage*, June 1984, p. 29). *'Night, Mother* falls squarely in the tradition of fourth-wall realism.

22. Jack Gilhooley, *Stage*, June 1984, p. 29; Humm., *Variety;* David Richards, *Washington Post*, May 15, 1983; Douglas Watts, *New York Daily News*, April 1, 1983, p. 3.

23. Robert Asahina, *Hudson Review* Vol. 37, No. 1 (Spring 1984), p. 101.

24. Robert Brustein, *New Republic*, May 2, 1983.

25. Trudy Scott, *Women & Performance Journal 1* Vol. 1, No. 1 (1983), p. 78.

26. Ibid. As a former editor of *Women & Performance Journal*, I have information about the reviewing context that would not be available to the average reader. Trudy Scott is a white woman in her fifties who was married and has children and grandchildren. These facts are only relevant to the extent that not many professional theatre critics share Scott's social background, which made her perspective unique. The point, of course, is that not all readers and spectators share the prominent reviewers' white, middle-class, heterosexual male background either, but because their perspectives are widely accessible and bear the power of print, they are cloaked in the universal guise.

27. Richard Gilman, *The Nation*, May 7, 1983, p. 586.

28. John Simon, *New York Magazine*, April 11, 1983, pp. 56–57; Walter Kerr, *New York Times*, April 10, 1983; Kissel, *Women's Wear Daily;* Brendan Gill, *New Yorker*, April 11, 1983, p. 10; Sy Syna, *News World*, April 1, 1983; Gilman, *Nation;* Asahina, *Hudson Review*.

29. Elizabeth Stone, "Playwright Marsha Norman," *Ms. Magazine*, July 1983, p. 56.

30. See Lynda Hart, "Doing Time: Hunger for Power in Marsha Norman's Plays," *Southern Quarterly* (Spring 1987).

31. See Kate Davy, "Buying and Selling a Look," *Parachute* (Spring 1986), for a relevant discussion of performers' influence on women's body size and the influence of performers' body size on spectator response. By way of comparison, although Jessie was condemned for her weight, the epilepsy factor got a much more positive press response. Although in Norman's script Jessie blames her epilepsy for her failure to secure or hold a job, Bruce Chadwick reported in the *Daily News* (February 14, 1984, p. 49) that organized groups of doctors were going to see *'night, Mother* for insight on how to treat their epileptic patients.

32. See E. Ann Kaplan, "Theories of Melodrama: A Feminist Perspective," *Women & Performance Journal 1* Vol. 1, No. 1 (1983) for a discussion of melodrama and female film spectatorship that has implications for the gender-biases of genre categories.

33. Colette Brooks, in Gayle Austin, ed., "The Woman Playwright Issue," p. 89.

34. Christine Froula, "When Eve Reads Milton: Undoing the Canonical Economy," in *Canons*, p. 164.

35. Barbara Herrnstein Smith, "Contingencies of Value," in *Canons*, p. 15.

36. Smith writes that canon validation "commonly takes the form of privileging absolutely—that is 'standard'-izing—the particular contingencies that govern the preferences of the members of the group and discounting or . . . pathologizing all other contingencies" (p. 22).

37. Kolodny, p. 8.

38. Frank Rich, *New York Times*, March 30, 1984; Edwin Wilson, *Wall Street Journal*, April 4, 1984; Douglas Watts, *New York Daily News*, March 30, 1984.

39. John Beaufort, *Christian Science Monitor*, March 30, 1984.

40. Lauter, p. 18.

41. Gilman, *The Nation*.

42. Kissel, *Women's Wear Daily*.

43. Syna, *News World*.

44. Richards, *Washington Post*.

45. Staiger, p. 10.

46. Humm., *Variety*.

47. Watts, *New York Daily News*, April 1, 1983.

48. Alan Wallach, *Newsday*, April 1, 1983.

49. Brustein, *New Republic*.

50. Asahina, *Hudson Review*.

51. Jill Dolan, *"'night, Mother," Women & Performance Journal 1* Vol. 1, No. 1 (1983), p. 79.

52. Ibid.

53. Sue-Ellen Case, "The Personal Is Not the Political," *Art & Cinema* Vol. 1, No. 3 (Fall 1987), p. 4.

54. Stone, p. 56.

55. Stone, p. 57.

56. Stone, p. 58.

57. Ibid.

58. Erving Goffman, in *Gender Advertisements* (New York: Harper & Row, 1976), analyzes the content of advertising displays to study how women are imaged. He finds that while women are frequently displayed out of context, against blank backgrounds, men are always placed in contexts and are usually active within them.

59. Gussow, *New York Times Sunday Magazine*, p. 22.

60. Gussow, p. 31.

61. Gussow, p. 22.

62. Gussow, p. 30.

63. Gussow, p. 31. Norman and Byck are now divorced.

64. Gussow, p. 22.

65. Gussow, p. 40.

66. Ibid.

67. Brooks, in Austin, p. 88.

68. Ibid., p. 90.

69. Staiger, p. 16.

70. Roberta Sklar, in Gayle Austin, ed., "The Woman Playwright Issue," p. 101.

71. Froula, p. 171.

Chapter 3

1. See John Berger, *Ways of Seeing* (New York: Penguin, 1972).

2. Herbert Blau, "Ideology and Performance," *Theatre Journal* Vol. 35, No. 4 (December 1983), p. 447.

3. Ibid., p. 448.

4. See Juliet Mitchell, *Psychoanalysis and Feminism* (New York: Pantheon, 1974); Nancy Chodorow, *The Reproduction of Mothering: Psychoanalysis and the Sociology of Gender* (Berkeley: University of California Press, 1978); and Jessica Benjamin, "Master and Slave: The Fantasy of Erotic Domination," in Ann Snitow, Christine Stansell, and Sharon Thompson, eds., *Powers of Desire: The Politics of Sexuality* (New York: Monthly Review Press, 1983), for examples

of feminist work in revising traditional psychoanalysis from the perspective of the female subject.

5. See Jane Gallop, *The Daughter's Seduction: Feminism and Psychoanalysis* (Ithaca: Cornell University Press, 1982), for a feminist explication of Lacanian psychoanalytic and French feminist language theory that helped coin this phrase. See also Kaja Silverman, *The Subject of Semiotics* (New York: Oxford University Press, 1983); Julia Kristeva, *Desire in Language* (New York: Columbia University Press, 1980); Luce Irigaray, *Speculum of the Other Woman,* translated by Gillian C. Gill (Ithaca: Cornell University Press, 1985); and Luce Irigaray, *This Sex Which is Not One,* translated by Catherine Porter (Ithaca: Cornell University Press, 1985), for further work on Lacan and feminist psychoanalysis.

6. See Frederic Jameson, "Postmodernism and Consumer Society," in Hal Foster, ed., *The Anti-Aesthetic: Essays on Postmodern Culture* (Washington, D.C.: Bay Press, 1983), for a pertinent discussion of the distinctions between modernism and postmodernism.

7. See Sue-Ellen Case and Jeanie Forte, "From Formalism to Feminism," *Theater* Vol. 16, No. 2 (Spring 1985), and my "Is the Postmodern Aesthetic Feminist?" *Art & Cinema* (Spring 1987), for fuller discussions of postmodern performance and politics. David Savran, in *The Wooster Group, 1975–1985: Breaking the Rules* (Ann Arbor: UMI Research Press, 1986), both accedes to and argues this point when he apologizes for using the male pronoun to describe the hypothetical Wooster Group spectator. He implies that gender has been one of the questions essayed by the Group in its investigation of "the disposition of theatrical forces and the status of the spectator" (p. 7).

8. For histories and analyses of the experimental theatre movement in the 1960s, see Margaret Croyden, *Lunatics, Lovers and Poets: The Contemporary Experimental Theatre* (New York: McGraw-Hill, 1974), particularly her chapter on "The Environmentalists and Some Others," pp. 193–228; Arthur Sainer, *The Radical Theatre Notebook* (New York: Avon, 1975); Karen Malpede Taylor, *People's Theatre in Amerika* (New York: Drama Book Specialists, 1972); and Richard Schechner, *The End of Humanism* (New York: Performing Arts Journal Publications, 1982). Savran's *The Wooster Group* includes historical material on Elizabeth LeCompte's disagreements with Schechner's methods in the Performance Group (pp. 2–4) that are relevant in terms of the American avant-garde's evolution from experimental to postmodern work.

9. Richard Foreman, tape recording of question-and-answer session, April 1984.

10. Ibid.

11. Richard Foreman, "Ontological-Hysteric Theatre Manifesto III" (June 1975), in Kate Davy, ed., *Richard Foreman: Plays and Manifestos* (New York: New York University Press, 1976), p. 191.

12. E. Ann Kaplan's essay "Is the Gaze Male?" in her *Women & Film: Both Sides of the Camera* (New York: Methuen, 1983), pp. 23–35, helped to phrase discussions of spectatorship in terms of analyzing the "male gaze." The term has since become part of the discourse of feminist film and performance criticism.

13. See Kate Davy, *Richard Foreman and the Ontological-Hysteric Theatre* (Ann Arbor: UMI Research Press, 1981), particularly chapter 2, "Foreman as Playwright," pp. 19–35, for discussion of Foreman's stylistic connection to Stein.

14. Davy, p. 194.

15. Richard Foreman, "Ontological-Hysteric Manifesto I," (April 1972), in Kate Davy, ed., *Richard Foreman: Plays and Manifestos*, p. 74.

16. Ibid., p. 73.

17. Foreman, tape recording.

18. Postmodern dance choreographers, of course, might take issue with that statement, since many were determined to work with nondancers performing ordinary movements or tasks. Foreman, too, worked with nonactors, in what Michael Kirby has called "not-acting" or "non-matrixed" performance (see "On Acting and Not-Acting," *Drama Review* Vol. 16, No. 1 [March 1972]). My argument is that regardless of the performers' training level or the nature of their behavior, their bodies become part of the system of representation and carry ideological weight.

19. See Davy's chapter, "Foreman as Scenographer: The Design and Use of the Physical Theatre," in *Richard Foreman and the Ontological-Hysteric Theatre*, pp. 37–58. She quotes Foreman as saying, "I do tend to think in a very frontal kind of picture-frame way" (p. 47).

20. Foreman, "Ontological-Hysteric Manifesto I," p. 72.

21. See Edmund Husserl, *Ideas: A General Introduction to Pure Phenomenology*, translated by W. R. Boyce Gibson, (New York: MacMillan, 1931) and Edmund Husserl, *The Idea of Phenomenology*, translated by William P. Alston and George Nakhnikian (The Hague: M. Nijhoff, 1964).

22. Davy frequently uses this word to describe the effort required of the spectator to fully experience Foreman's work.

23. Richard Foreman, "Ontological-Hysteric Manifesto II," (July 1974), in Kate Davy, ed., *Richard Foreman: Plays and Manifestos*, p. 138.

24. Ibid., p. 148.

25. Jameson, p. 120.

26. Ibid.

27. Bertolt Brecht, in John Willett, ed., *Brecht on Theatre* (New York: Hill and Wang, 1964), pp. 180–81.

28. See in particular Laura Mulvey, "Visual Pleasure and Narrative Cinema," *Screen* Vol. 16, No. 3 (Autumn 1975); E. Ann Kaplan, *Women & Film: Both Sides of the Camera;* and Mary Ann Doane, *The Desire to Desire: The Woman's Film of the 1940s* (Bloomington: Indiana University Press, 1987) for theoretical work on these issues.

29. Mulvey, Kaplan, and Doane use this Lacanian analysis of the viewing process to begin their critiques of film spectatorship.

30. Mulvey, p. 6.

31. Ibid., p. 7.

32. See Teresa de Lauretis, *Alice Doesn't: Feminism, Semiotics, Cinema* (Bloomington: Indiana University Press, 1984), particularly her chapters "Desire in Narrative," pp. 103–57, and "Semiotics and Experience," pp. 158–86 for detailed analyses of the workings of desire in the formation of subjectivity. See also Jessica Benjamin, "A Desire of One's Own: Psychoanalytic Feminism and Intersubjective Space," in Teresa de Lauretis, ed., *Feminist Studies/Critical Studies* (Bloomington: Indiana University Press, 1986), pp. 78–101.

33. See Claire Johnston's "Women's Cinema as Counter-Cinema," *Notes on Women's Cinema* (London: Society for Education in Film and Television, 1973), pp. 24–31 for an argument with this approach to feminist cinematic practice. Johnston feels "women's cinema must embody the working through of desire: such an objective demands the use of the entertainment film" (p. 31).

34. See Elin Diamond, "Brechtian Theory/Feminist Theory: Toward a Gestic Feminist Criticism," *Drama Review* Vol. 32, No. 1 (1988)—which is also incorporated into my discussion in chapter 6 below—for a reading of Mulvey in light of Brechtian aesthetics that has useful implications for materialist feminist performance practice.

35. Mulvey, p. 16.

36. Davy, *Richard Foreman and the Ontological-Hysteric Theatre*, p. 55.

37. Ibid., p. 214. See also the interview with Foreman and Manheim, as well as the text of a recent Foreman piece, in *Drama Review* (Winter 1987), which was unavailable at this writing.

38. Foreman, tape recording.

39. Ibid.

40. Photos and slides examined in Kate Davy's collection of materials from her books, and in the Billy Rose Theatre Collection at the Performing Arts Library at Lincoln Center in New York, New York. Admittedly, this work is now ten or more years old. My intent is to look at it almost as an historical example of the male gaze operating in avant-garde performance. Whether Foreman has significantly changed his attitude toward gender is debatable, although colleagues have argued that his more recent work in New York does confront gender issues in a more progressive way. I do not, in any case, mean to imply malicious intent on Foreman's part. But because he has been articulate about his work in published writings, and because so much of his work is preserved on video or in photographs, he is a productive example for my case study here.

41. Berger, p. 87.

42. See Gayle Rubin, "The Traffic in Women: Notes on the 'Political Economy' of Sex," in Rayna Reiter, ed. *Toward an Anthropology of Women* (New York: Monthly Review Press, 1978), for an explication of Lacanian theory and for a feminist revision of the structure of kinship systems proposed by Levi-Strauss. Rubin suggests that women are used as commodities—that is, traded between men—in a male economy in which they have no other value other than that gained by their exchange. See also Luce Irigaray, "When the Goods Get Together," in Isabelle de Courtivron and Elaine Marks, eds., *New French Feminisms* (New York: Schocken Books, 1981), for speculation on what might happen if women refused to participate in such an exchange.

43. Kate Davy, "Total Theatre: The Work of Richard Foreman," lectures, New York University, Spring 1984.

44. Foreman, tape recording.

45. Berger, p. 47.

46. See chapter 4 for a full discussion of women in pornography in terms of the discourse of representation, narrative, and desire, in which the gaze is adopted as a model of reception and the shared meanings between spectators/readers and performers/images.

47. Kate Davy, "Kate Manheim as Foreman's Rhoda," *Drama Review* Vol. 20, No. 3 (September 1976), p. 45.

48. Ibid., p. 47.

49. Lizzie Borden's film, *Working Girls* (1987), offers another example of women's bodies used as projection screens for male desire in a representational context. The prostitutes in Borden's film efface themselves for their clients, and construct personalities chosen by each individual man. (In a similar way, Manheim effaces herself to the desires of the spectators she imagines watching her.) As in Genet's *The Balcony*, the whorehouse becomes a theatre, or a representational space. In Borden's film, many of one of the women's clients want to meet her on the outside. But as Molly says in a scene with a particularly vicious man, their interaction would not work on the outside. Molly is a lesbian in "real life"—only in the liminal space of her working environment will she authorize the wielding of his male power so personally. When this man hurts her by calling her a whore, Molly is prompted to remove herself from the representational space that objectifies her; she quits her job as a prostitute. Unfortunately, Borden's film does not deal with the issue of representation in her use of the camera or the nude female body. Apparently, *Working Girls* became popular, particularly in Manhattan, as a highbrow kind of pornography.

50. Michelle Barrett, "Ideology and the Cultural Production of Gender," in Judith Newton and Deborah Rosenfelt, eds., *Feminist Criticism and Social Change: Sex, Class, and Race in Literature and Culture* (New York: Methuen, 1985), p. 70.

51. There are other times when the nude male represents a kind of homosocial exchange masked by the image of female sexuality. A spread in the June 1985 issue of *Hustler*, for example, involves two sailors having various kinds of sex with a female officer. In some instances, if the woman was dropped from the image, the men would essentially appear to be having sex with each other. The male homosexual potential in representation is, however, outside the realm of this discussion.

52. See, for example, Michael Kirby's "Richard Foreman's Ontological-Hysteric Theatre," *Drama Review* Vol. 17, No. 2 (June 1973), pp. 5–32, for a descriptive, documentary approach to the work.

53. Jameson, p. 114.

54. Davy, *Richard Foreman and the Ontological-Hysteric Theatre*, p. 183.

55. Richard Foreman, quoted in Robb Baker, "The Theater of Richard Foreman: Hysterical Cool," *Soho Weekly News*, January 9, 1975, as quoted in Kate Davy, *Richard Foreman and the Ontological-Hysteric Theatre*, p. 183.

56. Davy, *Richard Foreman and the Ontological-Hysteric Theatre*, pp. 22–23.

57. Roland Barthes, *Mythologies* (New York: Hill and Wang, 1972), pp. 109–10.

Chapter 4

1. See the "Sex Issue," *Heresies #12* Vol. 3, No. 4 (1981), for short articles expounding both views; Pat Califia, "Feminism and Sadomasochism," *Heresies #12*, pp. 30–35, for the manifesto of the most vocal proponent of lesbian s/m sexuality; *Coming to Power*, Samois Collective, eds. (revised ed., Boston: Alyson Publications, 1982), for articles and personal testimony on lesbian sadomasochistic practice; Andrea Dworkin, *Pornography: Men Possessing Women* (New York: Perigree Books, 1979) for the foremost antipornography feminist tract; and Susanne

Kappeler, *The Pornography of Representation* (Minneapolis: University of Minnesota Press, 1986) for an attempt to summarize both positions, as well as the anti censorship stance, with regard to issues of representation.

2. Alice Echols, "The Taming of the Id," in Carol S. Vance, ed., *Pleasure and Danger* (Boston: Routledge & Kegan Paul, 1984), p. 276.

3. Many feminist critics have taken issue with the reification of sexual difference prompted by this shift to a focus on gender. See in particular Teresea de Lauretis, "Issues, Terms, and Context," in de Lauretis, ed. *Feminist Studies/Critical Studies* (Bloomington: Indiana University Press, 1986); Linda Gordon, "What's New in Women's History," in *Feminist Studies/ Critical Studies;* and Sue-Ellen Case, "The Personal is Not the Political," in *Art & Cinema* Vol. 1, No. 3 (Fall 1987) for a discussion of the issue in terms of feminist theatre.

4. Sue-Ellen Case, "Towards a Butch/Femme Aesthetic," keynote address, Women and Theatre Program/ATHE, Chicago, August 2, 1987; forthcoming in Lynda Hart, ed., *Making a Spectacle: Feminist Essays on Contemporary Women's Theatre* (Ann Arbor: University of Michigan Press, 1988).

5. These two efforts are described in Janice Raymond, "A Genealogy of Female Friendship," *Trivia* Vol. 1, No. 1 (Fall 1982), and in Adrienne Rich, "Compulsory Heterosexuality and Lesbian Existence," *Signs* Vol. 5, No. 4 (Summer 1980), respectively.

6. "Excerpts from the Minneapolis Ordinance," in Varda Burstyn, ed. *Women Against Censorship* (Vancouver: Douglas & McIntyre, 1985), p. 206.

7. Quoted in Mary Kay Blakely, "Is One Woman's Sexuality Another Woman's Pornography?" *Ms. Magazine* April 1985, p. 46.

8. As I discussed in chapter 1, cultural feminism is sometimes called "radical feminism." I prefer the term "cultural feminism" because it articulates the desire to separate women's culture—both its art and its everyday experience—from the dominant culture. See Alice Echols, "The New Feminism of Yin and Yang" for a discussion and critique of cultural feminism in Ann Snitow, Christine Stansell, and Sharon Thompson, eds., *Powers of Desire* (New York: Monthly Review Press, 1983), pp. 439–59; Sue-Ellen Case, "The Personal is Not Political," for her definition and critique of radical feminism; and Alison Jaggar, *Feminist Politics and Human Nature* (Totowa, N.J.: Rowman and Allanheld, 1983), for an extensive definition of radical feminism's epistemology.

9. See E. Ann Kaplan, "Is the Gaze Male?" in *Women & Film: Both Sides of the Camera* (New York: Methuen, 1983). Kaplan argues that the dominance/submission patterns that inform sexual fantasies—catalogued by Nancy Friday—are the same impulses that operate in the cinematic apparatus to construct spectators according to gender roles and to provide spectatorial pleasure.

10. See Linda Gordon, "What's New in Women's History"; Gordon argues that the gender-polarized dominance/submission pattern can be replaced with a model of "domination/resistance" that implies at least the exercise of power against dominance.

11. Moira Roth, ed., *The Amazing Decade: Women and Performance Art in America 1970–1980* (Los Angeles: Astro Artz, 1983), p. 34.

12. Ibid.

13. "Politicizing Art: Hannah Wilke," *New Common Good* May 1985, p. 1.

14. Wilke interview, quoted from the catalog of the exhibition *American Women Artists* at the São Paulo Museum, July 1980, p. 10.

15. See Roth, *The Amazing Decade*, and Lucy Lippard, *From the Center: Feminist Essays on Women's Art* (New York: E. P. Dutton, 1976), particularly her chapter on European and American women's body art, pp. 121–38.

16. Lippard remarks, "It is difficult to find any positive images whatsoever of women in male body art," and mentions that Chris Burden, one of the first so-called performance artists, once threw burning matches on his wife's nude body in performance (p. 134). Lippard documents male masochism in performance as practiced by Burden, Vito Acconi, and Dennis Oppenheim, among others (p. 135).

17. For a full description of this piece, see Jeanie Forte, "Rachel Rosenthal: Feminism and Performance Art," *Women & Performance Journal 4* Vol. 2, No. 2 (1985), pp. 30–31.

18. For theoretical work on this position, see Monique Wittig's writings in *Feminist Issues*, particularly "The Category of Sex," Fall 1981.

19. See Rich, "Compulsory Heterosexuality and Lesbian Existence," and also Gayle Rubin, "The Traffic in Women: Notes on the 'Political Economy' of Sex," in Rayna Reiter, ed., *Towards an Anthropology of Women* (New York: Monthly Review Press, 1978).

20. See Case, "Towards a Butch/Femme Aesthetic," for a discussion of what she calls a "strategy of appearances" in which lesbian sexuality subverts traditional gender codes; see also my "Lesbian as Refusor, Lesbian as Creator: An Anti-Aesthetic," paper delivered at American Theatre Association convention, San Francisco, August 1984, for an analysis of the expression of lesbian sexuality through genderized costuming. The implications of lesbian sexuality as representation are discussed fully in chapter 6 below.

21. Gayle Rubin, "Thinking Sex: Notes for a Radical Theory of the Politics of Sexuality," in *Pleasure and Danger*, p. 276.

22. Rubin, "Thinking Sex," p. 308.

23. *Eidos* Vol. 1, No. 4 (Spring 1985).

24. See chapter 3 for an extended discussion of the ideological and semiotic differences between male and female nudity in the representational space.

25. Kaplan, "Is the Gaze Male?" p. 29.

26. C. Carr, "Unspeakable Practices, Unnatural Acts: The Taboo Art of Karen Finley," *Village Voice*, June 24, 1986.

27. See Bob Greene, "Bar Wars," *Esquire* (November 1986), pp. 61–62; describing a performance in a bar in which male spectators are invited, en masse, to shoot water guns at a passive female "performer." Greene quotes some of the men as fantasizing that the performer is responding only to them. See also my "Desire Cloaked in a Trenchcoat," forthcoming in *Drama Review* (1988) for a discussion of the operation of the male gaze in live sex show performances such as this one.

28. Carr, "Unspeakable Practices," p. 17.

29. Carr, "Unspeakable Practices," p. 86. See also Richard Schechner's interview with Karen Finley in *Drama Review* Spring 1988, which was not yet available at the time of this writing.

30. Ibid.

31. In a performance in Cologne in 1981, Finley and her husband Brian Routh (one of the Kipper Kids) performed as Adolf Hitler and Eva Braun. "Kipper goosestepped and saluted, naked from the waist down. Finley wore a corset and garter belt, and because she had diarrhea, periodically took a dump on one side of the stage. On one of the nights, Kipper sang a Johnny Mathis hit, then went to the bowl where Finley had been relieving herself and lapped up the shit" (Carr, p. 19). As Carr notes, this is clearly not mainstream sexuality.

32. See Teresa de Lauretis, "Desire and Narrative," in *Alice Doesn't: Feminism, Semiotics, Cinema* (Bloomington: Indiana University Press, 1984), pp. 103–57, for work on the relationship of desire to narrative structure. See also Kaplan, "Is the Gaze Male?" and Laura Mulvey, "Visual Pleasure and Narrative Cinema," *Screen* Vol. 16, No. 3 (Autumn, 1975), for one of the first psychoanalytical analyses of gender positions in representation.

33. The Spring 1985 issue of *Drama Review* Vol. 29, No. 1, is devoted to East Village performance. Each of the clubs prominent in the neighborhood in Fall 1984, just before most of them were closed, is profiled in detail. A multi-authored article called "30 November 1984" documents different performances happening on the same evening at clubs within walking distance of each other. WOW performers are profiled in several of the performances described. See also Alisa Solomon's article on the history of the WOW Cafe in the same issue.

34. Weaver and Troyano made these remarks on a panel about East Village performance held during the Women's Program (of the former American Theatre Association) preconvention on August 16, 1986, at New York University. Writer/performer Holly Hughes, who is also a core WOW member, joked that East Village art happened because the places people live in are so small they are forced to create social and artistic outlets simply to have somewhere else to go.

35. See Monique Wittig, "The Straight Mind," *Feminist Issues* (Summer 1980). Wittig argues, "'Woman' has meaning only in heterosexual systems of thought and heterosexual economic systems. Lesbians are not women" (p. 110).

36. See Sue-Ellen Case, "Gender as Play," *Women & Performance Journal 2* Vol. 1, No. 2 (Winter 1984), pp. 21–24. Case writes, "The drag role makes all gender roles appear fictitious."

37. Kate Davy, *"The Heart of the Scorpion* at the WOW Cafe," *Drama Review* Vol. 29, No. 1 (Spring 1985), p. 56.

38. Helen Krich Chinoy and Linda Walsh Jenkins, eds., *Women in American Theatre* (New York: Crown, 1981; revised ed., New York: Theatre Communications Group, 1987), pp. 303–5.

39. Shaw, who is quite tall, tends to wear shiny, 1950s-style suits, narrow ties, and black shoes with white socks. Weaver, whose hair is dyed platinum blonde à la Tammy Whynot, wears makeup, jewelry, and generally more feminine clothes. Seeing the couple and other WOW performers on the street, it is never quite clear whether they are heading to the theatre for a performance or simply going out to eat.

40. *Disgusting Songs and Pukey Images* at Theatre for the New City in 1985 was a revival piece, and marked the first time Spiderwoman and Split Britches had worked together since the split. History has it that Shaw and Weaver left Spiderwoman because of sexuality-based conflicts. It is important then, that the performance of lesbian desire was so prominent in the production the women chose to revive.

41. See the *Village Voice Literary Supplement* (December 1982), p. 16, for a discussion of the Barnard conference; Ann Snitow, Christine Stansell, and Sharon Thompson, eds., *Powers of Desire,* and the "Sex Issue," *Heresies #12* also contain materials from the Barnard conference.

42. Echols, "The Taming of the Id," p. 58.

43. Susie Bright, ed., *On Our Backs* Vol. 1, No. 4 (Spring 1985). All other references will appear in the text. *On Our Backs'* name satirizes *Off Our Backs,* one of the oldest cultural feminist newspapers in the country. Based in Washington, D.C., the monthly paper covers national and international conferences, news, and events. It reported on the Barnard conference in depth, and was the first feminist newspaper to offer a forum for discussing the pornography debate.

44. *Hustler,* June 1985, p. 28.

45. Seph Weene, "Venus," *Heresies #12,* p. 36.

46. See Priscilla Alexander and Frederique Delacoste, eds. *Sex Work: Writings by Women in the Sex Industry* (Pittsburgh: Cleis Press, 1987), for first-hand, personal accounts of women who work as strippers, a number of whom are lesbians. See also Laurie Bell, ed., *Good Girls, Bad Girls: Feminists and Sex Trade Workers Face to Face* (Seattle: Seal Press, 1987), a transcription of the conference "Challenging Our Images: The Politics of Pornography and Prostitution," which was held in Toronto in November 1985. This collection also includes first-hand accounts by sex workers.

47. Debi Sundahl, "Stripper," in *Sex Work,* pp. 175–80.

48. Robin Ruth Linden, Darlene R. Pagano, Diana E. H. Russell, Susan Leigh Star, eds., *Against Sadomasochism* (E. Palo Alto: Frog in the Well, 1982), p. 7.

49. Linden, *Against Sadomasochism,* p. 2.

Chapter 5

1. See Moira Roth, ed., *The Amazing Decade: Women and Performance Art in America, 1970–1980* (Los Angeles: Astro Artz, 1983), p. 130, for a brief description of Schneeman's performance, and Lucy Lippard, *From the Center: Feminist Essays on Women's Art* (New York: E. P. Dutton, 1976), p. 126. See also Jeanie Forte, "Female Body as Text in Women's Performance Art," in Helen Krich Chinoy and Linda Walsh Jenkins, eds., *Women in American Theatre* (New York: Crown, 1981; revised ed., New York: Theatre Communications Group, 1987), pp. 378–80.

2. Lippard, p. 126.

3. Catherine Belsey, "Constructing the Subject: Deconstructing the Text," in Judith Newton and Deborah Rosenfelt, eds., *Feminist Criticism and Social Change: Sex, Class and Race in Literature and Culture* (New York: Methuen, 1985), p. 53.

4. Ibid.

5. Rosemary Curb, "Re/cognition, Re/presentation, Re/creation in Woman-Conscious Drama: The Seer, The Seen, The Scene, The Obscene," *Theatre Journal* Vol. 37, No. 3 (October 1985), p. 304.

6. This position was advanced by several academic theatre women in response to a panel on "Feminism and Realism" which I organized for the Women and Theatre Program Conference held at Mundelein College in Chicago, August 2–4, 1987.

7. See Margaret Croyden, *Lunatics, Lovers and Poets: The Contemporary Experimental Theatre* (New York: McGraw-Hill, 1974); Arthur Sainer, *The Radical Theatre Notebook* (New York: Avon, 1975); Karen Malpede Taylor, *People's Theatre in Amerika* (New York: Drama Book

Specialists, 1972); and Richard Schechner, *The End of Humanism* (New York: Performing Arts Journal Publications, 1982).

8. For histories of cultural feminist theatres in America, see Chinoy and Jenkins, *Women in American Theatre;* Helene Keyssar, *Feminist Theatre* (New York: Grove Press, 1985); Karen Malpede, ed., *Women and Theatre: Compassion and Hope* (New York: Drama Book Publishers, 1983); Elizabeth J. Natalle, *Feminist Theatre: A Study in Persuasion* (Metuchen, N.J.: Scarecrow Press, 1985); Janet Brown, *Feminist Drama: Definitions and Critical Analysis* (Metuchen, N.J.: Scarecrow Press, 1980); and Dinah Leavitt, *Feminist Theatre Groups* (Jefferson, N.C.: McFarland, 1980).

9. See Alice Echols, "The New Feminism of Yin and Yang," in Ann Snitow, Christine Stansell, and Sharon Thompson, eds., *Powers of Desire: The Politics of Sexuality* (New York: Monthly Review Press, 1983), for an incisive critique of the cultural feminist ideology that informs this term.

10. See for example, Barbara Smith, ed., *Home Girls* (New York: Kitchen Table Press, 1983); Cherrie Moraga and Gloria Anzaldua, eds., *This Bridge Called My Back: Writings by Radical Women of Color* (New York: Kitchen Table Press, 1983); and Evelyn Torton Beck, ed., *Nice Jewish Girls* (New York: Crossing Press, 1982). These anthologies are collections of personal testimonies that follow the consciousness-raising model to encourage the awareness of racial and ethnic differences among women.

11. Judith Newton and Deborah Rosenfelt, "Toward a Materialist-Feminist Criticism," in their *Feminist Criticism and Social Change*, p. xxvi.

12. Echols, p. 444.

13. For work that distinguishes the more ambiguous term "French feminism," see Ann Jones, "Writing the Body: Toward an Understanding of *L'écriture féminine*," in *Feminist Criticism and Social Change;* Ann Jones, "Inscribing Femininity: French Theories of the Feminine," in Gayle Greene and Coppelia Kahn, eds., *Making a Difference: Feminist Literary Criticism* (New York: Methuen, 1985); and Toril Moi, *Sexual/Textual Politics* (New York: Methuen, 1985).

14. Hélène Cixous, "Aller à la Mer," *Modern Drama* Vol. 27, No. 4 (December 1984), p. 547.

15. Josette Feral, "Writing and Displacement: Women in Theatre," *Modern Drama* Vol. 27, No. 4 (December 1984), p. 554.

16. Linda Walsh Jenkins, "Locating the Language of Gender Experience," *Women & Performance Journal 3* Vol. 2, No. 1 (1984) pp. 6–7.

17. Jenkins, p. 8.

18. Annette Kolodny, "Dancing through the Minefield: Some Observations on the Theory, Practice, and Politics of a Feminist Literary Criticism," *Feminist Studies* Vol. 6, No. 1 (Spring 1980), p. 6.

19. Curb, p. 302.

20. Linda Gordon, "What's New in Women's History," in Teresea de Lauretis, ed., *Feminist Studies/Critical Studies* (Bloomington: Indiana University Press, 1986), p. 21.

21. Ibid.

22. See my masters thesis, "Toward a Critical Methodology of Lesbian Feminist Theatre," Performance Studies Department, New York University, 1983, for a cultural feminist analysis of WET's *Daughter's Cycle Trilogy* in the context of feminine writing theory. See also Roberta Sklar, "'Sisters,' or Never Trust Anyone Outside the Family," *Women & Performance Journal 1* Vol. 1, No. 1 (1983), for an interpretation of *Sister/Sister*, Part II of the *Cycle*. For more writings by WET, see also "Notes on the Women's Experimental Theatre," in *Women and Theatre*, pp. 235–44, and "The Women's Experimental Theatre," in *Women in American Theatre*, pp. 305–8.

23. Clare Coss, Sondra Segal, and Roberta Sklar, *Daughters, Part I, The Daughter's Cycle Trilogy*, unpublished manuscript (1977), p. 1; all other references will appear in the text. An abbreviated version of *The Daughter's Cycle Trilogy* appears in Coss, Segal, Sklar, "Separation and Survival: Mothers, Daughters, Sisters—The Women's Experimental Theatre," in Hester Eisenstein and Alice Jardine, eds., *The Future of Difference* (Boston: G. K. Hall, 1980), and an excerpt of *Daughters* was published in *Massachusetts Review* Vol. 24, No. 1 (Spring 1983).

24. Coss, Segal, Sklar, "Notes on the Women's Experimental Theatre," in *Women and Theatre*, p. 239.

25. Curb, p. 313.

26. Curb, p. 309.

27. Feral, p. 554.

28. Coss, Segal, and Sklar, "Separation and Survival," p. 194, quoted in Feral, p. 552.

29. Feral, p. 553.

30. Segal and Sklar, "The Women's Experimental Theatre," in *Women in American Theatre*, p. 307.

31. Ibid.

32. All of Phyllis Jane Rose's and the ATFM performers' remarks quoted or referred to here were made at the postperformance discussion of their presentation of *Raped* and *The Story of a Mother*, Monday, August 3, 1987, at the Women and Theatre Program conference, in Chicago. In Fall 1987, Rose resigned as artistic director of ATFM because of a dispute over artistic autonomy with the company's board of directors. Nayo-Barbara Watkins is now the managing director of the company, and artistic affairs are overseen by a triumvirate comprised of Jan Magrane—one of the theatre's founders—and Bernadette Hak Eun Cha and Rebecca Rice, two members of the acting ensemble. The company's new leadership reflects its mandate to develop a multicultural perspective. See Robert Collins, "A Feminist Theatre in Transition," *American Theatre* (February 1988), pp. 32–34.

33. Martha Boesing rarely appears at the Women and Theatre Program conferences, which have been held annually since the mid-1970s. But Rose frequently attends as ATFM's spokesperson, and continually refers to Boesing. Sue-Ellen Case called Boesing the "absent presence" at the Chicago 1987 conference. For historical information on At the Foot of the Mountain, see also Linda Walsh Jenkins, "At the Foot of the Mountain," in *Women in American Theatre*, pp. 302–3.

34. Promotional mailing, At the Foot of the Mountain, September 1987. See also "Other Voices," by Naomi Scheman, a sidebar to Collin's piece in *American Theatre*. Scheman is a board member of ATFM, and her short piece eloquently spells out the company's attempt to truly integrate race and class perspectives in their organization and their work. Scheman's and

Collin's reports clarify the difficulty of ATFM's slow, painful process of change. My intent here is certainly not to contradict their intentions, which are laudable and important, but to point out that the version of the work presented several months before Rose's departure and Watkins' arrival as managing director belied their intent from a critical perspective.

35. Curb, p. 305.

36. Sue-Ellen Case and Jeanie Forte, "From Formalism to Feminism," *Theater* Vol. 16, No. 2 (Spring 1985), p. 62.

37. Sue-Ellen Case, "Classic Drag: The Greek Creation of Female Parts," *Theatre Journal* Vol. 37, No. 3 (October 1985), p. 318.

38. Although this idea has been advanced in many contexts, I am quoting here from a remark made by Elin Diamond at the Women and Theatre Program conference "Feminism and Realism" panel in Chicago.

39. See my "Gender Impersonation Onstage: Destroying or Maintaining the Mirror of Gender Roles," *Women & Performance Journal 4* Vol. 2, No. 2 (1985), in which I argue, "It might be that sexual difference is too deeply embedded in the mimetic structure of theatrical representation. . . . [W]e might have to question the mirror as an apt analogy for theatre. Adjusting this analogy would mean adjusting a wealth of expectations. It would no longer be possible to attend theatre hoping for a truthful reflection of oneself. . . . If we stop considering the theatre as a mirror of reality, we can use it as a laboratory in which to construct new, non-genderized identities" (p. 10).

40. Curb, p. 316.

41. See Echols for an insightful critique of cultural feminism's antisexuality stance and the homophobia it implies.

42. Curb, p. 316.

43. Feral, p. 559.

Chapter 6

1. Teresa de Lauretis, *Alice Doesn't: Feminism, Semiotics, Cinema* (Bloomington: Indiana University Press, 1984), p. 13.

2. Julia Kristeva, "Woman Can Never Be Defined," in Isabelle de Courtivron and Elaine Marks, eds., *New French Feminisms* (New York: Schocken Books, 1981), pp. 137–38. See also Elin Diamond, "Refusing the Romanticism of Identity: Narrative Interventions in Churchill, Benmussa, Duras," *Theatre Journal* Vol. 38, No.3 (October 1985), p. 273, which also quotes Kristeva and unravels the implications of her statement for feminist theatre practice by Simone Benmussa, Caryl Churchill, and Marguerite Duras.

3. Teresa de Lauretis, "The Technology of Gender," in *Technologies of Gender: Essays on Theory, Film, and Fiction* (Bloomington: Indiana University Press, 1987), p. 20.

4. de Lauretis, "The Technology of Gender," p. 5.

5. Sue-Ellen Case, "Towards a Butch/Femme Aesthetic," keynote address, Women and Theatre Program conference, Chicago, August 2, 1987; forthcoming in Lynda Hart, ed., *Making a Spectacle: Feminist Essays on Contemporary Women's Theatre* (Ann Arbor: University of Michigan Press, 1988).

6. Sharon Willis, "Hélène Cixous' *Portrait de Dora:* The Unseen and the Un-scene," *Theatre Journal* Vol. 38, No. 3 (October 1985), p. 288.

7. See Simone Benmussa, *"Portrait of Dora:* Stagework and Dreamwork," in *Benmussa Directs: Playscript 91* (Dallas: Riverrun Press, 1979).

8. Willis, p. 289.

9. Willis, p. 290.

10. See Willis on interference effects, p. 289; for Freud's remark, see *Portrait of Dora* in *Benmussa Directs,* p. 53.

11. Hélène Cixous, "Aller à la Mer," *Modern Drama* Vol. 27, No. 4 (December 1984), p. 547.

12. de Lauretis, in "The Technology of Gender," explains that the "space-off" is "the space not visible in the frame but inferable from what the frame makes visible" (p. 26).

13. Willis, p. 292.

14. Catherine Belsey, "Constructing the Subject, Deconstructing the Text," in Judith Newton and Deborah Rosenfelt, eds., *Feminist Criticism and Social Change: Sex, Race, and Class in Literature and Culture* (New York: Methuen, 1985), p. 53.

15. Willis, p. 292.

16. Willis, p. 294.

17. Willis, p. 300.

18. Simone Benmussa, *The Singular Life of Albert Nobbs* in *Benmussa Directs,* p. 86.

19. Sue-Ellen Case, "Gender as Play: Simone Benmussa's *The Singular Life of Albert Nobbs,*" *Women & Performance Journal 2* Vol. 1, No. 2 (Winter 1984), p. 24.

20. Diamond, p. 283.

21. Terry Eagleton, *Marxism and Literary Criticism* (Berkeley: University of California Press, 1976), p. 64.

22. Bertolt Brecht in John Willett, ed., *Brecht on Theatre* (New York: Hill and Wang, 1964), p. 44.

23. Martin Esslin, *Brecht: The Man and His Work* (New York: Doubleday, 1960), p. 150.

24. Walter Benjamin, *Illuminations* (New York: Schocken Books, 1969), p. 150.

25. Brecht, in Willett, p. 92.

26. Diamond, p. 281.

27. Brecht, in Willett, p. 98.

28. See Janelle Reinelt, "Beyond Brecht: Britain's New Feminist Drama," *Theatre Journal* Vol. 38, No. 2 (May 1986).

29. Fornes is adamant about disassociating herself from feminism. In a taped interview conducted by Liz Hughes and Trudy Scott for "Pittsburgh Video Women Presents," June 19, 1987, Fornes bemoaned the fact that "no one wants to see what's there" in her plays; "They all want to apply it to their own theories." Nonetheless, despite Fornes' disclaimers, a feminist reading is clearly relevant.

30. All three Fornes plays are collected in *Maria Irene Fornes: Plays* (New York: Performing Arts Journal Publications, 1986).

31. There is some sense, both in lesbian plays and lesbian communities, that single women pose a threat to monogamous couples. As a result, a concerted effort is exerted to find them suitable mates. Perhaps because of the realist mode to which it subscribes, *Bluefish Cove*'s lesbian characters are coupled in "marriages."

32. Bonnie Marranca, *Theatrewritings* (New York: Performing Arts Journal Publications, 1984), p. 71.

33. Eagleton, p. 66.

34. Esslin, p. 134.

35. Brecht, in Willett, p. 197.

36. Gayle Rubin, "The Traffic in Women: Notes on the 'Political Economy' of Sex," in Rayna Reiter, ed., *Toward an Anthropology of Women* (New York: Monthly Review Press, 1978), p. 178.

37. Rubin, p. 180.

38. For a relevant discussion of the WOW Cafe's parody of genre conventions, see also my "Feminists, Lesbians, and Other Women in Theatre: Thoughts on the Politics of Performance," forthcoming in *Themes in Drama* Vol. 11 (1989).

39. Benjamin, p. 149.

40. Eagleton, p. 68.

41. Brecht, in Willett, p. 42.

42. Brecht, in Willett, p. 92.

43. Laura Mulvey, "Visual Pleasure and Narrative Cinema," *Screen* Vol. 16, No. 3 (Autumn 1975), p. 11.

44. Elin Diamond, "Brechtian Theory/Feminist Theory: Toward a Gestic Feminist Criticism," *Drama Review* Vol. 32, No. 1 (1988). I quote here from the unpublished manuscript, p. 14. An earlier version of this article was read at the American Theatre in Higher Education Conference in Chicago, August 1987, on a "New Directions in Feminist Research" panel.

45. Diamond, "Gestic Criticism," p. 16.

46. See also my "Desire Cloaked in a Trenchcoat," forthcoming in *Drama Review* (1988), for a further discussion of this moment in *Upwardly Mobile Home* in terms of female spectatorship and the exchange of meanings.

47. Brecht, in Willett, p. 92.

48. Brecht, in Willett, p. 137.

49. Brecht, in Willett, p. 191.

50. Diamond, "Gestic Criticism," p. 8.

51. Diamond, "Gestic Criticism," p. 14.

52. de Lauretis, "The Technology of Gender," p. 17.

53. de Lauretis, "The Technology of Gender," p. 25.

54. Ibid.

55. Dick Hebdige, *Subculture: The Meaning of Style* (New York: Methuen, 1979), pp. 90–91.

56. Case, "Towards a Butch/Femme Aesthetic."

57. Joan Nestle, "Butch/Femme Relationships in the 1950s" in the "Sex Issue" of *Heresies #12* Vol. 3, No. 4 (1981), p. 24.

58. Ibid.

Bibliography

Books and Articles

Alexander, Priscilla, and Frederique Delacoste, eds. *Sex Work: Writing by Women in the Sex Industry*. Pittsburgh: Cleis Press, 1987.

Austin, Gayle, ed. "The Woman Playwright Issue." *Performing Arts Journal 21*, Vol. 7, No. 3.

Barrett, Michelle. "Ideology and the Cultural Production of Gender." In *Feminist Criticism and Social Change: Sex, Class, and Race in Literature and Culture*, Judith Newton and Deborah Rosenfelt, eds. New York: Methuen, 1985.

Barthes, Roland. *Mythologies*. New York: Hill and Wang, 1972.

Beck, Evelyn Torton, ed. *Nice Jewish Girls*. New York: Crossing Press, 1982.

Bell, Laurie, ed. *Good Girls, Bad Girls: Feminists and Sex Trade Workers Face to Face*. Seattle: Seal Press, 1987.

Belsey, Catherine. "Constructing the Subject: Deconstructing the Text." In *Feminist Criticism and Social Change: Sex, Class, and Race in Literature and Culture*, Judith Newton and Deborah Rosenfelt, eds. New York: Methuen, 1985.

Benjamin, Jessica. "Master and Slave: The Fantasy of Erotic Domination." In *Powers of Desire: The Politics of Sexuality*, Ann Snitow, Christine Stansell, and Sharon Thompson, eds. New York: Monthly Review Press, 1983.

————. "A Desire of One's Own: Psychoanalytic Feminism and Intersubjective Space." In *Feminist Studies/Critical Studies*, Teresa de Lauretis, ed. Bloomington: Indiana University Press, 1986.

Benjamin, Walter. *Illuminations*. New York: Schocken Books, 1969.

Benmussa, Simone. *Benmussa Directs: Playscript 91*. Dallas: Riverrun Press, 1979.

Berger, John. *Ways of Seeing*. New York: Penguin, 1972.

Betsko, Kathleen, and Rachel Koenig, eds. *Interviews with Contemporary Women Playwrights*. New York: Beech Tree Books, 1987.

Blakely, Mary Kay. "Is One Woman's Sexuality Another Woman's Pornography?" *Ms. Magazine*, April 1985.

Blau, Herbert. "Ideology and Performance." *Theatre Journal* Vol. 35, No. 4 (December 1983).

Brecht, Bertholt. *Brecht on Theatre*. Edited by John Willett. New York: Hill and Wang, 1964.

Bright, Susie, ed. *On Our Backs* Vol. 1, No. 4 (Spring 1985).

Brown, Janet. *Feminist Drama: Definitions and Critical Analysis*. Metuchen, N.J.: Scarecrow Press, 1980.

Burstyn, Varda, ed. *Women Against Censorship*. Vancouver: Douglas & McIntyre, 1985.

Califia, Pat. "Feminism and Sadomasochism." "Sex Issue" of *Heresies #12* Vol. 3, No. 4 (1981).

Carr, C. "Unspeakable Practices, Unnatural Acts: The Taboo Art of Karen Finley." *Village Voice*, June 24, 1986.

Case, Sue-Ellen. "Reviewing Hrotsvit." *Theatre Journal* Vol. 35, No. 4 (December 1983).

——— . "Classic Drag: The Greek Creation of Female Parts." *Theatre Journal* Vol. 37, No. 3 (October 1985).

——— . "Gender as Play: Simone Benmussa's *The Singular Life of Albert Nobbs.*" *Women & Performance Journal 2* Vol. 1, No. 2 (Winter 1984).

——— . "Comment." *Theatre Journal* Vol. 38, No. 4 (December 1986).

——— . "The Personal is Not the Political." *Art & Cinema* Vol. 1, No. 3 (Fall 1987).

——— . "Toward a Butch/Femme Aesthetic." In *Making a Spectacle: Feminist Essays on Contemporary Women's Theatre.* Lynda Hart, ed. Ann Arbor: University of Michigan Press, 1988.

Case, Sue-Ellen, and Jeanie Forte. "From Formalism to Feminism." *Theater* Vol. 16, No. 2 (Spring 1985).

Chinoy, Helen Krich, and Linda Walsh Jenkins, eds. *Women in American Theatre.* New York: Crown, 1981; revised ed., New York: Theatre Communications Group, 1987.

Chodorow, Nancy. *The Reproduction of Mothering: Psychoanalysis and the Sociology of Gender.* Berkeley: University of California Press, 1978.

Cixous, Hélène. "Laugh of the Medusa." In *New French Feminisms,* Elaine Marks and Isabelle de Courtivron, eds. New York: Schocken Books, 1981.

——— . "Aller à la Mer." *Modern Drama* Vol. 27, No. 4 (December 1984).

Collins, Robert. "A Feminist Theatre in Transition." *American Theatre,* February 1988.

Coss, Clare, Sondra Segal, and Roberta Sklar. "Separation and Survival: Mothers, Daughters, Sisters—The Women's Experimental Theatre." In *The Future of Difference,* Hester Eisenstein and Alice Jardine, eds. Boston: G.K. Hall, 1980.

——— . *The Daughter's Cycle Trilogy.* Unpublished manuscript, 1977; excerpted in *The Massachusetts Review* Vol. 24, No. 1 (Spring 1983).

——— . "Notes on the Women's Experimental Theatre." In *Women and Theatre: Compassion and Hope,* Karen Malpede, ed. New York: Drama Book Publishers, 1983.

Croyden, Margaret. *Lunatics, Lovers, and Poets: The Contemporary Experimental Theatre.* New York: McGraw-Hill, 1974.

Curb, Rosemary. "Re/cognition, Re/presentation, Re/creation in Woman-Conscious Drama: The Seer, the Seen, the Scene, the Obscene." *Theatre Journal* Vol. 37, No. 3 (October 1985).

Davy, Kate . "Kate Manheim as Foreman's Rhoda." *Drama Review* Vol. 20, No. 3 (September 1976).

——— . *Richard Foreman and the Ontological-Hysteric Theatre.* Ann Arbor: UMI Research Press, 1981.

——— . "*The Heart of the Scorpion* at the WOW Cafe." *Drama Review* Vol. 29, No. 1 (Spring 1985).

——— . "Buying and Selling a Look." *Parachute* (Spring 1986).

de Courtivron, Isabelle, and Elaine Marks, eds. *New French Feminisms.* New York: Schocken Books, 1981.

de Lauretis, Theresa. *Alice Doesn't: Feminism, Semiotics, Cinema.* Bloomington: Indiana University Press, 1984.

——— . "Issues, Terms, Contexts." *Feminist Studies/Critical Studies,* Teresa de Lauretis, ed. Bloomington: Indiana University Press, 1986.

——— . *Technologies of Gender: Essays on Theory, Film, and Fiction.* Bloomington: Indiana University Press, 1987.

Diamond, Elin. "Refusing the Romanticism of Identity: Narrative Interventions in Churchill, Benmussa, Duras." *Theatre Journal* Vol. 38, No. 3 (October 1985).

——— . "Brechtian Theory/Feminist Theory: Toward a Gestic Feminist Criticism." *Drama Review* Vol. 32, No. 1 (1988).

Doane, Mary Ann. *The Desire to Desire: The Woman's Film of the 1940s.* Bloomington: Indiana University Press, 1986.

Dolan, Jill. "Toward a Critical Methodology of Lesbian Feminist Theatre." Unpublished Masters thesis, Performance Studies Department, New York University, 1983.

———. "'night, Mother." *Women & Performance Journal 1* Vol. 1, No. 1 (1983).

———. "Women's Theatre Program of the ATA: Creating a Feminist Forum." *Women & Performance Journal 3* Vol. 1, No. 2 (1984).

———. "Lesbian as Refuser, Lesbian as Creator: An Anti-Aesthetic." Paper presented at American Theatre Association convention, San Francisco, August 1984.

———. "Gender Impersonation Onstage: Destroying or Maintaining the Mirror of Gender Roles." *Women & Performance Journal 4* Vol. 2, No. 2 (1985).

———. "The Politics of Feminist Performance." *Theatre Times* Vol. 5, No. 6 (July/August 1986).

———. "Is the Postmodern Aesthetic Feminist?" *Art & Cinema* Vol. 1, No. 3 (Fall 1987).

———. "Desire Cloaked in a Trenchcoat." *Drama Review,* Fall 1988.

———. "Feminists, Lesbians, and Other Women in Theatre: Thoughts on the Politics of Performance." *Themes in Drama* Vol. 11 (1989).

Dworkin, Andrea. *Pornography: Men Possessing Women.* New York: Perigree Books, 1979.

Eagleton, Terry. *Marxism and Literary Criticism.* Berkeley: University of California Press, 1976.

———. *The Function of Criticism: From the Spectator to Post-Structuralism.* London: New Left Books, 1984.

Echols, Alice. "The New Feminism of Yin and Yang." In *Powers of Desire: The Politics of Sexuality,* Ann Snitow, Christine Stansell, and Sharon Thompson, eds. New York: Monthly Review Press, 1983.

———. "The Taming of the Id." In *Pleasure and Danger: Exploring Female Sexuality,* Carol S. Vance, ed. Boston: Routledge and Kegan Paul, 1984.

Eisenstein, Zillah. *The Radical Future of Liberal Feminism.* New York: Longman, 1981.

Esslin, Martin. *Brecht: The Man and His Work.* New York: Doubleday, 1960.

Feral, Josette. "Writing and Displacement: Women in Theatre." *Modern Drama* Vol. 27, No. 4 (December 1984).

Fetterley, Judith. *The Resisting Reader: A Feminist Approach to American Fiction.* Bloomington: Indiana University Press, 1978.

Finley, Karen. Interview by Richard Schechner. *Drama Review,* Spring 1988.

Foreman, Richard. *Plays and Manifestos.* Kate Davy, ed. New York: New York University Press, 1972.

Fornes, Maria Irene. *Maria Irene Fornes: Plays.* New York: Performing Arts Journal Publications, 1986.

Forte, Jeanie. "Female Body as Text in Women's Performance Art." In *Women in American Theatre* Helen Krich Chinoy and Linda Walsh Jenkins, eds. New York: Crown, 1981; revised ed. New York: Theatre Communications Group, 1987.

———. "Rachel Rosenthal: Feminism and Performance Art." *Women & Performance Journal 4* Vol. 2, No. 2 (1985).

Froula, Christine. "When Eve Reads Milton: Undoing the Canonical Economy." In *Canons,* Robert von Hallberg, ed. Chicago: University of Chicago Press, 1984.

Gallop, Jane. *The Daughter's Seduction: Feminism and Psychoanalysis.* Ithaca: Cornell University Press, 1982.

———. *Reading Lacan.* Ithaca: Cornell University Press, 1985.

Goffman, Erving. *Gender Advertisements.* New York: Harper & Row, 1976.

Gordon, Linda. "What's New in Women's History." In *Feminist Studies/Critical Studies,* Teresa de Lauretis, ed. Bloomington: Indiana University Press, 1986.

Greene, Bob. "Bar Wars." *Esquire,* November 1986.

Gussow, Mel. "Women Playwrights: New Voices in the Theatre." *New York Times Sunday Magazine,* May 1, 1983.

Hallberg, Robert von, ed. *Canons.* Chicago: University of Chicago Press, 1984.

Hart, Lynda. "Doing Time: Hunger for Power in Marsha Norman's Plays." *Southern Quarterly,* Spring 1987.

Hebdige, Dick. *Subculture: The Meaning of Style.* New York: Methuen, 1979.

Henley, Beth. *Crimes of the Heart.* New York: Penguin, 1982.

Holub, Robert. *Reception Theory: A Critical Introduction.* New York: Methuen, 1984.

Husserl, Edmund. *Ideas: A General Introduction of Pure Phenomenology.* Translated by W.R. Boyce Gibson. New York: MacMillan, 1931.

———. *The Idea of Phenomenology.* Translated by William P. Alston and George Nakhnikian. The Hague: M. Nijhoff, 1964.

Irigaray, Luce. "When the Goods Get Together." In *New French Feminisms,* Isabelle de Courtivron and Elaine Marks, eds. New York: Schocken Books, 1981.

———. *This Sex Which is Not One.* Translated by Catherine Porter. Ithaca: Cornell University Press, 1985.

———. *Speculum of the Other Woman.* Translated by Gillian C. Gill. Ithaca: Cornell University Press, 1985.

Jaggar, Alison. *Feminist Politics and Human Nature.* Totowa, N.J.: Rowman & Allanheld, 1983.

Jameson, Frederic. "Postmodernism and Consumer Society." In *The Anti-Aesthetic: Essays on Postmodern Culture,* Hal Foster, ed. Washington: Bay Press, 1983.

Jenkins, Linda Walsh. "At the Foot of the Mountain." *Women in American Theatre,* Helen Krich Chinoy and Linda Walsh Jenkins, eds. New York: Crown, 1981; revised ed. New York: Theatre Communications Group.

———. "Locating the Language of Gender Experience." *Women & Performance Journal 3* Vol. 2, No. 1 (1984).

Johnston, Claire. *Notes on Women's Cinema.* London: Society for Education in Film and Television, 1973.

Jones, Ann. "Writing the Body: Toward an Understanding of *L'écriture féminine.*" In *Feminist Criticism and Social Change: Sex, Class, and Race in Literature and Culture,* Deborah Rosenfelt and Judith Newton, eds. New York: Methuen, 1985.

———. "Inscribing Femininity: French Theories of the Feminine." In *Making a Difference: Feminist Literary Criticism,* Gayle Greene and Coppelia Kahn, eds. New York: Methuen, 1985.

Kaplan, E. Ann. *Women & Film: Both Sides of the Camera.* New York: Methuen, 1983.

———. "Theories of Melodrama: A Feminist Perspective." *Women & Performance Journal 1* Vol. 1, No. 1 (1983).

Kappeler, Susanne. *The Pornography of Representation.* Minneapolis: University of Minnesota Press, 1986.

Kendall. "On a Stage of One's Own." *The Women's Review of Books* Vol. 4, No. 10–11 (July/August 1987).

Keyssar, Helene. *Feminist Theatre.* New York: Grove Press, 1985.

Kirby, Michael. "On Acting and Not-Acting." *Drama Review* Vol. 16, No. 1 (March 1972).

———. "Richard Foreman's Ontological-Hysteric Theatre." *Drama Review* Vol. 17, No. 2 (June 1973).

Kolodny, Annette. "Dancing through the Minefield: Some Observations on the Theory, Practice, and Politics of a Feminist Literary Criticism." *Feminist Studies* Vol. 6, No. 1 (Spring 1980).

Kristeva, Julia. *Desire in Language.* New York: Columbia University Press, 1980.

———. "Woman Can Never Be Defined." In *New French Feminisms,* Isabelle de Courtivron and Elaine Marks, eds. New York: Schocken Books, 1981.

Lauter, Paul. "Race and Gender in the Shaping of the American Literary Canon: A Case Study from the Twenties." In *Feminist Criticism and Social Change: Sex, Race, and Class in Literature and Culture*, Judith Newton and Deborah Rosenfelt, eds. New York: Methuen, 1985.

Leavitt, Dinah. *Feminist Theatre Groups*. Jefferson, N.C.: McFarland, 1980.

Linden, Robin Ruth, Darlene R. Pagano, Diana E. H. Russell, and Susan Leigh Star, eds. *Against Sadomasochism*. E. Palo Alto: Frog in the Well, 1982.

Lippard, Lucy. *From the Center: Feminist Essays on Women's Art*. New York: E. P. Dutton, 1976.

Malnig, Julie. "The Women's Project: A Profile." *Women & Performance Journal 1* Vol. 1, No. 1 (1983).

Malpede (Taylor), Karen. *People's Theatre in Amerika*. New York: Dream Book Specialists, 1972.

Malpede, Karen, ed. *Women and Theatre: Compassion and Hope*. New York: Drama Book Publishers, 1983.

Marranca, Bonnie. *Theatrewritings*. New York: Performing Arts Journal Publications, 1984.

Miller, Jean Baker. *Psychoanalysis and Women*. New York: Penguin, 1973.

Mitchell, Juliet. *Psychoanalysis and Feminism*. New York: Pantheon, 1974.

Moi, Toril. *Sexual/Textual Politics*. New York: Methuen, 1985.

Moraga, Cherrie, and Gloria Anzaldua, eds. *This Bridge Called My Back: Writings by Radical Women of Color*. New York: Kitchen Table Press, 1983.

Mulvey, Laura. "Visual Pleasure and Narrative Cinema." *Screen* Vol. 16, No. 3 (Autumn 1975).

Natalle, Elizabeth J. *Feminist Theatre: A Study in Persuasion*. Metuchen, N.J.: Scarecrow Press, 1985.

Nestle, Joan. "Butch/Femme Relationships in the 1950s." "Sex Issue" of *Heresies #12* Vol. 3, No. 4 (1981).

Newton, Judith, and Deborah Rosenfelt. "Toward a Materialist-Feminist Criticism." In *Feminist Criticism and Social Change: Sex, Class, and Race in Literature and Culture*, Judith Newton and Deborah Rosenfelt, eds. New York: Methuen, 1985.

Norman, Marsha. *'night, Mother*. Acting Edition. New York: Dramatists Play Service, 1983.

Parker, Roszika, and Griselda Pollock. *Old Mistresses: Women, Art and Ideology*. New York: Pantheon, 1981.

Primus, Francesca. "Women's Theatres around Town: Feminist or Contemporary?" *Backstage*, December 6, 1985.

Raymond, Janice. "A Genealogy of Female Friendship." *Trivia* Vol. 1, No. 1 (Fall 1982).

Reinelt, Janelle. "Beyond Brecht: Britain's New Feminist Drama." *Theatre Journal* Vol. 38, No. 2 (May 1986).

Rich, Adrienne. *Of Woman Born: Motherhood as Experience and Institution*. New York: Bantam Books, 1976.

———. "Compulsory Heterosexuality and Lesbian Existence." *Signs* Vol. 5, No. 4 (Summer 1980).

Robinson, Lillian S. *Sex, Class, and Culture*. Bloomington: Indiana University Press, 1978; revised ed., New York: Methuen, 1986.

Roth, Moira, ed. *The Amazing Decade: Women and Performance Art in America, 1970–1980*. Los Angeles: Astro Artz, 1983.

Rubin, Gayle. "The Traffic in Women: Notes on the 'Political Economy' of Sex." In *Toward an Anthropology of Women*, Rayna Reiter, ed. New York: Monthly Review Press, 1978.

———. "Thinking Sex: Notes for a Radical Theory of the Politics of Sexuality." In *Pleasure and Danger: Exploring Female Sexuality*, Carol Vance, ed. Boston: Routledge & Kegan Paul, 1984.

Sainer, Arthur. *The Radical Theatre Notebook*. New York: Avon, 1975.

Samois Collective, eds. *Coming to Power*. Revised ed., Boston: Alyson Publications, 1982.

Savran, David. *The Wooster Group, 1975–1985: Breaking the Rules*. Ann Arbor: UMI Research Press, 1986; revised ed., New York: Theatre Communications Group, 1988.

Schechner, Richard. *The End of Humanism*. New York: Performing Arts Journal Publications, 1982.

Scott, Trudy. *"'night, Mother."* *Women & Performance Journal 1* Vol. 1, No. 1 (1983).

Segal, Sondra, and Roberta Sklar. "The Women's Experimental Theatre." In *Women in American Theatre*, Helen Krich Chinoy and Linda Walsh Jenkins, eds. New York: Crown, 1981; revised ed., New York: Theatre Communications Group, 1987.

Silverman, Kaja. *The Subject of Semiotics*. New York: Oxford University Press, 1983.

Sklar, Roberta. "'Sisters,' or Never Trust Anyone Outside the Family." *Women & Performance Journal 1* Vol. 1, No. 1 (1983).

Smith, Barbara, ed. *Home Girls*. New York: Kitchen Table Press, 1983.

Smith, Barbara Herrnstein. "Contingencies of Value." In *Canons*, Robert von Hallberg, ed. *Canons*. Chicago: University of Chicago Press, 1984.

Snitow, Ann, Christine Stansell, and Sharon Thompson, eds. *Powers of Desire: The Politics of Sexuality*. New York: Monthly Review Press, 1983.

Staiger, Janet. "The Politics of Film Canons." *Cinema Journal* Vol. 24, No. 3 (Spring 1985).

Stone, Elizabeth. "Playwright Marsha Norman." *Ms. Magazine*, July 1983.

Sundahl, Debi. "Stripper." In *Sex Work: Writings by Women in the Sex Industry*, Priscilla Alexander and Frederique Delacoste, eds. Pittsburgh: Cleis Press, 1987.

Vance, Carol, ed. *Pleasure and Danger: Exploring Female Sexuality*. Boston: Routledge & Kegan Paul, 1984.

Wandor, Michelene. *Carry On, Understudies*. New York: Routledge & Kegan Paul, 1986.

Weene, Seph. "Venus." "Sex Issue" of *Heresies #12* Vol. 3, No. 4 (1981).

Wilke, Hannah. Interview. Quoted in American Women Artists exhibition catalog, São Paulo Museum, July 1980.

Willis, Sharon. "Hélène Cixous' *Portrait de Dora:* The Unseen and the Un-scene." *Theatre Journal* Vol. 38, No. 3 (October 1985).

Wittig, Monique. "The Straight Mind." *Feminist Issues*, Summer 1980.

––––––. "The Category of Sex." *Feminist Issues*, Fall 1981.

Nontextual Sources

Clippings and photographs, Billy Rose Theatre Collection, Lincoln Center Library for the Performing Arts.

Davy, Kate. "Total Theatre: The Work of Richard Foreman." Lectures, New York University, Spring, 1984.

Foreman, Richard. Tape recording of question and answer session, April 1984.

Index

Acting technique: Brechtian, 114; experimental theatre and, 85; realism and, 61; Stanislavskian, 84

Actors Theatre of Louisville, 24, 38

Age of Invention (Skipitares), 111

American drama: canonization, 19–20; father/son relationships, 33–36, 91–92; genre categorization, 32; mainstream theatre, 120

American Repertory Theatre, 21

American Theatre in Higher Education (American Theatre Association), 4

Anthropology in women's theatre, 90–91

Apparatus: in postmodern performance, 43; in theory, 83, 95, 101–13

Aristotle, 34, 38

Artaud, Antonin, 8, 85, 97, 106

At the Foot of the Mountain: company statement, 8, 85; at Women and Theatre Program Conference (1987), 92–95, 97

Audience: participation, 94, 120; support, 92

Autobiography in performance, 62

Banal, Sherry Blakey, 92

Barnard Conference on Sexuality (1982), 77

Barthes, Roland, 57

Bates, Kathy, 24, 30

Benmussa, Simone, 101–2, 103–6, 107–8

Berger, John, 52, 54

Birth rituals, 90

Blau, Herbert, 41

Body image: in lesbian theatre, 110; in *'night, Mother*, 31–33; in performance art, 62–63. *See also* character appearance

Boesing, Martha, 92–95

Bonsoir, Dr. Schon (Rosenthal), 62

Book of Splendors (Foreman), 55–58

Brecht, Bertolt, 13, 14, 84; acting technique, 114; cultural feminist theatre and, 90; epic theatre, 106–8; and Richard Foreman, 44–48; gestus, 108, 116; historicization, 111–13; not

... but, 114–15

Brooks, Collette, 31, 39

Brustein, Robert, 21, 28

Busch, Charles, 120

Butch/femme: in 1920s-1950s, 105; in lesbian performance, 69, 73, 76–77; as representation, 116, 119. *See also* role-playing

Camp, 112

Canonization: 5; deconstruction and, 39–40; female countercanons, 7, 21, 36; genre categories and, 31–34; in theatre, 19–21

Carr, C., 65–66

Case, Sue-Ellen: on canonization, 20, 96; on cultural feminism, 8–9, 59–60; on liberal feminism, 4–5; on strategy of appearance, 101, 116

Casting, 24, 110

Cha, Bernadette Hak Eun, 92

Chambers, Jane, 68, 109

Character: appearance, 24, 31–33, 110; in postmodernism, 42–43

Chekhov, Anton, 111–12

Chit Chat with Carmelita (Troyano), 69–70

Cinema, psychoanalysis and, 13–14, 49

Cixous, Hélène: Artaud and, 8; feminine aesthetic and, 87; *Portrait of Dora*, 101–3

Class, 93, 108

Club Chandalier, 68

Club performance, 68

Commodification: Karen Finley and, 67; of men, 55; striptease and, 65; of women, 52

Community theatre, 69

Conduct of Life (Fornes), 108

Consciousness-raising: cultural feminist theatre and, 85–86; performance art and, 62; radical feminism and, 7

Coss, Clare, 88

Crimes of the Heart (Henley), 25–26, 35

Criticism: Aristotelian, 20, 34; mainstream, 19;

value judgments and, 17
Cronenberg, David, 67
Cultural feminism: character and, 113; definition of, 3, 5–10; experimental theatre and, 85–86; 'night, Mother and, 35; woman-identification and, 83–95. See also radical feminism
Cultural nationalism, 86
Curb, Rosemary, 7, 84, 87, 95

Daughter's Cycle Trilogy, The (Women's Experimental Theatre), 88–91
Daughters (Women's Experimental Theatre), 88–91
Davy, Kate, 45, 50, 52
Death of a Salesman (Miller), 5, 31–33
Defenders of the Code (Skipitares), 111
de Lauretis, Teresa: on gender technology, 99–101; on materialist feminism, 10; on narrative, 13; on representation, 115–16, 119
Desert Hearts (Dietch), 71
Desire: in Albert Nobbs, 103–6; cultural feminism and, 60–61, 63–64; in Foreman, 49, 53; Lacan and, 42; lesbians and, 78
Diamond, Elin, 105, 115
Direct address: in cultural feminist theatre, 89, 93; in lesbian performance, 73; in materialist feminist performance, 112; in realism, 110
Dietch, Donna, 71
Doane, Mary Ann, 13, 48
Documentary in cultural feminist theatre, 93, 96
Drag, 70, 104, 116. See also gender impersonation
Dramaturgy in American theatre, 22
Dress Suits for Hire (Weaver, Shaw, Hughes), 120
Dworkin, Andrea, 60

Echols, Alice, 5, 59, 79
Ecriture féminine and the feminine aesthetic, 8, 99, 101–2
Eidos, 64–65
Electra Speaks (Women's Experimental Theatre), 91
Erotica, 64–65
Esslin, Martin, 106
Ethnicity: Spiderwoman Theatre and, 71; Split Britches and, 76, 86
Evening of Disgusting Songs and Pukey Images, An (Spiderwoman), 71–72
Exception and the Rule, The (Brecht), 92
Experimental theatre: cultural feminism and, 85; Richard Foreman and, 43–44
Expressionism, 85

Family: in American drama, 26, 33; in cultural feminist theatre, 89–90, 91–92; in lesbian theatre, 108; in performance art, 62
Fantasy, 59, 67–78
Fatale, Fanny, 79
Fear of Laughing (Forrester), 113
Feast or Famine (Women's Experimental Theatre), 91
Feminism: definition of, 3. See also cultural feminism, liberal feminism, materialist feminism
Feral, Josette, 87, 89, 97
Fetishism: in film theory, 13, 48; Foreman and, 56
Film noir, 107
Finley, Karen, 65–67
Fly, The (Cronenberg), 67
Food (Women's Experimental Theatre), 91
Foodtalk (Women's Experimental Theatre), 91
Foreman, Richard, 12, 15; Brecht and, 48; nudity and, 49–50, 52–53; political theatre and, 43–44; pornography and, 54; scenography and, 48, 49–50; texts and, 47–48
Fornes, Maria Irene, 101, 108, 110
Forrester, Allice, 71, 113
Forte, Jeanie, 96
Freud, Sigmund, 11; fetishism and, 48; subjectivity and, 41–42

Gaze: the male, 14; Richard Foreman and, 45–58; materialist feminism and, 114; psychoanalysis and, 102; striptease and, 65
Gender: definition of, 10, 63; as representation, 99, 116–17
Gender impersonation, 70, 71; in Albert Nobbs, 103–6. See also drag
Genre categorization, 31–34
Gordon, Linda, 3, 6, 88
Grotowski, Jerzy, 85
Gussow, Mel, 19, 37–39

Hart, Lynda, 30
Heart of the Scorpion (Forrester), 71
Henley, Beth, 4, 25
Hopper, Edward, 28
Howe, Tina, 37
Hughes, Holly, 70, 107, 120
Hustler, 78–79

Identity: in Hélène Cixous, 103; mimesis and, 96; in postmodern performance, 42
Identity politics, 86, 92
Intertextuality, 70

Jameson, Frederic, 47–48, 55
Jenkins, Linda Walsh, 87
Jory, John, 38

Kaplan, E. Ann, 13, 48
Kitchen, The, 65

Kolodny, Annette, 32, 87–88
Kristeva, Julia, 99

LaMama, 68
Labowitz, Leslie, 61
Lacan, Jacques, 12, 83; desire and, 49; Richard Foreman and, 56; subjectivity and, 42
Lady Dick (Hughes), 107, 117
Landesman, Heidi, 27
Last Summer at Bluefish Cove (Chambers), 109–10
LeCompte, Elizabeth, 42
Lesbian playwrights, 73
Lesbians: coming-out stories, 109–10; cultural feminist theatre and, 97; desire and, 63, 70, 78; performance and, 67–77; pornography and, 77–80; as representation, 115–17; sexuality and, 59, 67–81, 119
Lévi-Strauss, Claude: division of labor, 112; kinship, 12
Liberal feminism: character and, 113; definition of, 4, 10; realism and, 84–85
Lippard, Lucy, 62
Living Theatre, The, 43, 85

MacKinnon, Catherine, 60
Maher, Antoinette, T., 92
Manheim, Kate, 50, 51–52, 52
Manheim, Nora, 50, 52
Mann, Emily, 4
Margolin, Deborah, 71, 72–76
Marranca, Bonnie, 110
Masquerade, 119
Materialist feminism: definition of, 3, 10–16; and psychoanalysis, 11–13; visual pleasure and, 115
Matrilineage, 88, 93
Mayo, Lisa, 71
Miguel, Gloria, 71
Miguel, Muriel, 71
Miller, Arthur, 5, 31–33
Mimesis: in cultural feminist theatre, 83, 86, 89, 95–97; and ideology, 16
Moore, Tom, 23, 37
Mother/daughter relationships in cultural feminist theatre, 9, 86, 88–89, 93; in *'night, Mother*, 22, 33
Ms. Magazine, 30, 35, 36
Mud (Fornes), 108–9
Mulvey, Laura: psychoanalysis and, 12–13; visual pleasure and, 48–49, 114
Multiculturalism, 92–95
Music, 107
Myth: in cultural feminist theatre, 86; Spiderwoman Theatre and, 71; woman as, 57

Narrative: closure, 84, 103, 110; epic theatre and, 106–7; in *Portrait of Dora*, 102–3; postmodernism and, 42–43
Native Americans, 71, 72
Nestle, Joan, 117, 119
New Age, 114
New Right, 59
New York Magazine, 30
New York Times, 19, 27
'night, Mother, 19–40
Norman, Marsha: 19–40; liberal feminism and, 4
Nudity: Richard Foreman and, 50; men and, 54–55; in performance art, 63, 77

On Our Backs, 79
Ontological-Hysteric Theatre, 43
Open Theatre, The, 43, 85

PAIN(T) (Foreman), 50, 53–54
Painting Churches, (Howe), 37
Parody, 55, 68–73
Pastiche, 55
Performance art: cultural feminism and, 60–68; men and, 62
Performance Group, The, 43, 85
Performing Arts Journal, 39
Persona, 67–77
Phallologocentrism, 12, 43, 91, 101
Phenomenology, 46–47, 57
Pitoniak, Anne, 24
Pluralism, 3, 21, 121
Popular culture, 24, 113
Pornography: antipornography feminism, 59–60, 80; Karen Finley and, 65; Richard Foreman and, 55; heterosexual females and, 63–64; lesbians and, 76–80; men and, 53–54
Portrait of Dora (Cixous), 102
Postmodernism: performance and, 15, 42; voyeurism and, 55
Power: Karen Finley and, 65–67; pornography and, 60, 76–79
Production: cultural, 15; feminism and, 120; modes of, 113
Proscenium staging, 46
Psychoanalysis: feminist film theory and, 12–14; identification and, 14, 72; materialist feminism and, 11–12; *Portrait of Dora* and, 101; subjectivity and, 42
Pulitzer Prize, 20, 22, 25, 32, 35
Puppets, 110, 111

Race, 86, 91, 95, 108, 112
Radical feminism: definition of, 6. *See also* cultural feminism
Rape, 93

Raped (At the Foot of the Mountain), 92–93
Realism: in American drama, 84; Brecht and, 106–7, 109; quotational, 110
Reception theory: author's intent, 22–23, 95, 121; gender biases and, 19–21, 27–34; horizon of expectations, 19, 23; process of, 121
Reinelt, Janelle, 108
Rhoda in Potatoland (Foreman), 45, 55–56
Rice, Rebecca, 92, 95
Rich, Frank, 19, 28, 32
Ritual, 43, 89–95
Role-playing: gender and, 63; pornography and, 77–80
Rosario, Carmen Maria, 92, 95
Rose, Phyllis Jane, 92–95
Rosenthal, Rachel, 62
Roth, Moira, 61
Rubin, Gayle, 6, 19, 63

Sadomasochism, 65, 77–80
Samois, 77
Sarita (Fornes), 108
Schechner, Richard, 43
Schneeman, Carolee, 83
Scopophilia, 13, 48
Scott, Trudy, 28, 35
Seduction: butch/femme and, 116; in *Pukey Images,* 72; textual, 111
Segal, Sondra, 88, 90, 97
Semiotics: female body as sign, 62, 83, 87, 99
Sexuality: compulsory heterosexuality, 11, 63, 112, 116; definition of, 10, 63; in heterosexual cultural feminist performance art, 61–67; lesbians and, 67–81; sexual preference, 67–68
Shaw, Peggy, 71–72, 114
Simon, John, 30
Singular Life of Albert Nobbs, The (Benmussa), 103–6, 108
Skipitares, Theodora, 72, 111
Sklar, Roberta, 39; *Last Summer at Bluefish Cove* and, 109–10; Women's Experimental Theatre and, 85, 88, 91
Sophia = (Wisdom) Part 3: The Cliffs (Foreman), 45, 51–52
Spiderwoman Theatre, 71, 102, 111, 114
Spirituality, 61, 64, 81
Split Britches (Split Britches), 72
Split Britches, 71, 72–76, 101
Sproutime (Labowitz), 61
Stein, Gertrude, 45
Story of a Mother II, The (At the Foot of the Mountain), 93–94, 97
Storytelling, 71, 93, 101, 104
Striptease, 65, 68, 77–80

Subjectivity: cultural feminist theatre and, 92; performance art and, 63; psychoanalysis and, 12; subject-formation, 42

Terkel, Studs, 93
Terry, Megan, 89
Theatre for the New City, 72
Themes in Drama Conference (1987), 10
Three Sisters, The (Chekhov), 111
Three Sisters from Here to There, The (Spiderwoman), 111–12
Transvestism, 120
Troyano, Alina (Carmelita Tropicana), 69, 69–70

Universality: canonization and, 20; cultural feminist theatre and, 92–95; *'night, Mother* and, 25–34; performance art and, 62
Up to and Including Her Limits (Schneeman), 83
Upwardly Mobile Home (Split Britches), 70, 72, 114

Vampire Lesbians of Sodom (Busch), 120
Village Voice, 65
Violence against women, 61, 67
Visual pleasure: Brecht and, 114; cultural feminist theatre and, 90; film theory and, 13; Richard Foreman and, 48–53; materialist feminism and, 114
Visualization, 94
von Gandersheim, Hrotsvit, 20
Voyeurism, 13, 50, 55

Weaver, Lois, 68, 71–72, 120
Wilke, Hannah, 61–62
Wilson, Robert, 42
Woman-conscious drama: definition of, 7; mimesis and, 95–97; woman-identification and, 83
Woman's Body and Other Natural Resources (Women's Experimental Theatre), 91
Women & Performance Journal, 35
Women and Theatre Program, 4; Chicago conference (1987), 92–95
Women of color, 9, 15, 92–95
Women playwrights, 37–40, 84
Women's Experimental Theatre, 85, 88–92, 97, 110
Women's Interart Theatre Center, 39, 91
Women's Project, 4
Women's theatre, 37, 83
Working (Terkel), 93
WOW Cafe, 67, 70, 71, 101, 114, 119